THIRD PARTY LIABILITY IN TORT

Non-vicarious liability for the acts of third parties is distinguishable from the traditional doctrine of vicarious liability insofar as it relates to a form of primary liability predicated upon the personal fault of the defendant. More conveniently termed 'third party liability', it is a novel category of tortious liability that has evolved from a collection of disparate and isolated judicial decisions setting out, on an entirely ad hoc basis, individualised exceptions to the entrenched common law rules against liability for omissions and liability for the acts of others. As a result of the improvised nature of its development, the current law on third party liability is unstructured, unprincipled and incoherent. The specific purpose of this book is to seek out the foundational principles governing the various existing instances of third party liability, with a view to identifying a coherent legal basis upon which such liability can develop in the future.

Third Party Liability in Tort

CLAIRE McIVOR

•HART•
PUBLISHING

OXFORD AND PORTLAND, OREGON
2006

HART PUBLISHING
Bloomsbury Publishing Plc
Kemp House, Chawley Park, Cumnor Hill, Oxford, OX2 9PH, UK

HART PUBLISHING, the Hart/Stag logo, BLOOMSBURY and the Diana logo are trademarks of Bloomsbury Publishing Plc
First published in Great Britain 2006

A catalogue record for this book is available from the British Library.

ISBN: 978-1-84113-552-6

Typeset by Forewords, Oxford

Acknowledgements

I owe a huge debt of gratitude to Margaret Brazier and Tony Dugdale for the instrumental role that they have played in the realisation of this book, and to Richard Hart for having the confidence in me to publish it. For the many ways in which she helped, I am also extremely grateful to Sangeeta Shah. Stephen Bailey deserves a special mention for the invaluable comments that he made on Chapter 6, as do my colleagues at Durham Law Department for their help and encouragement throughout the writing process. Most of all, however, I wish to thank Harvey Teff, who has been my mentor for the last seven years. Without his constant guidance and support, I would not be where I am today and this book would never have come into being.

Contents

Table of Cases

UK Cases

Commonwealth Cases

ECtHR Cases

US Cases

French Cases

Introduction

THIRD PARTY LIABILITY is a novel category of tortious liability which has crept very quietly into English tort law. More precisely described as non-vicarious liability for the acts of others, it differs from the traditional doctrine of vicarious liability in being a form of primary liability based on the personal fault of the defendant.[1] Third party liability was never consciously conceived as a separate category of liability in its own right. Rather, it has evolved from a collection of disparate and isolated judicial decisions setting out ad hoc exceptions to the entrenched common law rules against liability for omissions and liability for the acts of others. Apart from *Home Office v Dorset Yacht*,[2] these decisions have generally had a very low profile, and it is not until recently that any, even loose, connections have been made between them. However, over the past decade, the incremental process of expanding the range of exceptional circumstances in which some form of third party liability is judicially recognised has gathered considerable pace, such that there now exists a sizeable pool of cases from which it is possible to identify individual strands of such liability.

Identifying the individual strands is, however, the easy part, for the cases can be very naturally categorised by reference to their common factual scenarios. It is in determining the legal principles that lie at the heart of these sub-categories that the real difficulties lie. Unfortunately, in third party actions, there has been a systematic failure to articulate with any degree of precision the actual grounds of decisions. Often the relevant issues are not properly isolated and individual decisions are typically arrived at without detailed reference to other related third party liability cases, and with little or no exploration of the inter-relationships between them.

Consequently, the current law on third party liability is unstructured, unprincipled and incoherent. It has also been largely ignored by legal academics and has not been the subject of any sustained analytical treatment. Although, in response to the burgeoning case law in this area over the past few years, the main tort law textbooks have started to include, within their chapters on the duty of care, a specific sub-section on liability for the acts of others, their treatment of the topic still tends to be rather brief and rudimentary. The specific purpose of this book is

[1] In the well-known case of *Home Office v Dorset Yacht* [1970] AC 1004, for example, the Home Office was held vicariously liable for the borstal officers whose negligence in allowing the borstal boys to escape and cause damage attracted third party liability.

[2] *Ibid.*

to seek out the foundational principles governing the various existing instances of third party liability, with a view to identifying a more coherent and controlled legal basis upon which it can develop in the future.

It is recognised, however, that insofar as it presupposes the legitimacy of a regime of third party liability within English tort law, the validity of this stated purpose needs to be specifically justified. For in view of its obvious conflict with the moral notion of individual responsibility, it may be questioned whether, as a matter of basic principle, third party liability should actually be recognised by the law. And more specifically, even if this question is to be answered in the affirmative, is there a place within the current English system for a regime of third party liability?

In response, it is necessary first of all to emphasise the entirely exceptional nature of the regime of third party liability being advocated. There can be no denying that, as a general rule, the very idea of holding one person liable for harm committed by another will be both incompatible with basic moral and legal principles, and contrary to the normative structure of English tort law. However, it is argued that there are specific instances of third party liability which can be independently justified, not just as a matter of principle, but also within the specific context of the tort system. Indeed, due to the particular nature of the relationships involved, it is argued that, paradoxically, some forms of third party responsibility may actually be seen to promote the concept of individual moral responsibility and to further the normative purpose of the tort system. As regards the moral responsibility issue, take, by way of example, the House of Lords decision in *Home Office v Dorset Yacht*. To the average person on the street, the imposition of liability on the borstal officers for the harm caused by the unsupervised borstal boys will be seen as wholly appropriate, such legal responsibility being viewed as a mere facet of the officers' ordinary personal responsibility, stemming from their position of authority in relation to the young harm-doers. To explain how such a decision fits within the tort system is, however, a much more complicated task which requires some account of what tort law is supposed to be all about.

(i) The Normative Purpose of Tort Law

Most tort lawyers agree that English tort law is essentially based upon the principles of corrective justice. That is not to say, however, that the tort system is to be understood exclusively in corrective justice terms, for it is in adhering too rigidly to traditional corrective justice theory that the main shortcomings of the standard philosophical explanations of tort law are to be identified.

There are numerous different theories of corrective justice which all vary to a greater or lesser extent as regards the content and demands of the doctrine.[3]

[3] See more generally, the collection of essays contained in DG Owens (ed), *Philosophical Foundations of Tort Law* (Clarendon Press, 1995).

However, it is possible to identify three core elements of Aristotelian/Kantian justice that are common to the main accounts of corrective justice: (1) wrongful conduct; (2) personal responsibility; and (3) correlativity of right and obligation.

The element of wrongful conduct relates to the basic corrective justice principle that there can be no liability without fault. Corrective justice is concerned with the fairness of interactions between individuals which result in imbalances in the proportional holdings of persons. The function of the law, according to corrective theory, is thus to decide in which cases it should intervene in order to rectify resulting inequalities, and the criterion it uses to measure the fairness of such transactions is the wrongfulness of the defendant's conduct. The operation of the fault doctrine in the law of tort gives effect to the moral principle that the stigma attached to a finding of liability should be imposed only in cases where the behaviour of the defendant is deserving of such a sanction.

As regards the element of personal responsibility, Coleman points out that it is the idea that the defendant is personally responsible for having caused the victim's loss that distinguishes the legal duty to compensate in corrective justice from the moral duties associated with the ordinary norms of decency and civility.[4] Correlativity refers to the fact that the claimant has a right to recover against the particular defendant in question because of the nature of the relationship between them. The victim's right to compensation is linked to the defendant's duty to compensate, and it arises out of the fact that the defendant has used up the victim's resources for his own ends. In other words, it is the fact that the defendant caused harm to the victim that places the defendant, specifically, under an obligation to ensure that reparation is provided, and the fact that the victim was the specific subject of this harm that gives rise to the victim's right to demand compensation. For Weinrib, perhaps the most well-known of all the corrective justice theorists, it is this idea of organising the world in terms of bilateral relationships between individuals which sets apart not just tort law but the whole of private law as a normatively distinct mode of legal ordering, and which makes it internally intelligible.[5]

Critics of the corrective justice explanation of tort law argue that it does not provide a full and realistic account of modern tort law. In terms of their practical operation, modern tort regimes are significantly influenced by distributive justice principles, which are said to be inherently incompatible with corrective justice theory. Atiyah, for instance, points to the fact that tort actions are generally no longer brought against individuals, but instead against liability insurers, employers and corporations, to dispute the idea that tort law is concerned with personal responsibility.[6] It is not to be denied that insurance and the doctrine of vicarious liability represent real obstacles to the corrective justice view. Corrective justice theorists may be quick to point out that the payment of damages via

[4] JL Coleman, 'The Practice of Corrective Justice', in *ibid*, p 57.

[5] EJ Weinrib, *The Idea of Private Law* (Harvard University Press, 1995).

[6] PS Atiyah, 'Personal Injuries in the Twenty First Century: Thinking the Unthinkable', in P Birks (ed), *Wrongs and Remedies in the Twenty First Century* (Clarendon Press, 1996).

insurance is not incompatible with corrective justice principles, since they govern only the creation of the defendant's responsibility for compensation and are unconcerned with the actual mechanism by which it is ultimately discharged.[7] However, they fail to address the other more pervasive aspects of the impact of insurance on tort law. As Lewis very clearly points out, insurers dominate the tort system.[8] Not only are they its 'paymasters', they also control the litigation process, control much of the legal representation and determine tactics that will be used in individual proceedings.[9] As a result of the way in which they exercise their settlement decisions, insurers are also able to decide precisely which cases will actually end up reaching the courts.[10] For reasons of cost and administrative efficiency, insurers will often settle minor claims without engaging in any detailed investigation of blame. Indeed, it is said that they routinely settle claims that are entirely devoid of legal merit according to the rules of tort law.[11] Of relevance also in this context is the impact of the new system of contingency fee agreements on individual law firms and claims management companies, in terms of making them much more selective about the cases they take on.

In the same way, the doctrine of vicarious liability is also to be described as a classic manifestation of distributive justice theory. Although Weinrib does attempt to fit vicarious liability within the principles of corrective justice, he does so by resorting to legal fictions, for he treats the principles of employer's liability as an application of the old master's tort theory.[12] According to this theory, the whole act of the employee is directly attributed to the employer so that, for all intents and purposes, the employer is regarded as being personally responsible for his own tort.

To the extent that they fail to recognise distributionist influences, the integrity of the main corrective justice explanations of tort law must be regarded as severely compromised. But it is submitted that this does not necessitate the abandonment of the corrective justice approach. It means simply that a more measured corrective justice explanation of the tort system is required. In this respect, the general theoretical approach of Peter Cane is to be supported. For Cane argues cogently that distributive justice principles have a supplementary role to play in tort, in the sense that such principles are sometimes necessary in order to achieve corrective justice outcomes.[13] In his view, while corrective justice forms the structure of tort law and constitutes the basis of all decisions regarding liability, it alone cannot provide an adequate explanation of this area of law. The law of tort has a dual function in that, in addition to regulating disputes between

[7] Weinrib, above n 5, p 13–36; RW Wright, 'Right, Justice and Tort Law', in DG Owens, above n 3, p 178; T. Honoré, 'The Morality of Tort Law – Questions and Answers', in DG Owens, above n 3, p 79.

[8] R Lewis, 'Insurance and the tort system' (2005) 25 LS 85 at 87.

[9] *Ibid*, at 88.

[10] *Ibid*, at 89.

[11] *Ibid.*

[12] *The Idea of Private Law*, n 5 above, pp 185–87.

[13] 'Corrective Justice and Correlativity in Private Law' (1996) 16 OJLS 471.

individuals, it also provides guidelines for future conduct.[14] This involves placing tort in its broader legal and social context, and it is here that distributional criteria become relevant.

As a result of the doctrine of precedent, the relevance of court decisions extends beyond the individual parties actually involved in the dispute. Using *Donoghue v Stevenson*[15] as an example, Cane explains how a corrective justice decision can significantly alter the distribution of wealth in society by transferring resources in the form of rights from one group to another, in that particular case from manufacturers to consumers.[16] Similarly, the concept of the duty of care in negligence may be said to implement distributive considerations[17] as a result of the way in which it is regularly used by the courts to avoid the imposition of liability in cases where this would be considered morally unjust or where political criteria deem it inappropriate. Indeed, the 'fair, just and reasonable' requirement of the standard duty of care test was specially conceived for this very purpose. As such, distributive justice notions are sometimes required in order to avoid the excesses of a pure theory of corrective justice.

This book is thus predicated upon the view that the primary purpose of tort law is to achieve corrective justice outcomes, but that in order to do so resort to distributive justice notions is sometimes required. Frequently, these corrective justice outcomes will also produce incidental distributive justice consequences and, occasionally, distributive justice principles will even form the basis of tort law decisions, but only to the extent of avoiding liability that would otherwise be imposed on a corrective justice basis. What all of this basically means is that fault and personal responsibility are regarded as the core guiding principles of tortious liability. The role played by the insurance industry in facilitating the discharge of obligations created through the imposition of fault-based liability is both necessary and appropriate. Given that the practical operation of the tort system depends upon the availability of liability insurance, it simply has to be accepted as inevitable that insurers will exert additional significant influence over the management of tort claims. Under no circumstances, however, should the existence of an insurance policy ever be used as a reason to impose liability. To the extent that it relied on the existence of compulsory liability insurance to justify the imposition of a high standard of care on learner drivers, the Court of Appeal decision in *Nettleship v Weston*[18] is therefore to be condemned.

The doctrine of vicarious liability is problematic. It is recognised that, like insurance, it performs a valuable role in the operation of the tort system. Insofar as its existence can be justified on the specific distributive justice grounds of enterprise liability and economic efficiency, its inclusion within the tort system again has to be accepted as necessary and appropriate. However, it is argued that

14 P Cane, *The Anatomy of Tort Law* (Hart Publishing, 1997), p 18.
15 [1932] AC 562.
16 Above n 14, at 482.
17 *Ibid*, at 485.
18 [1971] 3 WLR 370, CA.

the recent developments in vicarious liability, extending the notion of the 'course of employment' and bringing intentional torts within the remit of the doctrine, are entirely insupportable in that they have been expressly justified on very vague and unspecified policy grounds, and not on the basis of legitimate distributive justice principles.[19] While policy can sometimes be invoked as a reason for denying the existence of liability, for example in the context of the negligence liability of a particular public body, it should never be used as a basis for imposing liability. Moreover, where policy arguments are employed to avoid liability, their exact nature and substance needs to be explicitly revealed, examined and specifically justified in the context of the prevailing circumstances.

(ii) Identifying a Place within the Tort System for a Regime of Third Party Liability

Within the vision of tort law as just described, there is undoubtedly a place for a regime of third party liability, provided that its scope is strictly limited. The general rule against third party liability must continue to retain its full vigour, for in the vast majority of cases the basic idea of holding one person liable for harm committed by another will be quite clearly contrary to the normative structure of tort law. Nevertheless, it must be recognised that there are specific and exceptional instances of third party liability which are entirely compatible with the core corrective justice principles of fault and personal responsibility, the existence of which within our tort system it is possible to legally justify. To date, the courts have been rather indiscriminate in their approach, and their lack of direction in this area of the law has resulted in the emergence of some legally unjustifiable forms of third party liability. Moreover, all of the existing instances of third party liability are susceptible to further unwarranted expansions, for the concept of such liability is obviously prone to being misused as a mechanism for the promulgation of collective welfare ideals. The normatively acceptable forms of third party liability thus need to be identified, and the principles underlying them elucidated, so that in future the law in this area can be developed, not just coherently, but also judiciously. It is, therefore, a case of clarifying the law so as to be able to control it.

(iii) The Organisation of the Chapters

Before looking at any of the existing strands of third party liability, it is first necessary to contend with a specific conceptual difficulty that is inherent in the issue of third party liability as a whole: that of liability for omissions. Chapter One thus addresses the evident confusion that surrounds the law on omissions

[19] See *Lister v Hesley Hall Ltd* [2001] UKHL 22, and *Majrowski v Guy's and St Thomas's NHS Trust* [2005] EWCA Civ 251.

and attempts to clarify the fundamental nature of its application to the law on third party liability.

Chapter Two looks at the most widely recognised form of third party liability. Stemming from the seminal House of Lords decision in *Home Office v Dorset Yacht*, it relates to the defendant's occupation of a position of authority and control over an irresponsible other. Of obvious applicability to persons in charge of children and incompetent adults, the parent/child relationship is widely assumed to constitute the paradigm example of such liability. Contesting this assumption, this chapter focuses on the parental position and demonstrates that, in this specific context, application of the *Dorset Yacht* principles has been tempered for public policy reasons. Parents are thus less likely to be held liable on a third party basis than other carers of irresponsible charges.

Chapter Three looks at the third party liability of property owners, and deals with liability in both nuisance and negligence. Chapters Four and Five are concerned with the more novel forms of third party liability to have emerged in recent years, namely liability in respect of the intoxicated, and third party liability in the context of sport. Chapter Six then looks specifically at third party liability actions against public authorities, for they are subject to special legal principles and considerations that warrant separate treatment.

Finally, for comparative purposes, Chapter Seven examines the French law on liability for the acts of others. The French system stands out in this respect because it operates an extremely advanced regime of third party liability that is both well established and well documented. That it has been the subject of a number of very recent and dramatic developments means, moreover, that it is also an area of particularly current importance. In terms of identifying a rational basis for the development of the English law on third party liability, it is hoped that this foray into the French experience will provide some useful pointers.

1

Omissions

CENTRAL TO THE issue of third party liability is the so-called 'no-duty-for-omissions' rule, that is, essentially, that the law of tort does not recognise a duty of care for omissions. Itself being a source of much confusion in the law, it is submitted that fundamental misconceptions surrounding the proper application of this rule lie at the heart of the current state of unintelligibility of the law on third party liability. Logic therefore dictates that by addressing these misconceptions concerning omissions, greater clarity may be imported into the law on third party liability. To this end, not only will the current rules on omissions be clarified, but the purpose and utility of the general principle against liability for omissions will also be considered. Specific focus will obviously also be placed on its particular relevance to the issue of third party liability.

I. CLARIFICATION OF THE CURRENT RULES ON OMISSIONS

(i) Distinction Between Misfeasance And Nonfeasance

The confusion surrounding the omissions issue may, first of all, be traced to a deep and widespread misunderstanding of the essence of the actual distinction between misfeasance and nonfeasance. While the problem is, to a large extent, merely terminological and may be tackled by restating the distinction using very strict and precise terms, at its core there would appear also to exist fundamental conceptual misapprehensions surrounding its nature and substance.

The most basic explanation that can be given of the misfeasance/nonfeasance distinction is that it relates to the difference between, on the one hand, making things worse and, on the other, simply failing to make things better. That this is not a straightforward application of the distinction to be drawn between the notions of activity and passivity is a point that cannot be overemphasised. The greatest mistake to make about legal omissions, and indeed the one that is most commonly made, is to assume that the categorisation of a given factual scenario as an instance of either misfeasance or nonfeasance is determined solely on the basis of whether or not the defendant can be said to have acted, in the sense of having engaged in positive bodily movement. Such an inquiry can provide an appropriate answer only in the simplest of cases, where the claim clearly relates either to positive misconduct on the part of the defendant directly resulting in the harm complained of or to an outright failure on his or her part to take a certain course of action to prevent the harm. Where, on the other hand, the relevant course of conduct contains elements of both action and inaction and there are other factors at play, such as the intervention of a third party, which prevent the harm from being linked so clearly and neatly to the defendant, this line of inquiry is utterly useless.

(ii) Specifying the Terms of the Claim

In these problem cases, it is necessary to approach the question of how to qualify the defendant's behaviour from a completely different angle. Rather than launching straight into the issue of how the defendant's overall conduct is to be categorised, the initial focus should instead be on the nature of the allegation of negligence made by the claimant. To what aspect of the defendant's wider course of conduct does the claim actually relate? What is the crux of the allegation? If he or she is to stand any chance of succeeding in court, the claimant must be able to state in concrete terms what exactly it is that the defendant has done or has failed to do that has resulted in the harm complained of and for which the claimant seeks to hold him or her liable. Given the way in which they interrelate, the rules governing duty, fault and causation can meaningfully be applied by judges only if they have in mind specific allegations and can consequently direct their attention to relevant instances of action or inaction.

This contention is, in turn, based upon a very strict view of the way in which the duty concept is supposed to work. It is submitted that the duty question must be framed in very specific terms relating to the type of harm suffered by the claimant and to the way in which it was inflicted. For example, was the defendant under a duty to take reasonable care not to cause the claimant personal injury by serving her a bottle of ginger beer containing a decomposing snail? Was the defendant under a duty to take reasonable care not to cause the claimant economic loss through the preparation of inaccurate company accounts upon which the claimant would later rely to make financial decisions? Was the defendant under a duty to take reasonable care to ensure that adequate security measures were in place to prevent a small child in its care from wandering out of the premises, onto a nearby road and into the path of the claimant's lorry, thus causing the claimant to suffer personal injury?

An insistence on such precision at this stage will oblige claimants to exercise great care over the way in which they frame a negligence action. Obviously, it would be in their best interests to avoid the notorious omissions rules altogether. If they can base their legal arguments upon something that the defendant has actually done, that is, if they can isolate conduct that is exclusively positive and in relation to which they are reasonably confident that they can satisfy the requirements of duty, breach and causation, then they should go ahead and make this conduct the sole focus of their claim. In this way, the liability rules governing negligent acts can be applied by the court to determine the duty issue. If, however, the defendant's positive conduct is not in itself capable of forming the basis of a sustainable claim, in that it would not satisfy all the elements of negligence, perhaps because it is too far removed from the actual harm complained of, then the claim will be dependent upon the further argument that, in the particular circumstances, there was also something that the defendant should have done that he or she did not do. If this is the case, then the rules governing omissions must apply. These hybrid cases will differ from those involving 'pure' omissions, that is, those in which the negligence allegations centre solely on the defendant's failure to take a particular course of action, in that the existence of the background positive conduct may make it easier to justify the imposition of a duty of affirmative action.

If, as has just been argued, the term 'omission' should be reserved exclusively for the purpose of referring to the alleged source of the defendant's negligence and so to the type of liability at stake, rather than that of characterising his or her actual conduct, then it would seem prudent to set out specific terms that could be used to describe the actual conduct involved. To this end, it is suggested that appropriate descriptive labels may be derived from the idea of viewing conduct as being either positive or negative in accordance with the nature of its causal relationship to the victim's injury. Active bodily movement that results in the direct infliction of harm or in the exacerbation of existing harm may be referred to as a positive act. It will, of necessity, give rise to the application of the rules governing liability for negligent acts. Movement that is positive only in the sense that it has contributed in some way to the creation of the risk of harm, so that it forms only an indirect causal link with the harm, may be described as positive contributory conduct. It corresponds with the active conduct involved in the hybrid category of negligence just discussed and will clearly give rise to the application of the rules governing negligent omissions. Finally, the conduct involved in 'pure' omissions cases, consisting as it will do of a complete failure to act, will then obviously be described as negative conduct, since it will have only a negative effect on the causation of the harm.

(iii) Clarifying the Duty of Care

Having established what an omission is and when the rules governing liability for omissions will apply, it is proposed to address one more source of terminological confusion in this domain before moving on to look at the actual substance of these rules and how they apply in practice. The issue in question is that of the proper categorisation of the kind of duty of care at stake in an omissions case. In general terms, the duty may always be accurately referred to as one of affirmative action. At a more specific level, however, it is possible to distinguish between different types of affirmative duties on the basis of the circumstances from which they derive. The tendency in academic circles, however, has been to refer indiscriminately to all affirmative duties as examples of a duty to rescue. For the sake of accuracy and clarity, it is submitted that the use of the term 'duty to rescue' should be confined to true rescue cases which, applying the ordinary commonsense definition of rescue, means those involving a sense of urgency and immediacy. To cover non-emergency situations, other terms better describing the type of affirmative duty in issue should be used.

In deciding which terms would be most appropriate in this respect, it is necessary first of all to have regard to the type of situations that commonly give rise to duties of affirmative action. In this respect, it is suggested that a broad distinction may be drawn between those cases in which it is sought to hold the defendant liable for failing to protect the claimant from some particular type of harm, the scope of the duty being determined by the nature of the relationship between them, and those cases in which the defendant is being sued for failing to control a third party who subsequently causes harm to the claimant. This latter duty may either be based upon a special relationship of control between the defendant and the third party or it may arise out of the third party's use of either real or personal property belonging to the defendant or over which the defendant exercises control.

In the first category, the affirmative duty in question may be properly described as a duty to protect. The crucial relationship upon which all such duty questions will centre is therefore that which exists between the defendant and the claimant. The duty to rescue may be regarded as one specific form of this broader duty to protect. In the second category, the duty is clearly one to control, and the crucial duty-forming relationship is therefore that existing between the defendant and the third party.

II. PURPOSE AND UTILITY OF THE NON-LIABILITY RULE FOR OMISSIONS

Addressing then the question of the substantive juridical significance of designating a claim as one concerning an omission, the first point that would have to be made is that, superficially, the law on omissions appears very simple and straightforward. There is really only one rule, and that is that the law of tort does not recognise a duty of care for omissions. As is well known, the effect of such a blanket denial of the existence of a duty of care is to render claims of the type in question non-justiciable. This should, in theory, send out a message to all potential claimants whose allegation of negligence is based upon an omission that there is no point in bringing a claim before the courts because it is simply not going to succeed. The reason that this is not what happens in practice is that this general rule against liability for omissions is subject to a plethora of exceptions which have been established on a very gradual and ad hoc basis. This is encapsulated by the vague generalisations employed to signify when an exception will be recognised. The most common is that of the infamous, undefined 'special relationship'. Claimants rely on this lack of coherency to bring their omissions claims, in the hope that they will be able to fit theirs into one of the established categories of exception, or indeed, even to create a new one.

The stage has now been reached where the exceptions appear to be all but submerging the rule. This has prompted many academics to call into question the utility of retaining it. Indeed, in recent years, the rule has been the subject of some particularly fierce criticism.[1] To address this criticism it is necessary to analyse the arguments that are traditionally put forward in support of the non-liability rule. In making his case for the formulation of a duty to warn, Logie provides a neat summary of these arguments.[2] The first to which he makes reference concerns the role played by the misfeasance/nonfeasance dichotomy in maintaining fundamental distinctions between law and morality.[3] The strength of this argument will clearly be determined by the degree of importance to be attached to the segregation of law and morality in the first place. To Smith and Burns, it constitutes the 'hallmark of English jurisprudence',[4] for they subscribe to the school of thought that advocates the complete separation of the two. This view is founded upon a very strict interpretation of the basic principle that it is not the function of the law to enforce moral values. The obvious criticism to be levelled here is that such an interpretation is too narrow and unnecessarily rigid. Insofar as the law is an instrument of social ordering, the importance of recognising its independence of morality cannot be disputed. For if it is to operate properly in this respect, its content has to be determined by application of sound legal principles which have themselves been formulated in accordance with its overall aims and objectives. That these legal principles may well conflict with moral norms is clearly exemplified by the operation in tort law of the objective notion of fault. However, all that this really means is that law must not be dictated by morality. It does not mean that the two are necessarily incompatible. One need not look too far for evidence demonstrating that often they will coincide. This argument about the rule against liability for omissions playing a vital role in preserving the distinction between law and morality can, therefore, only apply with any force in cases where the sole reason for imposing an affirmative duty is to compel good samaritanism. Where there is an independent legal basis for the duty, it is of little significance.

[1] See, eg, B Markesinis, 'Negligence, Nuisance and Affirmative Duties of Action' (1989) 105 LQR 104.

[2] J Logie, 'Affirmative Action in the Law of Tort: The Case of the Duty to Warn' [1989] CLJ 115.

[3] *Ibid*, at 118.

[4] JC Smith and P Burns, '*Donoghue v Stevenson* – The Not So Golden Anniversary' (1983) 46 MLR 147, at 163.

The second argument detailed by Logie concerns the extent to which affirmative duties restrict the individual's right to liberty. It is said that, by contrast with obligations not to inflict harm, insistence on positive action to benefit others is morally objectionable in that it permits an unjustifiably high level of interference with freedom of action. However, whether this is true in any given case is essentially an empirical matter. What counts as 'justifiable' interference may plausibly be seen in utilitarian terms. From this perspective, a duty of positive action is not unduly restrictive where the overall effect is to maximise liberty. Moreover, as Smith and Burns have pointed out, a positive duty which flows from a specific *voluntary* commitment, or from a particular role or function *voluntarily* assumed, is not, by definition, an unjustifiable limitation on agency.[5] For present purposes, the significance to be taken from this is that the argument about freedom of action clearly does allow for the recognition of a number of legitimate exceptions to the general no-duty-for-omissions rule.

A further, related argument is that the imposition of a duty of positive action may require significant expenditure in terms of time, money and effort. While, again, this may be said to be justified in the case of a commission by the voluntary nature of the defendant's decision to act in the first place, that is, there is implied in this decision a voluntary assumption of all associated burdens and responsibilities, the same cannot be said of an omission. Put in economic terms, in relation to commissions, such expenditure may be properly regarded as part and parcel of the defendant's activity and, moreover, as necessary for the assessment of the true cost of the activity. Economic efficiency requires that activities bear their own costs. Since obligations of affirmative action will often absorb the costs of other harm-producing activities, they are said to create a situation of economic inefficiency. This very argument was discussed by Lord Hoffmann in *Stovin v Wise*.[6] It is significant, however, that although he appeared to attach much credence to it, he recognised that it would not apply to those situations in which the affirmative duty is based upon a particular undertaking on the part of the defendant with concomitant reliance.[7]

The third argument dealt with by Logie centres upon causation. First, it is questioned whether a failure to act can be said to have 'caused' anything at all. Second, the problem of identification of the defendant may be invoked. Generally, the defendant is identified via a direct causal link between his or her negligent behaviour and the claimant's injury. How is this to be done in the absence of such a link? Indeed, the defendant might just be one of a large group of people who were in a position to take positive steps to assist the claimant but failed to do so. However, while such arguments may look good on paper, the practical reality is that they would not even arise for consideration in the vast majority of omissions cases reaching the courts. The reason why the particular defendant has been targeted by the litigation will be self-evident, for it will most

[5] *Ibid*, at 157 (emphasis added).
[6] [1996] 3 All ER 801, at 819.
[7] *Ibid*.

probably form the basis of the claimant's duty arguments. Moreover, the courts have come to accept as sufficient, proof of causation of an indirect nature. Again, therefore, such arguments can be used only, in a fairly abstract way, to justify the absence in our tort system of a general duty to rescue. Otherwise, they are of little substance and by no means cast any doubt upon the large number of exceptions to the rule that are currently in existence.

There is one other important reason, not expressly covered by Logie, behind the general reluctance of our tort system to impose liability for omissions. It is the popular notion that omissions are simply less culpable than commissions. Clearly this argument presupposes that culpability is an essential element of civil responsibility. If it is accepted that the doctrine of corrective justice forms the primary structure of the English law of tort, this is not problematic, although it would perhaps be more accurate to speak in terms of moral blameworthiness rather than culpability. For present purposes, it is fortunate that the matter has already been considered in great detail by Honoré.[8]

Put in very simple terms, Honoré's basic premise is that the degree of blameworthiness to be attached to an omission will be determined by the character of the norm that it violates. Ordinarily, it is worse to violate a norm through a positive act than it is to do so through negative conduct. However, Honoré maintains that it is possible to designate certain norms, which he refers to as 'norms imposing distinct duties', as being so important that their violation by whatever means will attract reproach. On this 'distinct-duties' theory, an omission violating such a norm will be just as blameworthy as a commission in the same instance. This begs the question of how a norm imposing a distinct duty is to be identified in the first place. According to Honoré, one distinction to be made between a distinct duty and a mere background duty imposed by an ordinary norm is that the former is owed to specific persons as dictated by the particular circumstances of the individual agent involved, whereas the latter is owed by each to all. Examples provided of distinct duties are those owed by parents to children,[9] those owed by citizens to their state, and those owed by persons who create dangers to those endangered. The broad conclusion to be drawn from this is that distinct duties are high-ranking social or moral duties in relation to which strong arguments may be advanced in support of their translation into legal duties. The list of such arguments drawn up by Honoré in this respect is fairly typical of that contained in the majority of academic accounts on the subject.[10]

(1) The agent has positively created a risk of harm.
(2) The agent occupies an office or position of responsibility.

[8] T Honoré, 'Are Omissions Less Culpable?', in P Cane and J Stapleton (eds), *The Law of Obligations: Essays for Patrick Atiyah* (Oxford, Clarendon Press, 1991), p 33.

[9] As far as omissions are concerned, exception may be taken to this particular example. See C McIvor, 'Expelling the Myth of the Parental Duty to Rescue' [2000] CFLQ 229.

[10] See, eg, J Logie, above n 2, at 121; JC Smith and P Burns, above n 4, at 157; D Howarth, *Textbook on Tort* (Butterworths, 1995), p 173; MA Jones, *Textbook on Torts* (OUP, 2002), p 53.

(3) The agent is well placed to meet a need, such position creating a situation of dependency.
(4) The agent is the recipient of a benefit.
(5) The agent has given an undertaking.

Honoré's discussion of the relationship between omissions and the notion of blameworthiness serves to reaffirm the conclusions drawn from the analyses of each of the other arguments in support of the omissions rule: that the basic rule against liability for omissions is entirely valid and justifiable, but that against this rule a large number of exceptions must be recognised. It is clear then that the main problem that we are left with concerning the law on omissions is that there is no obvious underlying theme connecting the established exceptions.

Highly critical of this whole area of the law, Markesinis has advocated that the basic rule be dispensed with altogether and that the ordinary principles of negligence be employed to exclude from the liability regime the majority of omissions-based claims.[11] This could usually be done at the duty stage, most notably by stringent application of a specially formulated and tightly construed concept of proximity. Although essentially a sound proposition, such a move would perhaps appear too radical for the English judiciary, given its longstanding and steadfast attachment to the non-liability principle. The alternative would be to entirely rework the exceptions, clearly setting out what the grounds for each of the acceptable exceptions are and ruthlessly rejecting all those scenarios not fitting within those parameters. This would involve methodically going through all the existing case law in which a duty of affirmative action has been recognised and trying to extract the precise grounds on which each one has been based, with the ultimate aim of establishing general categories of exception to the non-liability for omissions rule. Obviously this would be a huge task. Each case in which it was sought to hold the defendant liable for harm which he or she did not directly cause, whether because the harm had been inflicted either by a third party or by an object, or as a result of a natural occurrence, would be relevant. Fortunately, for present purposes, the remit of such a search can be narrowed down significantly, for it would be limited solely to third party liability cases. In effect, then, this is largely what will be attempted in the remainder of this book for, although not all third party liability actions will necessarily involve omissions,[12] it is undoubtedly the case that by far the vast majority, and certainly the most contentious, will.

[11] Above n 1.

[12] As Lunney and Oliphant point out, if the defendant were to provide the third party with the means to injure the claimant, for example, then it is possible that such misfeasance could constitute the sole focus of a negligence action: *Tort Law: Text and Materials* (OUP, 2003), p 441.

2

The *Dorset Yacht* Principles of Third Party Liability and the Exceptional Position of Parents

THE HOUSE OF Lords decision in *Home Office v Dorset Yacht*[1] is widely regarded as the founding case on third party liability. Although not the earliest imposition of such liability, it does constitute the first detailed and explicit discussion of third party liability issues by a superior English court. Often mistakenly interpreted as the main legal authority on third party liability issues generally, the ratio of *Dorset Yacht* in actual fact applies only to persons occupying a position of authority and control over an irresponsible third party, so as to place them under an obligation to control the conduct of that third party and thereby to protect those in close proximity. To this extent, the application of the *Dorset Yacht* principles of third party liability is thus strictly limited. In terms of identifying common examples of control-based relationships to which the *Dorset Yacht* principles could feasibly be applied, it is the parent/child relationship that springs most immediately to mind. However, it will be demonstrated that, in practice, the parental position is actually to be distinguished in this respect. For policy reasons, the courts make special concessions towards parents in an attempt to protect them, as far as possible, from liability in respect of their children. Unlike other custodians of irresponsible charges, therefore, parents are not subject to a straightforward application of the *Dorset Yacht* principles of third party liability.

I. THE *DORSET YACHT* PRINCIPLES OF THIRD PARTY LIABILITY

The claim in *Home Office v Dorset Yacht Co Ltd* arose out of property damage caused by a group of rampaging borstal trainees. Under the supervision and control of three borstal officers, the trainees in question had been taken to

[1] [1970] AC 1004.

Brownsea Island in Poole Harbour to work. During the night when, contrary to their instructions, the officers had allegedly gone to bed and left the boys to their own devices, some of the group sneaked out, stole a yacht and promptly crashed it into another boat. The owners of the damaged boat argued that the officers had been negligent in failing properly to supervise the trainees and duly sued the Home Office, as their employer, on the grounds that it was vicariously liable for their tortious conduct.

In holding the Home Office liable, a majority of the House of Lords (Lords Reid, Morris, Pearson and Diplock, with Viscount Dilhorne dissenting) considered that the particular facts of this case justified the recognition of an exception to the general rule against holding one person liable for the acts of another. Of the five speeches given, it is arguably Lord Diplock's that provides the clearest explanation of the legal basis for the third party liability of the officers. According to Lord Diplock, it was specifically the combination of two special relationships of close proximity (one between the officers and the trainees, and another between the officers and the claimants) and the very high degree of foreseeability that the particular resultant harm would be caused to the specific victims in question that warranted the exceptional imposition of an affirmative duty of care in this case. While the officers' special relationship with the boys was obviously based on notions of authority and control,[2] the special relationship with the claimants was said rather to arise from the proximate location of their boats to the place where the trainees were staying and the fact that this set them apart from members of the public at large by exposing them to a particularly high degree of risk in the not unlikely event of the boys escaping. The officers' relationship with the trainees thus warranted the imposition on the officers of the basic obligation to control the trainees' conduct, and their relationship with the boat owners then justified the specific application of this obligation to the claimants. On the facts, breach of duty was then very easily established.

Lord Reid, rather confusingly, discussed the claim wholly in terms of remoteness issues. It is submitted that this was incorrect on his part. There is a clear distinction to be drawn between the roles of duty and legal causation requirements in third party liability actions. In essence, the relevance of these requirements will differ depending on the nature of the third party claim against the defendant. Where the defendant is being sued for failing to prevent harm that has been wholly inflicted by a third party, it will be duty arguments that take centre-stage, for the main issue to be determined is whether there are sufficient grounds linking the defendant with the third party and the victim, so as to make the defendant the main target for legal responsibility as opposed to anyone else. Such actions may be defined as standard third party liability claims. Where, however, the defendant in question has already wrongfully caused some identifiable harm to the claimant prior to the intervention of the third party harm-doer,

[2] Lord Pearson explicitly stating that '[t]he borstal boys were under the control of the Home Office's officers, and control imports responsibility', at 1055.

and the issue to be determined is whether the defendant can be made liable for any *additional* harm that has been caused by the third party to the claimant,[3] it is the *novus actus interveniens* principles of legal causation that need to be applied. As the claim in *Dorset Yacht* clearly fell within the former category, the main issue to be determined was accordingly that of duty.

Although Lord Reid confused the duty and causation issues in *Dorset Yacht,* he is nevertheless to be credited with establishing the current test for determining whether a third party intervention amounts to a *novus actus,* namely, the 'high likelihood' test. In the words of Lord Reid:

> [W]here human action forms one of the links between the original wrongdoing of the defendant and the loss suffered by the claimant, that action must at least have been something very likely to happen if it is not to be regarded as a *novus actus interveniens* breaking the chain of causation.[4]

It must be recognised, however, that this causation principle is specifically excluded by Lord Diplock's duty of care analysis, in that it would be nonsensical to decide that there is a duty to control the acts of a third party but then to hold that the third party conduct breaks the chain of causation. Therefore, in third party liability claims involving a specific affirmative duty of control, it will not be open to the defendant to raise a *novus actus* argument.[5] At the legal causation stage, therefore, the only issues for discussion will be that of ordinary remoteness, that is, reasonable foreseeability of the type of harm, or *novus actus* arguments concerning either a natural event or conduct on the part of the claimant or an outside party other than the third party perpetrator in question.

To sum up *Dorset Yacht,* it may be said to provide authority for the existence of a duty to control the actions of a third party in situations where it can be demonstrated:

(1) that there is a very strong relationship of authority and control between the 'responsible' defendant and the 'irresponsible' third party perpetrator;
(2) that the claimant comes within a narrowly defined class of potential victims; and
(3) that the harm-causing conduct of the third party was highly foreseeable in the circumstances.

In terms of applying this *ratio decidendi* to other relationships of authority and control over an irresponsible other, and leaving aside potential public authority defendants, who will be dealt with separately in chapter 6, the obvious subjects

[3] See, eg, *Lamb v Camden London Borough Council* [1981] QB 625.
[4] [1970] AC 1004 at 1030.
[5] In the same vein, note that in *Reeves v Commissioner of Police of the Metropolis* [1999] 3 WLR 363, the House of Lords held that where a specific duty is owed to prevent an act of suicide, it would be 'self-contradictory' to decide that such an occurrence could then amount to a *novus actus interveniens.*

would be private carers of children or mentally impaired adults.[6] As has been stated already, while it may be thought that the parental position would provide the paradigm example of this form of third party liability, in practice it turns out that parents are actually to be distinguished from other custodians of irresponsible charges. It is to the parental position that the focus of this chapter will now turn.

II. THE LIABILITY OF PARENTS IN RESPECT OF THEIR CHILDREN

Characterised as it is by notions of responsibility, authority and control, the parental role would seem to provide a strong foundation for the imposition of two distinct duties of affirmative action involving their children: (1) to protect them from harm caused by third parties; and (2) to control them in order to prevent harm to third parties. That such duties do exist as a matter of law is a perception shared by many legal academics.[7] An analysis of the relevant case law, however, reveals a different picture. The whole idea of parental liability is quite exceptional in English tort law, with such judicial reticence being seemingly explicable on the basis of policy considerations. There is a general belief that the domain of family life is one area of social interaction where the negative consequences of strict legal regulation are likely to outweigh the associated benefits. This is because the family unit is regarded as one of the foundational institutions underpinning society, with family harmony accordingly being treated as sacrosanct. Concerned to promote this ideal, the courts have reasoned that by refusing to intrude into family affairs in the absence of compelling reasons to do so, they will effectively be encouraging and protecting the existence of stable family relationships. Clearly such reasoning can be criticised as overly simplistic. Nevertheless, it has to be recognised that it underlies the current English approach to parental liability.

To analyse in detail the law on the third party liability of parents in respect of their children, it is necessary to approach separately the two different types of such liability. For, as mentioned above, the duty to protect the child from third parties and the duty to protect third parties from the child are two entirely distinct and independent duties. It is of crucial importance at the outset to realise that the law does not treat these obligations as inextricably linked, in that the recognition of one will not necessarily indicate the existence of the other.

[6] See, eg, *Bye v Bates* (1989) 51 SASR 67 (duty of neighbour to protect child in his temporary care); *Arnold v Teno* (1978) 83 DLR (3d) 609 (duty of ice-cream vendor to protect four-year-old customer from oncoming traffic); *Slater v Buckinghamshire County Council* [2004] EWCA Civ 1478 (duty of minibus operator in collecting disabled passenger to protect that passenger from oncoming traffic).

[7] See, eg, D Howarth, *Textbook on Torts* (Butterworths, 1995), p. 173; JG Fleming, *The Law of Torts* (Sydney Law Book Co, 1998), p 171 and; MA Jones, *Textbook on Tort* (Oxford University Press, 2002), p 59.

(i) The Liability of Parents to their Own Children for Harm Committed by Others[8]

The paucity of authority on the issue of the duty of parents to protect their children is a point of significance in itself.[9] In the space of nearly 300 years, there have been just two reported English decisions in which a parent has been sued in respect of injuries sustained by his or her own child.[10] The first is the seventeenth-century case of *Ash v Ash*,[11] in which a mother was successfully sued by her daughter for the torts of assault, battery and false imprisonment. It is, however, of little relevance to the present discussion for it merely provides authority for the undisputed proposition that parents may be liable to their children for intentional torts perpetrated directly by *them* on the child. In such cases, a specific duty is owed and the liability of the parent is the same as that of any stranger, the relationship of parenthood being merely incidental.[12] Whether parents are under a positive duty to protect their children at all times from foreseeable dangers relates rather to the general issue of liability for negligence, based on a failure to prevent injury being sustained by the child. Fortunately, this issue is directly addressed by the second reported decision.

In *Surtees v Kingston-upon-Thames Borough Council*,[13] the adult claimant brought an action in negligence against her former foster parents[14] and against the local authority that had placed her with them, for serious injuries sustained to her foot when she was just two years old.[15] It had been clearly established that the injuries had been sustained through immersion in water hot enough to cause third degree burns, but the facts as to the actual circumstances surrounding the injury were unclear. The claimant alleged that while left unattended she must have placed her foot in a basin containing hot water, whereas the foster parents

[8] For a more detailed discussion of this subject, see C McIvor, 'Expelling the myth of the parental duty to rescue' [2000] CFLQ 229.

[9] Yeo has suggested that the main reason why children rarely sue their parents is that parents are not usually insured against liability, since most household policies exclude liability to members of the insured's family residing with him or her: 'Am I My Child's Keeper? Parental Liability in Negligence' 1998 AJFL Lexis 12, at 2. As Yeo also points out, this insurance issue was indeed noted by the South Australian Court of Appeal in its rejection of a parental liability claim in *Robertson v Swincer* (1989) 52 SASR 356.

[10] In *S v Ward & Another* [1995] 1 FLR 862, the claimant brought an action in negligence against her mother for failing to protect her from the abuse she suffered as a child at the hands of her father. The matter was never substantively litigated, however, for the only issue to actually come before the court was that of statutory limitation. There is also the Scottish case of *Young v Rankin* [1934] SC 499, in which an infant claimant brought an action against his father for injuries sustained due to his negligent driving.

[11] (1696) Comb 357.

[12] See the dictum of Lucas J to this effect in the Australian case *Cameron v Commissioner for Railways* (1974) Qd R 480.

[13] [1991] 2 FLR 559.

[14] The court accepted that the duty owed by a foster parent is the same as that owed by an ordinary parent.

[15] In the case of children, the ordinary limitation period of three years applicable to tort claims does not start to run until the age of majority has been attained: Limitation Act 1980, s 28.

argued that she had somehow activated the hot tap herself after placing her foot in the wash basin.

However, the significance of the decision, for present purposes, relates to the unanimous finding that the parental duty of care is not an automatic duty and that its existence must be determined on a case-by-case basis, the appropriate test being reasonable foreseeability of injury of the type sustained. In finding that the foster mother was subject to a duty of care, the Court of Appeal considered it to be of crucial importance that she had been in a position to exercise de facto control over the claimant, which suggests that the question of control may, in itself, be a determinative factor. The natural conclusion is that the parental duty of protection arises solely in certain circumstances and is not recognised as a general duty.

Indeed, it seems that even where such a duty is held to exist, it may be so easily fulfilled as to make it almost incapable of giving rise to liability for 'negligent parenting'. In *Surtees*, the majority avoided holding the foster mother liable on the basis that the injury was too remote to be attributed to any fault on her part. In their refusal to characterise as negligent 'the care which ordinary, loving and careful mothers are able to give to individual children, given the rough and tumble of home life',[16] the judges were evidently motivated by a desire to avoid the imposition of an 'impossibly high' standard of care on parents and to preserve family harmony.

(a) A Commonwealth Perspective

In the absence of any other English authority on the subject, it is instructive to consider at this point how the question has been dealt with by other Commonwealth courts, as, having been confronted with the issue in a greater number of cases, they have had the opportunity to give it more detailed examination. It is worthy of note that in the cases about to be discussed, the action in negligence against a parent was actually instigated by a third party, usually an insurance company, in the form of contribution proceedings. The general pattern is that a child victim sues a third party for injuries sustained and this first defendant, in seeking a contribution to any damages payable, alleges that the parents are also partly responsible because they negligently failed to protect the child.[17] This is an important point because it has been suggested that one of the main policy arguments against holding parents liable in negligence to their children is that, in practice, to allow such actions would actually operate to the financial detriment of the child.[18] For, if such allegations were to arise in contribution proceedings, it cannot be denied that to uphold these claims against parents would effectively be

[16] [1991] 2 FLR 559 at 583, 584 per Browne-Wilkinson V-C.

[17] In England and Wales, this issue is governed by s 1(1) of the Civil Liability (Contribution) Act 1978.

[18] Yeo, above n 9, p 22.

to reduce the award of damages to which the child victim would otherwise be entitled.

The two leading Commonwealth decisions on the parental duty of care are that of the New Zealand Court of Appeal in *McCallion v Dodd*[19] and that of the High Court of Australia in *Hahn v Conley*.[20] In *McCallion v Dodd*, the four-year-old claimant was struck by a car as he walked along the roadside with his parents, in the dark and against the flow of traffic. While the claimant was to the outside, being led by the hand by his mother, his father was on the inside carrying the baby. The claimant sued the defendant motorist whose insurance company claimed contribution from the boy's father, alleging negligence on his part. In considering the nature of the duty of care owed by the father to his son, the judges offered differing opinions. North P considered that the mere presence of the parent at the scene, coupled with the relationship of parenthood, placed him under a legal duty to ensure the child's safety, whereas Turner and McCarthy JJ approved the Australian view that the basis of the parent's duty of care is no different to that of a stranger and arises only where the parent has assumed responsibility for the child in a particular situation.[21] McCarthy J, in particular, stated that there is no legal duty on a parent *qua* parent to protect and control a child, only unenforceable moral duties.

In ordinary cases, the application of these rules would mean that the fact that the child was in the physical control of one parent at the time of the injury, as where a child is led by the hand, would suffice to exonerate the other parent. In *McCallion*, however, there were special circumstances to be considered because the mother was deaf and the father knew that she was not wearing her hearing aid at the time. In the view of the court, this meant that the father still retained some responsibility towards the child, which imposed upon him a duty of care, which he had failed to discharge.

The judgment of McCarthy J was approved by the majority of the High Court of Australia in *Hahn v Conley*. The case concerned a three-year-old girl who was knocked down by a car as she crossed a road to see her grandfather who was on the other side. The child brought an action in negligence against the motorist, whose insurance company duly claimed contribution from the grandfather, alleging negligence on his part in failing, first of all, to prevent her from wandering onto the road and then in failing to come to her aid when she called out to him from the other side.

While all the judges agreed that the existence of a duty of care depended solely on the particular factual situation, and not on the blood relationship, there was great divergence of opinion as to the significance of the particular facts of the case and the actual application of the concept of foreseeability. In the end, the decision reached by a three-to-two majority was that the grandfather was not

19 [1966] NZLR 710.

20 (1971) 126 CLR 276.

21 See *Cameron v Commissioner for Railways* (1964) Qd R 480 and *DJ Collett v Hutchins* (1964) Qd R 495.

under a duty to the child. Barwick and McTiernan JJ held that, in the circumstances, no legal duty could be imposed in the absence of some positive action on the part of the grandfather, such as calling the child over to him and so leading her into danger. As it stood, all that he could be admonished for was a nonfeasance. Windeyer J disagreed to the extent that he did consider that a duty of care arose, but he concurred in the overall decision not to impose liability because he held that the duty had not been breached.

In their dissenting judgments, Menzies and Walsh JJ held that the grandfather was under a duty and that he had breached it since, as a familiar figure to the child, he should have foreseen that she would attempt to cross the road to reach him.[22]

It is clear from this case that if the relationship of parenthood cannot constitute the source of a duty then the only way in which it can be relevant is in so far as it may influence the nature and extent of the steps necessary to discharge any duty which arises. This means that it can only go to questions of breach and not duty. Typically, it would make little or no difference but, nevertheless, it remains the only way in which the liability of parents towards their children is capable of differing from that of strangers.

Commenting on these decisions, Jane Wright suggests that, in comparison with that of the English courts, the Commonwealth approach to the circumstances giving rise to a parental duty is much narrower. In *Surtees,* the Court of Appeal was at least prepared to accept that having de facto care of a child is enough to place a parent under an obligation of protection.[23] Nevertheless, for present purposes, the most important point is that, even in English law, parents are not held to be under a *general* legal duty to protect their children from foreseeable harm and that if, exceptionally, such a duty does arise, it will rarely lead to liability because fault will be so difficult to establish. Moreover, the much stricter approach adopted by the High Court of Australia in *Hahn* has been largely affirmed in subsequent decisions of the Supreme Court of South Australia and in other Australian jurisdictions.[24]

(ii) The Liability of Parents for Harm Committed by their Children upon Others

The first point of reference in any inquiry on the law governing the liability of parents for the acts of their children has to be the following statement made by Willes J in the nineteenth-century case *Moon v Towers*:

[22] See also J Wright, 'Negligent Parenting. Can My Child Sue?' (1994) JCL 104 at 106 and 107.
[23] *Ibid*, at 107.
[24] *Robertson v Swincer* (1989) 52 SASR 356 and *Towart v Adler* (1989) 52 SASR 373 (SA); *Darcy v Nominal Defendant* (1985) 2 MVR 447 (Queensland); *Anderson v Smith* (1990) 101 FLR 34 (NT); *Kerr v Allen* (1995) *Aust Torts Reports* 81-323 (NSW). All citations are taken from S Yeo, above n 9.

> I am not aware of any such relationship as between a father and a son though the son be living with his father as a member of his family, as will make the actions of the son more binding upon the father than the actions of anybody else.[25]

This sets out the basic rule against general parental liability for a child's conduct in English law. No duty arises on the part of parents to prevent their children from causing harm to third parties simply out of the fact of their parenthood. This is no more than is to be expected, in keeping with the judiciary's traditional aversion to any kind of liability for omissions. Indeed, all that it really confirms is that parents will not be automatically held liable for the wrongdoings of their children. Of more interest, for present purposes, are the exceptions to this basic rule. In this respect, reference must be made to the famous statement of Dixon J in the Australian case *Smith v Leurs*,[26] which is regarded as the seminal judicial pronouncement relating to parental liability. In it, he affirms the absence of any general duty to control the actions of another, but goes on to say that there could be extraordinary circumstances in which 'special relations' give rise to such a duty, the relationship between parent and child in some instances falling into this category:

> [I]t is incumbent upon a parent who maintains control over a young child to take reasonable care so to exercise that control as to avoid conduct on his part exposing the person or property of another to unreasonable danger. Parental control, *where it exists*, must be exercised with due care to prevent the child inflicting intentional damage on others or causing damage by conduct involving an unreasonable risk of injury to others.[27]

From this statement, it is clear that any duty of care owed by parents to third parties will be based on the exercise of parental control. Unfortunately, however, Dixon J does not elaborate any further upon the meaning or content of this notion of control. It is clear that he does not consider parental control to exist in all relationships between a parent and child, so that what he is referring to is not something that arises automatically upon attainment of parenthood. He could be referring to the legal duty to control imposed upon parents as part of their statutorily recognised 'parental responsibility'. If so, then, in the current English context, duties of affirmative action in respect of a child would be imposed only upon persons exercising such responsibility, as a matter of law, under section 3(1) of the Children Act 1989. Alternatively, he could be referring simply to parents who, in a given situation, are able to exercise de facto control over their children. It would then have to be further questioned what degree of de facto control would be required in any given scenario to found a duty of affirmative action. Or perhaps he means to limit such duties to persons who have both parental

25 (1860) 141 ER 1306.
26 (1945) 70 CLR 256.
27 *Ibid*, at 262 (emphasis added).

responsibility and de facto control at the relevant time. A further complicating factor is that Dixon J gives no indication of the particular form such a duty would take, in terms of nature and extent. What would it involve? Mere supervision or something more?

To fill in these gaps it is necessary to turn to the case law. The House of Lords decision in *Carmarthenshire County Council v Lewis*[28] is commonly regarded as the leading English authority on the parental duty to control. This interpretation of the case is, however, to be disputed. The case involved a young child who, as a result of an unlocked gate, was able to stray from the playground of his nursery school, onto a busy road, and to thereby cause the death of a lorry driver who swerved to avoid him. The wife of the deceased brought an action for damages against the education authority responsible for the nursery, alleging that it was either directly or vicariously liable for the death. While the direct liability argument was based on the duty of the authority to ensure that there was adequate security to prevent nursery children getting onto the road, its alleged vicarious liability was said to stem from the negligence of the teacher involved in leaving the child unattended and enabling him to wander off. It is crucially important to recognise that only the direct liability argument succeeded and that, in this context, the House went to some lengths to distinguish the potential dangers of the school setting from that of the home, with Lord Goddard specifically stating that '[t]here is no analogy between a school playground and the home in this respect'.[29] If any analogy with the parental position were to be drawn in the circumstances, it would be with the position of the teacher and, for present purposes, the unanimity of the Law Lords that she was not to be regarded as negligent in the circumstances is thus highly significant. Referring once again to Lord Goddard's speech, he described her duty as being that of a careful parent, and expressly stated that it would not have been negligent for a mother in similar circumstances to have left her child momentarily unattended.[30] Moreover, a claim against a parent arising out of a very similar scenario has since arisen for consideration before Birmingham County Court. In *Palmer v Lawley*,[31] a child escaped onto the street from an unlocked gate at his house and caused a road accident in which the claimant was injured. Declining to hold the mother liable, the district judge held that liability would impose too high a burden on parents and would be contrary to public policy.

The dearth of English authority on the subject thus makes it necessary, as before, to take the analysis further afield and include the jurisprudence of the Commonwealth courts. It is significant that all the cases that deal directly with the issue of parental liability are based on a similar factual scenario, for this may lead to the conclusion that it is the only type of situation in which parental liability may arise. This is where a child has caused harm to the claimant through

[28] [1955] AC 549.
[29] *Ibid*, at 562.
[30] *Ibid*, at 561.
[31] [2003] CLY 2976.

the misuse of a dangerous object, and an action in negligence has been brought against the parents for allowing the child to have possession of the object and then exercising inadequate supervision. It appears that, in determining whether a parent is under a duty of care in such circumstances and whether or not his or her conduct is to be construed as constituting a breach of duty, the courts are generally influenced by a number of common factors. These are, in particular: the circumstances in which the child obtained the object; the nature of the object; and the age and general disposition of the child. It is possible to divide the cases into three separate categories, from which a series of patterns can be seen to emerge. The categories are:

(a) Entrustment;
(b) Accessibility; and
(c) Unknown possession.

(a) Entrustment

Entrustment refers to cases in which the defendant parent either gave the object to the child or was aware that the child had the object and allowed him or her to retain possession of it. It is in these cases that the liability of the parent is most likely to be established. This stands to reason, since entrustment can quite easily be construed as amounting to a clear and positive contribution to the risk of the harm occurring, which in turn makes a duty to control easier to establish. In assessing breach of duty, the most important consideration for the courts appears to be the nature of the object involved. Whether a finding of fault will be made therefore depends to a large extent on whether the object is to be classified as one that is dangerous per se or merely as being potentially dangerous if misused. The entrustment cases may, therefore, be further subdivided according to this classification of the instrument causing the harm.

An example of an object that the courts consider to be dangerous per se is a gun. Where such an object is involved, the liability of the parent is often established on the mere fact of allowing the child to be in possession of the weapon, without anything more. In *Newton v Edgerley*,[32] a 12-year-old boy bought a shotgun with his father's approval and, in direct disobedience to his father's orders not to use the gun outside their farm, he took it with him on an outing with some friends. Walking along, another boy tried to take the gun off him and, in the process, accidentally pulled the trigger with the result that the claimant was shot in the leg. The father of the boy who owned the gun was held to have been negligent in that either he should have forbidden the use of the gun altogether or else, anticipating his son's disobedience, he should have given careful instruction to the boy as to the use of the weapon to ensure that he did not represent a danger to others. It is difficult to gauge what level of instruction would have been needed to satisfy the court that the boy had been rendered totally safe in the use

[32] [1959] 1 WLR 1031.

of the gun. It is submitted that, even if the father had given further safety instructions, the same result would have been reached. Such a conclusion is supported by a much earlier decision in which a master was held liable for injuries caused by his maidservant through her use of a gun.[33] The court considered that either he should have rendered the weapon totally harmless before entrusting it to her or he should have prevented her from using it altogether. Waller considers that had it been the defendant's own *child* who had caused the harm, the same principle would have applied.[34]

A further decision in this respect is that of the British Columbia Court of Appeal in *Edwards v Smith*.[35] In this case, a father who bought a spring gun for his children was held liable for the actions of his son in injuring the claimant through the use of the gun. This was so despite the fact that the son had acted in direct disobedience to his father's orders not to use the gun unsupervised. More active control on the part of the father was required to discharge the duty, such as, presumably, the taking of positive steps to ensure that the boy was not able to use the gun unsupervised. O'Halloran JA stated that the father incurred such responsibility 'as he permitted a dangerous thing to come into the hands of an immature boy without control under circumstances in which he should have anticipated … that harm might be done to the … third party'.[36] The duty to control was directly linked to the tender age and immaturity of the child perpetrator. In this context, reference must be made to the speech of Goodman J in the Canadian case of *Ryan v Hickson*.[37] Referring specifically to cases of the type being described, he said that the parents are liable because they are to be regarded, in the circumstances, as having direct control of the object causing the harm. This makes them personally responsible to the victim. In support of this, the decision in *North v Wood*[38] may be cited. The claimant's puppy was attacked and killed by a dog owned by the defendant's daughter. The dog was known to be savage and had previously attacked other dogs. The action in negligence against the father failed. His daughter was aged 17 at the time and was considered by the courts to be old enough to exercise control over the dog herself. The implication is that if she had been younger the decision might have been different.

That the liability of parents in allowing their children to be in possession of dangerous objects is no different from the liability of a stranger in this respect is exemplified by the decision in *Burfitt v Kille*.[39] In this case, a shopkeeper who sold a pistol and some cartridges to a 12-year-old boy was held liable for injuries occasioned to a third party by the boy through the use of the weapon. His liability was based on the sole fact of having made the sale. The court held that, while in

[33] *Dixon v Bell* (1816) 5 M & S 198.

[34] PL Waller, 'Visiting the Sins of Children: The Liability of Parents for Injuries Caused by Their Children' (1963) 4 Melbourne University Law Review 17 at 26.

[35] (1941) 1 DLR 736.

[36] *Ibid*, at 745.

[37] (1974) 55 DLR (3d) 196.

[38] [1914] 1 KB 629.

[39] [1939] 2 All ER 372.

ordinary cases where dangerous articles are sold, the seller is under a duty to third parties likely to be injured by such weapons to warn buyers of the potential dangers involved in the use of the object, where the customer is a young child, the matter is taken one step further in that the seller must refrain from selling the article at all. This establishes the age of the child as a decisive factor in the determination of liability.

Similarly, in the Australian case of *Curmi v McLennan*,[40] a father who allowed his son and some of his friends to stay unsupervised in a boathouse which was owned by him and in which he kept a loaded gun was held liable for the actions of *both* his son *and* another boy in using the gun to injure a third party. His duty of care obviously arose out of his actions in providing the boys with a dangerous object.

Where the object inflicting the damage is not dangerous in itself but rather has the potential to be dangerous if mishandled by its user, different considerations apply, with a lesser duty of care being imposed upon the parents. It would seem to consist of a simple obligation to warn and instruct, usually without the further need to supervise. Typical instruments falling into this category are airguns, pellet guns and catapults. In *Beebee v Sales*,[41] a 15-year-old boy using an airgun shot and blinded the claimant in one eye. The boy's father was held liable for the harm. It is significant, however, that there was no negligence alleged on his part in allowing his son to be in possession of the weapon. The particulars of the claim related rather to his actions in permitting his son to continue to use it after he had received a warning about the potential hazards, for a neighbour whose window had been broken by the boy through the use of the gun had already made a complaint to the father. Thus it would appear that, even if Lush J was 'far from saying that even if the father had not been warned beforehand, there would have been no negligence on his part',[42] this factor, if it was not decisive of liability, at least influenced to a large extent the decision of the court. Several subsequent decisions lend support to this proposition.

In the famous Australian case *Smith v Leurs*,[43] the parents of a boy younger than the defendant's son in *Beebee* were held not liable for the eye injury sustained by the victim as a result of an accident caused by their son's use of a catapult. Although the court held that the knowledge of the defendants that their son was in possession of such a weapon placed them under a duty to third parties to control his actions, this duty was discharged by the simple act of issuing warnings to the boy about the dangers of using the catapult and receiving assurances from him that he would only use it against the house wall.

Similarly, in *Donaldson v McNiven*,[44] a boy who was again younger than the defendant's son in *Beebee* also blinded his victim using an airgun, and his father

40 [1994] 1 VR 513.
41 (1916) 32 TLR 413.
42 *Ibid.*
43 Above n 26.
44 [1952] 2 All ER 691.

was held not to have been negligent. The father's duty to take care for the safety of third parties by supervising and controlling his son was also fulfilled by the simple act of exacting a promise from the boy that he would only use the gun in the cellar. The statement of Lord Goddard CJ that '[h]e cannot be watching his son all day and everyday, nor is there any obligation on him to do so'[45] illustrates clearly the reluctance of the courts to impose onerous duties on parents.

It is instructive to draw a contrast here between the decision in *Donaldson* and that in *Newton v Edgerley.*[46] In the latter case, an express prohibition issued by the father did not suffice to exonerate him from liability, since the weapon involved was classified as inherently dangerous. The differences in the ages and character of the children involved in both cases provided a further ground upon which the House of Lords in *Donaldson* was able to distinguish *Newton,* in that in *Donaldson* the boy in question was older and more mature. This evidently made it more reasonable for the defendant father to rely on the promise given by him.

Gorely v Codd[47] similarly involved an injury caused by the improper use of an airgun, although this time by a mentally impaired 16½-year-old boy. The action against the father was based on his alleged negligence in allowing his mentally incompetent son to possess such a weapon and then failing adequately to supervise him or instruct him in the use of it. True to form, the court took a very lenient approach to the question of the father's liability. It held that his conduct was not unreasonable because, although his son was academically impaired, in all other respects he was a normal boy. Indeed, Nield J appeared to be particularly persuaded by the good character of the youth, describing him at one point as a 'decent young person' who was not prone to violence. This seemed to make the judge more favourably disposed toward the defendant father, as though these attributes of the son were necessarily an accurate reflection of the father's good parenting skills. He thus held that sufficient instruction had been given and that, incredibly, supervision was not necessary.[48]

Thus the English cases indicate that, in the absence of special circumstances, the duty of care placed on parents by reason of allowing their children to be in possession of potentially dangerous objects is very easily discharged. Commonwealth courts would appear to adopt a more stringent approach.[49] In *Starr v Crone,*[50] a British Columbia case, an 11-year-old boy who had been given an airgun by his father wilfully shot and injured the claimant in the eye. After carefully reviewing the existing authority on the subject, Wilson J summed up the

[45] *Ibid,* at 692.

[46] Above n 32.

[47] [1967] 1 WLR 19.

[48] See also, *Rogers v Wilkinson* (1963) *The Times,* January 19 (airgun, father not liable).

[49] For example, in *LaPlante v LaPlante* (1995) 125 DLR (4th) 569, a father who allowed his inexperienced son to drive a car in treacherous icy conditions with some of his younger children in the back was held liable for the injuries suffered by the children when the car crashed. The defendant's liability was, however, based specifically on a breach of the duty of care he owed to the victims as his children to protect them, rather than on a breach of any duty to control the actions of his son.

[50] (1950) 4 DLR 433.

legal position as being that it is negligent to entrust a dangerous weapon to a young boy unless it is proved: (a) that he was properly and thoroughly trained in the use of the weapon, with particular regard to using it safely and carefully; and (b) that the boy was of an age, character and intelligence such that the father might safely assume that he would understand and obey the instructions.

In ordinary cases, where the injury has been caused by a simple act of carelessness on the part of the child, the giving of detailed instructions is generally enough to satisfy the court of the reasonableness of a parent's conduct. The actual decision in *Starr*, however, demonstrates that additional principles apply where the child has demonstrated some form of malice. In such cases, parental liability is more likely to be established. Wilson J considered that such a gross misuse of the weapon gave rise to a strong initial presumption that the boy in question was not of a character and mentality to understand the instructions given.[51] In order to rebut the presumption, express evidence to the contrary was required, and it was not forthcoming in this case. In particular, Wilson J stated that he would have liked the boy to have appeared as a witness in court so that he could have had the opportunity to assess him personally.

The notion of being under a duty to give detailed instructions as to the use of a dangerous object, and further to ensure that the child is capable of following them, was also taken up by the Ontario Supreme Court in *Ryan v Hickson*.[52] In this case, two fathers were held liable for the damage caused by their children in driving snowmobiles. In considering whether their children were sufficiently trained in the safe operation of such machines, the defendants should have taken into account 'the ordinary character of boys twelve to fourteen years of age, their general aptitude for mischief, their desire for excitement, their lack of good and mature judgment and propensity for irresponsible acts in the use of motorised vehicles.'[53] This case would also suggest that the Canadian courts place parents under a stricter duty of supervision than their English counterparts.[54]

That the nature of the object being entrusted to a child similarly affects the liability of strangers is evidenced by *Ricketts v Erith Borough Council*.[55] Like *Burfitt v Kille*,[56] it was concerned with the liability of a shopkeeper for selling to a child an object subsequently used to injure a third party. In this case, however, the object in question was a bow and arrow, which was not considered to be dangerous per se. The court, in consequence, held that the shopkeeper was not under any duty of care, either to the boy or any other person. This case also provides an example of the rather ridiculous lengths to which the courts are

[51] Indeed, in holding the defendant father liable, Wilson J distinguished the facts of the case from an earlier decision, *Turner v Snider* (1906) 16 Man R 79, in which a father who had entrusted a shotgun and some shells to his son was exonerated. He pointed to the fact that in *Turner* the act committed by the boy was one of mere negligence and not a wilful assault.

[52] (1974) 55 DLR (3d) 196.

[53] *Ibid*, at 207.

[54] See also, *Ingram v Lowe* (1975) 55 DLR (3d) 292.

[55] [1943] 2 All ER 629.

[56] Above n 39.

sometimes prepared to go in treating the perceived disposition of the child as being relevant to questions of breach and duty. In arriving at his decision, Tucker J made a point of saying that the young boy in question was 'intelligent and bright-looking'.[57] This was evidently meant to imply that he would have given the defendant no cause for concern in selling him the bow and arrow. It is extremely doubtful whether the defendant would have been able to make such an assessment of the boy in the space of a single transaction, or that he would even have been inclined to, for that matter. As such, it is unrealistic to think that this influenced in any way his decision to sell the weapon to the boy. It must also be questioned how it is possible to discern that someone is 'bright-looking', and whether there is necessarily any direct correlation between the facial expressions of a child and his or her behaviour. Indeed, are not bright children often the most mischievous?

(b) Accessibility

The category of accessibility deals with cases in which parents leave objects in places where they are accessible to children. The children then get hold of the object for themselves and use it to cause harm to a third party. Since the behaviour of parents in this category is, by comparison with cases of entrustment, less reproachable in that their contribution to the creation of the risk of harm will have been much more indirect, it stands to reason that their liability is more difficult to establish. Indeed, the cases show that, in such circumstances, the duty of care placed on parents is less onerous again and, more unexpectedly, that it depends to an even greater extent on the nature of the child's character.

In *Hatfield v Pearson*,[58] a 13-year-old boy, in direct defiance of his father's orders and unknown to him, took a rifle that was kept in the house and subsequently injured the claimant as a result of his misuse of it. The British Columbia Supreme Court held that the imputed mischievous nature of young boys made it foreseeable that the defendant's son might meddle with the gun, and this imposed on the defendant a duty to remove it from the boy's physical reach, either by locking it away or hiding it. This decision was, however, overturned by the Court of Appeal, which held that such a duty only arises in special circumstances in which the child in question has previously demonstrated a propensity to 'intermeddle' going beyond that of a generally obedient boy of average intelligence. Otherwise, the placing of a simple moral restraint on the child by giving an order not to touch the dangerous article and securing a promise to that effect is apparently all that a reasonable parent would be expected to do.

Indeed, although it was set out by Lord Esher MR in *Williams v Eady*[59] that, as a general rule, in carrying out their duty of care to children, parents are 'bound to take notice of the ordinary nature of young boys, their tendency to do

[57] *Ricketts v Erith Borough Council*, above n 55, at 631.
[58] (1957) 6 DLR (2d) 593.
[59] (1893) 19 TLR 41.

mischievous actions and their propensity to meddle with anything that [comes] in their way,'[60] it would appear that the courts tend not to apply this principle. It is only really where a child has demonstrated a particular propensity to misbehave that a heightened duty of care is placed on parents. In *Smith v Leurs*, Dixon J considered that society would only expect a parent to take steps to prevent conduct that was reprehensible, for otherwise, the causing of harm by children was simply to be regarded as an 'unavoidable or reasonable incident of vigorous boyhood'.[61]

Waller would also suggest that, despite the constant refusal of the courts to equate children with animals, the fact that they are more inclined to impose liability on parents for harm caused by children shown to be of bad character indicates that the English and Australian courts are influenced, to some extent at least, by considerations similar to those governing the doctrine of *scienter*.[62] He also points out that there is a clear application of the doctrine in several American cases, which he terms the 'vicious child cases'.[63]

That the bad character of the child operates to impose a greater duty on parents to supervise and control is justified on the basis that such parental knowledge, actual or imputed, makes the risk of injury more foreseeable. Should this mean, however, that parents of children who are of generally good character be relieved of all need to take any real steps to control them? As the cases illustrate, harm is just as likely to be caused by obedient children as by mischievous ones. Harm is often caused by children just being children and, hence, irresponsible. Unintentional torts are torts no less than those that are caused intentionally or recklessly and can often be easily prevented through the exercise of adequate supervision and control.

(c) Unknown Possession

This final category deals with cases in which the parents are unaware that the child is in possession of the object causing the harm. Here, it would seem that if parents are placed under any duty of care at all, it is no more than a very slight duty of supervision. *Walmsley v Humenick*[64] illustrates the point. In this British Columbia case, the parents of a five-year-old boy who had shot an arrow from a bow and struck another child in the eye were held to be exempt from liability on the basis that they did not know that their son had such an object. While the mother, who had seen her son whittling the sticks which were later used as arrows, was deemed under a duty to supervise her children as a result, this involved little more than glancing at them through the window from time to time. Indeed, it would seem that, but for the fact of her witnessing this activity,

60 *Ibid*, at 42.

61 (1945) 70 CLR 256 at 263.

62 Starke J in *Smith v Leurs* stated that '[y]oung boys, despite their mischievous tendencies, cannot be classed as wild animals': *ibid*, at 260.

63 Waller, above n 34, at 29.

64 (1954) 2 DLR 232.

there would have been no duty of care at all. In any event, there was none placed on the father. This can only be explained on the basis that all that the father could have been reproached for was a pure omission.

It would also appear that, in these cases, the nature of the child's character is even more significant and that parents are subject to a much lower standard of care. In *Streifel v Strotz*,[65] the British Columbia Supreme Court held that the parents of two youths aged 14 and 15 were not liable for damage caused by their sons arising out of their theft of a car, since the boys had not previously demonstrated a propensity to steal cars. Whittaker J went on to say that even if the parents had known of such a tendency, the onus was then on the claimant to show that there was some reasonable step the parents could have taken to prevent the theft which they had negligently failed to take. He also pointed to the fact that it had not been proved that the parents in question had been 'more than ordinarily lax'[66] in training or supervising their children. The obvious implication is that ordinary carelessness is an acceptable standard of parental care. To establish a breach of duty, therefore, it would seem that claimants are required to show that the conduct complained of was extraordinarily unreasonable rather than just unreasonable. Thus parents, like professionals and public bodies, are set apart as a special category of defendant.

III. CONCLUSION

The courts routinely employ a number of artificial control devices in order to limit as far as possible the liability of parents for the acts of their children. First of all, a rather stringent test of foreseeability of harm is utilised, for liability has been largely confined to cases in which parents were aware of their child's participation in a hazardous activity. By exonerating parents who are oblivious to their children's activities, without making any real inquiry as to whether they should have been more aware in the circumstances, the courts are effectively excluding the ordinary tortious concept of reasonable foreseeability and replacing it with a requirement that amounts almost to inevitability.

To like effect is the implied rule that parents of children of bad character are more likely to be held liable than those whose offspring are said to be generally obedient. Arguably, this view of the relevancy of the general disposition of a child harm-doer is seriously misguided.

Such observations suggest that the courts are willing to impose a duty of care only on persons who are in a position to exercise de facto control, construed not just in the sense of being physically able to take appropriate action at the relevant time but also in the sense of being actually aware of the need to intervene in the

[65] (1958) 11 DLR 667.
[66] *Ibid*, at 668.

first place. Unfortunately, the analysis reveals little else about any additional criteria relating to parental status that the courts consider to be a prerequisite to liability. It is submitted that this is because there are no defined criteria, the courts proceeding rather on an ad hoc basis and, in the majority of cases, applying whatever principles they deem necessary to preclude liability.

Finally, the cases show that even where the courts do recognise a duty, the relevant standard of care is set so low and is so easily discharged as to make it nigh on impossible, in the absence of special circumstances, for a claimant to succeed in an action based on parental negligence. Thus, although the idea of imposing liability for the acts of others may be much more easily justified in the context of the parent/child relationship than in relation to many of the other recognised categories of such liability, parental liability is, paradoxically, probably the most difficult form of third party liability to establish in practice. This is due to the important role played by policy in this domain.

In the context of other similar relationships of authority and control over an irresponsible other which would not be subject to such policy considerations, however, third party liability will be much more easily established in practice. Thus, the potential liability of temporary carers of children, for example, in respect of harm both to their charges and by their charges, is probably much greater than that of the actual parents in question.

3

Third Party Liability of Property Owners

THE EXALTED STATUS of the proprietary right is a defining feature of English private law. Indeed, so heightened is the protection given to this type of interest that the legal system of England and Wales could even be accused of valuing the notion of property more highly than that of personal physical integrity.[1] In view of this heightened protection, the fact that, correlatively, the ownership or control of property also imports a number of responsibilities, to ensure that the property does not, in itself, represent a danger to others, is uncontroversial. Thus, for example, occupiers of land are bound by the occupiers' liability legislation to ensure that their premises are reasonably safe for persons permitted to use them, with an attenuated form of this duty even extending to trespassers.[2]

What is controversial, however, is the idea that the legal responsibilities of property owners[3] can extend to the actions of independent third parties in using the property, so as to give rise to liability in tort for harm caused by these third parties. Common law duties of this nature have, nevertheless, long been recognised in nuisance. More recently, attempts have also been made to establish wider third party proprietary duties in negligence, albeit that these have been largely unsuccessful. Unfortunately, the law in both respects is in a rather confused state, due to the failure of the courts in dealing with these types of claims to put forward consistent lines of reasoning. Indeed, prevalent throughout all of the cases in this domain is a distinct lack of understanding about the normative foundation of these particular forms of third party liability. Crucially, ratios have been misinterpreted and misapplied, and the true nature of the interrelationships between the relevant cases has been obscured. However, a thorough analysis of the case law reveals that a coherent body of founding principles justifying limited instances of third party property liability both in nuisance and in negligence can be identified.

1 See, eg, P Cane, *The Anatomy of Tort Law* (Hart Publishing, 1997), p 131, and P Cane, '"What a Nuisance!"' (1997) 113 LQR 515 at 519.

2 Occupiers' Liability Act 1984.

3 This term is used in the broad sense to refer to any party with a legal interest in land.

I. THIRD PARTY PROPERTY LIABILITY IN NUISANCE

(i) General Principles

There are three basic grounds upon which the liability in nuisance of a property owner who is not directly and personally responsible for the creation of a nuisance may be based:

(1) authorisation of the nuisance;
(2) adoption of the nuisance; and
(3) continuation of the nuisance.

Viewed abstractly, each of these grounds appears relatively straightforward. A property owner is said to authorise a nuisance if he permits to take place on his property an activity which he ought to realise is likely to constitute a nuisance. Thus, in *Tetley v Chitty*,[4] a local authority which granted a lease of its land to a third party, knowing that the land was to be used as a go-karting track, was held liable for authorising the noise nuisance which ensued. Similarly, a property owner 'adopts' a nuisance quite simply if he makes use of it. And lastly, he will be said to continue it if, with actual or constructive knowledge of its existence, he fails reasonably to abate it. In true legal fashion, however, each ground has proven to be rather difficult to apply in practice.

From the descriptions just provided, it is clear that, in the case of either authorisation or adoption, it is at least notionally possible to point to some kind of active involvement on the part of the defendant in the infliction of the harm complained of, and hence to some degree of moral fault, which arguably serves to make a finding of liability against him or her more justifiable in terms of ordinary notions of fairness. The concept of continuation, however, cannot be reconciled with the doctrine of individual responsibility for actions, for liability in such instances is, at its most basic level, predicated purely upon status. Thus, while it may ultimately be determined by notions of fault, it is not founded on fault. Clearly the most contentious of the three grounds, continuation is also the basis of liability with potentially the widest scope, for it can be argued against a property owner who has quite simply done nothing at all. By contrast, the criteria of liability for the other two grounds are more clearly defined. Continuation is, therefore, the ground most likely to be used to argue third party property liability and indeed, over time, to extend its remit.

It is not surprising, therefore, that the courts have tended to apply the concept of continuation rather restrictively. Indeed, it seems that continuation is alone subject to a special rule concerning the nature of the defendant's interest in the land concerned, although this rule is by no means obvious from the case law, the

[4] [1986] 1 All ER 663.

courts having for some reason failed to articulate it clearly. The rule is that only those in legal possession of the land can be liable for continuing a nuisance.[5] In the case of land subject to a lease, therefore, regardless of whether the third party causing the nuisance is a tenant, a trespasser or a mere licensee, the landlord will have no duty to abate and could only be held liable on the basis of authorisation or adoption. What this effectively means is that the concept of continuation will serve to benefit claimants subject to a nuisance caused by a trespasser or a licensee, only insofar as it will give them a choice of parties to sue – either the creator or the occupier. By contrast, where the creator is the occupier, he alone can be sued for a failure to abate.

It is ventured that the rationale behind this distinction may have something to do with the fact that, in practice, unlike the tenant creator, it will generally be difficult to track down the trespasser or the licensee in order to sue them personally. Thus, the victim would be left without any viable course of action at all were he unable to sue the occupier instead. Thus, it may be that this particular rule relating to continuation is motivated to some extent by basic considerations of justice and fairness towards the claimant. Presumably, the issue of ability to abate is also relevant.

In practical terms, it is a simple rule yet clearly an important one. It is to be expected, therefore, that the courts would have no difficulty in applying it consistently. Not so. In *Chartered Trust Plc v Davies*,[6] the landlord of a shopping mall was held liable for continuing a nuisance created by one of its tenants, without any discussion of the fact that occupation is supposed to be a prerequisite to liability on this basis. Perhaps more surprisingly, however, when this case was later drawn to the attention of the Court of Appeal in the important case of *Hussain v Lancaster City Council*,[7] the court affirmed the propriety of the rule but refused to condemn this particular instance of blatant circumvention, instead explaining it away, rather unconvincingly, on the basis that it was a case that involved special facts. It is submitted that the only ground of third party property liability which could feasibly have been argued in this case was that of authorisation.

Furthermore, while it is clear that all three grounds are separate and distinct, there can be identified on the part of both the judiciary and some legal academics a pronounced tendency to elide the distinction between them. Such elision is most evident in relation to the concepts of adoption and continuation. More specifically, the notion of adoption is often referred to as though it were the same thing as continuation.[8] It is submitted that one of the main sources of this error

5 The principal authority for this rule would appear to be *Smith v Scott* [1973] 1 QB 314, as applied in *Hussain v Lancaster City Council* [2000] QB 1.

6 [1997] 2 EGLR 83.

7 [2000] QB 1 at 18–20.

8 See *Lippiatt v South Gloucestershire Council* [2000] QB 51; M Lunney and K Oliphant, *Tort Law, Text and Materials* (OUP, 2003), p 610; and R Bagshaw, 'Private Nuisance By Third Parties' (2000) 8 Tort LR 165.

is a misreading of *Sedleigh-Denfield v O'Callaghan*,[9] a case which will be discussed in detail presently. Suffice to say here that it is regarded as the leading authority on continuation and, as such, is always cited in this context. However, while the principal basis of liability in this case was, undoubtedly, the defendants' failure to abate, there was also evidence of adoption, as the defendants had made use of the source of the nuisance for some considerable time before it actually caused any harm to the victim. It is, therefore, strictly correct to refer to *Sedleigh-Denfield* in terms of both. Presumably, 'continuation and adoption' has simply become a familiar and convenient phrase commonly associated with this case, to such an extent that it is used, unwittingly, even when the case is being discussed solely in terms of continuation. This in turn has led to the use of the phrase in other contexts in which only the concept of continuation is appropriate, and has thus given rise to the misconception that adoption is just another word for continuation.

Such confusion has arguably been further compounded by the decision of the Court of Appeal in *Page Motors Ltd v Epsom and Ewell Borough Council*.[10] This case involved a claim in nuisance against a local authority in respect of a nuisance created on its land by a number of travellers who had for a number of years been camping there illegally. Although it had the legal power to do so, the defendant authority had deliberately refrained from ejecting the offending parties, since to have done so would have been simply to have transferred the problem elsewhere within the area. Clearly, from the point of view of its civic responsibilities, this would not have achieved anything and, indeed, it actually suited the authority to have the travellers remain on the land in question at that time as it gave it a chance to work out how to contain the borough's recognised traveller problem properly and to make the necessary alternative arrangements.

On the facts, this was clearly a classic case of continuation. The authority, as legal occupier, had a duty to abate the undisputed nuisance existing on its property, and this it had failed absolutely to do. That should have been the end of the matter. However, Ackner LJ's legal sensibilities were clearly offended by the authority's rather self-serving attitude, and this seemingly impelled him to reinforce the finding of liability against it. Relying specifically on its admitted motivation for not removing the travellers, he reasoned that, in obtaining a temporal advantage from their continued presence on this particular site, the council was in fact making use of the nuisance complained of so that it could also be regarded as having adopted it. This is clearly erroneous. To adopt a nuisance, a defendant must actively take advantage of the *actual* nuisance or of the source of the nuisance in order to obtain a concrete benefit from it. Here, however, any benefit obtained was not related at all, in any direct sense, to the activities of the travellers constituting the nuisance. Rather it was merely ancillary to its failure to abate. The council exploited the general situation rather than the actual nuisance.

[9] [1940] AC 880.
[10] (1981) 80 LGR 337.

To deliberately decide, in the interests of personal gain, to ignore one's legal obligations is hardly laudable, but it does not amount to active and specific use of particular sources of harm to others.

Quite simply, Ackner LJ tried to stretch the notion of adoption too far. What is most worrying about this is that he appears to have succeeded, for this aspect of the decision has never been challenged. The result is that an essentially straightforward concept has become unnecessarily complicated. Construed so broadly, its scope is now vulnerable to further inappropriate manipulations.

Finally, it is necessary to mention one other operational difficulty which appears to afflict all three grounds of liability but which has arisen for discussion particularly in relation to continuation. This is the issue of whether the nuisance complained of must actually take place on the property owner's land. Rather unhelpfully, the case law on this point is blatantly contradictory.

(ii) The Nuisance Cases

The concept of third party liability in nuisance is long established. For example, in *Attorney-General v Corke*,[11] a property owner was successfully sued by his neighbours in respect of the conduct of a group of travellers occupying his land. Although technically categorised as a *Rylands v Fletcher* decision, *Corke* is often discussed in a nuisance context as most of the judgment handed down was actually concerned with the applicability of nuisance principles. It was a common fact that the conduct in question was of a serious and substantial nature and that it was, in itself, capable of constituting a nuisance. For Bennett J, the principal difficulty as regards making the defendant liable for this nuisance was rather that this conduct had not been carried out on the defendant's land. Obviously, therefore, the judge had assumed this to be a necessary precondition of liability in nuisance. Rather surprisingly, however, he did not actually discuss the basis for the defendant's liability in this instance. He made no mention at all of the notions of authorisation, adoption or continuation, and so it is not clear upon which of these grounds he was actually considering the claim in nuisance. It is submitted that this was a fundamental error which, as regards nuisance, deprived his judgment of all legal substance.

There are tenable grounds for arguing both authorisation and continuation in this case. In his rather short judgment, Bennett J made marked reference to the high degree of foreseeability that the presence of the travellers on the defendant's land would result in the harm complained of in this case. This, taken in conjunction with the fact that the defendant had given the offending parties permission to be there, had provided them with some limited facilities and was moreover making a commercial profit out of them, arguably provided a strong case for authorisation. On the other hand, the general tenor of the judgment would seem

[11] [1933] Ch 89.

to suggest that Bennett J was rather more concerned with the issue of whether there was a duty on the part of the defendant to abate the nuisance, and indeed subsequent courts considering the decision have tended to treat it as an instance of continuation.[12] Either way, for Bennett J, liability was precluded by the fact that the acts complained of had not taken place on the defendant's land. However, having demonstrated himself to be particularly unfavourably disposed towards members of the travelling community generally, he was clearly sympathetic towards the concerns of the claimants and did wish to provide them with a remedy. So he, rather ingeniously, overcame this spatial obstacle by grounding liability instead on the rule in *Rylands v Fletcher*,[13] which sets out a form of strict liability for isolated escapes from property. A triumph of judicial innovation this may have been, but he forfeited any legitimacy the decision may have had by once again failing to elaborate. He did not even explain what the rule was, let alone how it actually applied in this particular instance.

Given that the defendant had brought the travellers onto his land for profit, it could plausibly be argued that there was accumulation for the purposes of *Rylands v Fletcher*, and given his allusion to the high degree of foreseeability that the travellers would cause offence to those in neighbouring properties, it is even possible to see how Bennett J was able to construe them as 'things likely to do mischief if they escape'. But it has to be questioned whether the element of escape can be meaningfully satisfied in this type of scenario. The duty of the defendant under *Rylands v Fletcher* is to prevent an escape, which in itself presupposes a power and an ability to control the thing in question. It is highly debatable whether the defendant in this case had any authority over the travellers so as to control any of their movements at all.[14] That is the difficulty with applying the rule in respect of independent persons, as they are necessarily free agents.

Although the decision has not been openly criticised by another court, it has been rather coolly received. Certainly the *Rylands v Fletcher* interpretation of it has not been used to found any further actions, and indeed subsequent courts have conveniently side-stepped the issue of the propriety of the decision in this respect by following the lead of Pennycuick VC in *Smith v Scott*[15] and construing it as a case of continuation. But, of course, this then brings the spatial issue back into play, for if it is indeed a condition of continuance liability that the nuisance take place on the defendant's land, then obviously the decision in *Corke* cannot stand on this basis either. This would lead inevitably to the conclusion that the case had simply been wrongly decided.

[12] See, eg, *Smith v Scott* [1973] 1 QB 314 at 321, 322, and *Lippiatt v South Gloucestershire Council* [2000] QB 51 at 58.

[13] The rule in *Rylands v Fletcher* provides that 'the person who for his own purposes brings on his lands and collects and keeps there anything likely to do mischief if it escapes, must keep it at his peril, and, if he does not do so, is prima facie answerable for all the damage which is the natural consequence of its escape' (per Blackburn J (1866) LR 1 Ex 265).

[14] It is recognised, however, that, as the *Rylands v Fletcher* rule was, in that era, more clearly seen as a strict liability concept, this may simply not have been considered as a relevant issue at the time.

[15] Above n 12.

It is perhaps of some significance in this respect that *A-G v Corke* was not even cited in the leading case on third party property liability, *Sedleigh-Denfield v O'Callaghan.*[16] There, the local council, in what transpired to be an act of trespass, constructed a culvert in the line of a ditch on the defendants' property. Unfortunately, it installed in the wrong place a grid designed to catch pieces of debris, with the result that the pipe was liable to become blocked. Although several years passed without incident, eventually, after a heavy storm, the culvert did become blocked and water from the ditch flooded the claimant's neighbouring property causing considerable damage. The crux of the claim against the defendants was that they should have been aware of the risk of harm posed by the improperly protected culvert and that, as occupiers of the property, they had a responsibility to remove this risk. In other words, the damage caused by the flooding was to be regarded as a nuisance stemming from an existing state of affairs on the defendants' property which the defendants had a duty to abate. The principal basis of liability was therefore continuation of the nuisance.

Prior to *Sedleigh-Denfield*, the legal position adopted by the courts had quite clearly been that an occupier would not be liable for a nuisance created by a trespasser unless he had allowed it to continue by his act or default. Crucially, mere refusal or neglect was said not to amount to a default for this purpose.[17] In holding the defendants liable in this case, the House of Lords departed dramatically from this position. It is clear from their speeches, however, that the Law Lords were still keen to preserve some link between liability and personal responsibility, or at least some loose idea of fault,[18] and they achieved this in part by making knowledge of the existence of the nuisance a key precondition of liability. Thus, in *Sedleigh-Denfield* itself, if it had not been for the fact that the defendants' employees had been known to have periodically cleaned out the ditch after the culvert had been inserted, the defendants may well have been able to avoid liability by simply disclaiming all knowledge of the existence of the nuisance.

A further concession made by the House in the interests of moral responsibility was its inclusion of the issue of ability to abate as a factor relevant to liability.[19] Having already established that the actual duty to abate would arise on a rather strict basis, what the Law Lords were trying to do here was ensure that the defendant would not be unduly burdened. Thus in determining whether this duty had been fulfilled, the defendant's conduct would be assessed according to a standard of reasonableness. While this test clearly bears a striking resemblance to that arising in ordinary negligence cases, a crucial distinction between the two is that the concept of fault being applied in this particular nuisance context is subjective rather than objective. This means that both the physical and material resources of the defendant will be taken into account, and clearly this should

[16] [1940] AC 880.
[17] *Job Edwards Ltd v Birmingham Navigations Proprietors* [1924] 1 KB 341.
[18] See, in particular, dicta of Lord Atkin at 897.
[19] *Ibid.*

operate to his or her advantage in most cases. Liability for continuation is therefore far from strict.

Clearly, the reason why the idea of holding a property owner liable for a nuisance created by a third party is unpalatable is that it would seem much more appropriate to sue the third party instead, as it is obviously more responsible for the harm. It is submitted, however, that the reason why the decision to impose liability on the property owner in *Sedleigh-Denfield* was so easily reached was that it was not particularly objectionable in this sense to begin with, for the role played by the third party here, although clearly instrumental, was rather remote from the actual harm and was just one of a combination of factors leading to the nuisance. In particular, the heavy rainfall played a crucial role. Moreover, as pointed out by Bright,[20] there is a difference between making a property owner liable for the conduct of a third party which affects the physical state of the land and consequently gives rise to harm to others, and making the defendant liable for the simple bad behaviour of a third party present on the land. Clearly it is much easier to justify the liability of the defendant in relation to the condition of the land.

However, the courts have made it very clear that they regard such distinctions as being of absolutely no relevance to the law on continuation. In *Leakey v National Trust*,[21] the Court of Appeal, affirming what had already been decided by the Privy Council a number of years earlier,[22] stated emphatically that the principles established by *Sedleigh-Denfield* would apply to all cases of continuation, regardless of whether the nuisance was caused by nature or by human agency. And indeed, in *Page Motors Ltd v Epsom and Ewell Borough Council*,[23] a case with no other complicating factors, the Court of Appeal had no hesitation in holding the defendant council liable for the anti-social conduct of travellers camped illegally on its property.

It is submitted that the judiciary has adopted the correct approach in this respect. Property owners should be made to act responsibly as regards every aspect of their property and its use, in terms of how it is likely to affect their neighbours. As regards third party nuisances taking place on their property, it is the property owners who are in the best position to prevent or abate them, for, at least in theory, they should have the legal power to remove such persons.[24] This duty to abate must simply be regarded as one of the burdens of ownership/occupation.

Susan Bright does not agree. Obviously concerned to keep this branch of the law firmly grounded in the notion of individual moral responsibility for one's actions, she has argued that the only situation in which a property owner should

[20] S Bright, 'Liability for the Bad Behaviour of Others' (2001) 21 OJLS 311 at 315.

[21] [1980] 1 QB 485.

[22] *Goldman v Hargrave* [1967] 1 AC 645.

[23] (1981) 80 LGR 337.

[24] The fact that they will generally be able to insure themselves against such risks cannot be ignored either.

be liable in nuisance for the conduct of someone else is where he or she has expressly or impliedly authorised the behaviour in question.[25] To support her argument, she reanalyses some of the existing cases with a view to demonstrating how easily they could be reinterpreted as instances of authorisation rather than continuation. In *Page Motors,* for example, she maintains that the provision of services to the travellers by the defendants, such as a water supply and waste disposal skips, could be said to amount to implicit authorisation. It is submitted that this is to construe the notion of authorisation in terms that are too wide and too vague. If it is to serve any useful purpose, it must be specific to the actual source of the nuisance.

In relation to another case, Bright relies on the precise wording of the following dicta, in particular, the use of the verb 'to allow':

> It may be that the correct analysis, where it is alleged that the owner/occupier of the land is liable for the activities of his licensees, is that he is liable, if at all, for a nuisance which he has created by *allowing* the troublemakers to occupy his land and to use it as a base for causing unlawful disturbance to his neighbours.[26]

Here, she would appear to be reading too much into the judge's particular choice of vocabulary. Given that the defendants had not consented to the presence of the troublemakers on their land in the first place,[27] simply failing to remove them once they found out they were there could clearly not, in itself, be said to amount to authorisation. It is just too weak an argument. It is, moreover, contradicted by authority. The decision in *Smith v Scott*[28] would indicate that it is only in exceptional circumstances that the courts will uphold a claim of authorisation in cases involving third parties, the test being virtual certainty that the nuisance will occur, and not just high likelihood. The case itself involved an action against a local authority landlord in respect of the conduct of a problem family that it had housed next to the claimants. Representatives of the council openly admitted in court that they had known that the family in question had a reputation for engaging in extremely anti-social behaviour and that it had actually been anticipated that they would cause a nuisance at this address. It was nevertheless held that this did not justify a finding that the council had authorised the nuisance.

Moreover, it may be questioned whether there is anything to be achieved by reinterpreting these cases as instances of authorisation. By stretching the notion of authorisation to the extent that it more or less mirrors the standard interpretation of continuation, Bright is arguably ensuring that the outcomes will always remain the same regardless of which route is taken. This will go no way towards

[25] Above n 20, at 320.

[26] *Lippiatt v South Gloucestershire Council* [2000] QB 51 at 61 per Evans LJ (her emphasis).

[27] Contrast *A-G v Corke,* in which the defendant had given the offending third parties express permission to be on his land.

[28] [1973] 1 QB 314.

achieving her stated aim of reducing the number of instances of property owner liability for the acts of third parties.

If, however, liability for the bad behaviour of trespassers and licensees is to be admitted, it will need to be very tightly controlled. The property owner's legal responsibilities must remain strictly linked to the use of the land. It is submitted that, considered in this context, the answer to the question posed earlier as to whether the existence of the nuisance on the defendant's property is to be regarded as a prerequisite to liability has clearly to be 'yes'. To permit otherwise would simply result in the tort of nuisance becoming dangerously denaturised. Ample proof of this is provided by two recent cases.

The nuisance action in *Hussain v Lancaster City Council*[29] revolved around an orchestrated campaign of violence and harassment perpetrated against the owners of a small shop situated on a housing estate. The owners sought to hold the local council liable in nuisance[30] for the harm they suffered as a result of this campaign on the basis that most of the culprits were either tenants of the council living on the estate or else persons living with tenants. Such relationships, they argued, placed the council under a duty to abate the nuisance, with particular emphasis being placed in this respect on the council's power, as landlord, to evict the troublemakers.

Before moving on to discuss the decision of the Court of Appeal, it is necessary to address briefly the significance of the defendant's status as a public authority. It is submitted that most of the academic commentaries on this case have accorded undue weight to this factor, and that this has resulted in unnecessary obfuscation of matters that are, in essence, entirely straightforward. Although this was in no way implied by the Court of Appeal in the case, it appears to have been assumed by some academics that special principles concerning the liability of public bodies in respect of the use of their statutory powers, such as those derived from *X & ors v Bedfordshire County Council & ors*,[31] would have to be applied in this case in order to determine whether the nuisance claim was even justiciable in the first place.[32] But in *Hussain*, the defendant council was not being sued in respect of its exercise of a public law function. It was being sued rather in its essentially private law capacity as a landlord, and as such was merely subject to the same rules in nuisance as any private landlord, at least as regards the existence of its basic obligations. It is recognised, however, that policy concerns may have a role to play in relation to the fulfilment of these

[29] [2000] QB 1. For a (not altogether convincing) criticism of the *Hussain* decision, and in particular the rule limiting liability for continuing a nuisance to occupiers, see J Morgan, 'Nuisance and the Unruly Tenant' (2001) 60 CLJ 382.

[30] They also brought an action in negligence against the council, but this was dismissed, rather perfunctorily it may be said, on the ground that it would not be fair, just and reasonable to impose a duty of care in the circumstances. Indeed, the judgments on this issue were so mundane and routine as to be of little or no academic interest.

[31] [1995] 3 All ER 353.

[32] See, for example, J O'Sullivan, 'Nuisance, Local Authorities and Neighbours from Hell' (2000) 59 CLJ 11.

obligations in terms of the standard of reasonableness to be applied. Indeed, comments to this effect were made by Ackner LJ in *Page Motors*.

Moreover, resort to control devices inspired by public law to avoid the liability of the council in this case were entirely unnecessary anyway, for the claim was always bound to fail on the basis of ordinary nuisance principles. The first factor in this respect, which was indeed determinative in itself, was that the council was being sued as a landlord for continuing the nuisance. However, as was stated earlier, it is an established rule of nuisance law that landlords cannot be sued on this basis, since the duty to abate arises only on the part of occupiers. As there were no grounds for arguing that the council had authorised or adopted the nuisance, there simply was no legal basis at all for holding it liable for a nuisance not of its own creation.

Secondly, none of the third party conduct constituting the nuisance actually took place on the tenanted property. In the Court of Appeal, this was the main point of contention, and Hirst LJ clearly stated that it was indeed a necessary condition of liability in this instance that the nuisance consist of an unreasonable user of the defendant's land. Such a decisive judgment on this issue would have gone a long way towards clarifying this particular aspect of the law, had not a differently composed Court of Appeal insisted on derogating from this position a mere couple of weeks later.

In *Lippiatt v South Gloucestershire Council*,[33] it was, once again, the activities of a group of travellers that were at the centre of a nuisance action. The travellers in question had established an encampment on an area of land owned by the local council. The claimants were tenant farmers of neighbouring land who complained that, among other things, the travellers trespassed onto their land, left rubbish and excrement on it, stole timber and fences, damaged crops and a stone wall and allowed their dogs to chase the claimants' sheep. They duly sued the council, as landowner, for failing to abate this nuisance behaviour.

The case came before the Court of Appeal as a striking-out action, the defendant arguing that, in view of *Hussain*, the claim had no reasonable prospect of success, since the acts amounting to the nuisance had not actually been carried out on the defendant's land. This was true, and should have been the end of the matter. The Court of Appeal, however, disagreed. Although recognising that they were bound by *Hussain*, all three judges considered the claimants in this case to be highly meritorious and desired to find some way of providing them with a remedy. They did this by taking out of context dicta of Lord Goff in *Hunter v Canary Wharf*[34] and transforming them into a veritable statement of principle which met their own purposes. They were thus able artificially to distinguish *Hussain*.

The comment in question by Lord Goff was to the effect that, in nuisance

[33] [2000] QB 51.
[34] [1997] AC 655.

cases, some form of emanation from the defendant's land is generally required.[35] He was, however, referring specifically to cases in which the defendant is being sued for *creating* a nuisance. Given that such cases are generally dealt with in an entirely different manner to third party cases, it does not follow that the comment would necessarily apply to the latter. Moreover, it was not intended as, and indeed has not otherwise been treated as, a statement of authority. In fact, it has long been a matter of debate in creation cases whether the nuisance must actually come from the defendant's land because, although it has never been formally articulated as a condition of liability, in practice most nuisance actions are between neighbours, and this has given rise to the suggestion that it is actually an unspoken rule. The balance of authority, however, would seem to indicate otherwise. There have been many successful actions against non-proprietary defendants.[36] What Lord Goff appeared to be doing in *Hunter* was effecting some kind of compromise between these two positions which could, in a vague and non-committal way, be used to explain the bulk of existing case law in a consistent manner. So he adopted the term 'emanation', which was clearly broad enough to fit this purpose, for it could be used to refer to any kind of loose connection between the nuisance and the defendant's property.

In *Lippiatt*, Evans LJ seized upon this notion of emanation, treated it as a bona fide and all-embracing principle, and applied it to the facts at hand to conclude that what had emanated in this case was the travellers themselves.[37] Similarly, Mummery LJ described the travellers as having used the defendant's land as a 'launching pad' or as a 'base' from which to commit the acts of nuisance on the claimants' property.[38] By way of distinction, in *Hussain*, the conduct of the perpetrators 'was not in any sense linked to, nor did it emanate from, the homes where they lived'.[39]

What is most worrying about this particular development is that it has been wholeheartedly endorsed by academic commentators.[40] It is submitted, however, that their endorsement is not so much of the decision itself, but relates rather to the fact that it represents a departure from *Hussain*, which they had roundly condemned. Bagshaw, for instance, accuses the Court of Appeal in *Hussain* of having made two serious errors of analysis. He disagrees with the rule that the nuisance must take place on the defendant's land and supports this view with a sizeable list of cases in which defendants were held liable for nuisances not on their own land. However, for the same reason just discussed in relation to the judgment of Evans LJ in *Lippiatt*, it is submitted that the argument is seriously flawed. The cases he refers to are all creation cases and, as already stated, there is a

[35] *Ibid* at 700.

[36] See list of cases drawn up by Bagshaw, above n 8, p 167. The textbooks are also in agreement on this point: D Howarth, *Textbook on Tort* (Butterworths, 1995), p 516; MA Jones, *Textbook on Torts* (OUP, 2002), p 360, P Giliker and S Beckwith, *Tort* (Sweet & Maxwell, 2004), p 290.

[37] [2000] QB 51 at 60.

[38] *Ibid*, at 64.

[39] *Ibid*, at 61 per Evans LJ.

[40] See, eg, Bagshaw, above n 8, and O'Sullivan, above n 32, at 16.

clear distinction to be drawn between these and third party liability cases in this respect. As confirmed by the House of Lords in *Hunter*, nuisance is solely a tort against land. Its function is to protect the rights of property owners, or more specifically, their rights to use and enjoy their property. It is therefore really only necessary that claimants prove their entitlement to this protection by asserting their proprietary interests. The defendant is identified as the appropriate party to sue by his actions, by the fact that he has positively created the nuisance. By contrast, in the third party nuisance cases, it is purely the property owner's status that forms the basis of his liability. Clearly, if the creator is an independent third party, the only thing linking the defendant to the nuisance can be the land. His legal responsibilities arise out of the land, not out of his control of the third parties. Any duties to control them are, rather, only ancillary to these duties in respect of the property itself. It is therefore crucial that this spatial factor be considered a necessary condition of liability. In the absence of this connection, there is no real reason for making the defendant any more responsible than anybody else for the nuisance. Moreover, the notion of emanation is much too loose a concept and would provide too tenuous a link, as it could be easily manipulated and distorted.

Obviously, the property owner has played some kind of role in the affair in facilitating the presence of the third parties in the area, thus enabling them to target the particular claimants in question. However, as regards the actual commission of the nuisance, in terms of cause and effect, this facilitative role could only be described as circumstantial rather than instrumental, and clearly this would not be enough, in itself, to justify the imposition of legal obligations. Of course, it would be desirable to compel property owners to act considerately in deciding who can make use of their land, so as to ensure that such persons would not engage in activities off the land which would be likely to annoy those in the surrounding area, but it is not appropriate to try and do this through the law of nuisance, for it has simply not been designed for this purpose.

The second error of analysis, according to Bagshaw,[41] was that instead of focusing their attentions on the tenants' land, the Court of Appeal should have been asking whether there was a state of affairs on the defendant council's land which amounted to a nuisance. The reason this error was an important one was that many of the alleged incidents took place on open spaces on the estate that were owned by the council and also on the highway. Since the council was technically the occupier of these areas, the second ground given by the court for dismissing the claim, the rule that landlords cannot be liable for continuing a nuisance, would no longer apply and there would be nothing then to bar its liability. It is submitted, however, that this is not a feasible argument. It would, in theory, make the council liable for nuisances caused by anyone and everyone in these areas. In particular, there would be nothing to link the council to the perpetrators of the harm in this instance *as council tenants*, which is crucial here

[41] Bagshaw, above n 8, at 167.

precisely because the claimants' principal argument against the council was that its duty to abate consisted largely in evicting these tenants from their council homes.

The reason why the decision in *Hussain* would appear unsatisfactory, particularly to the layperson, is that the victims in this case were genuinely meritorious. They had endured an appalling litany of abuse and intimidation spanning a number of years, which the police had been unable to contain. Bright comments that, by comparison with the claimants in *Page Motors*, who had actually succeeded, the victims in *Hussain* were obviously much more in need of legal protection.[42] However, this is because she obviously conceives of the law of nuisance as having among its functions to curb anti-social behaviour. A brief reference to *Hunter v Canary Wharf*, in terms of its categorical reaffirmation of the link between nuisance and land, is enough to demonstrate just how fallacious this view is.

As pointed out by Thorpe LJ in his very short judgment in *Hussain*,[43] the simple truth of the matter is that, by its nature, the claim in question fell more appropriately within the domain of criminal law. The fact that, up until that point, it had failed to provide the victims with an adequate remedy was unfortunate, but it did not justify the denaturisation of the law of nuisance.

II. THIRD PARTY PROPERTY LIABILITY IN NEGLIGENCE

(i) General Principles

The action in negligence against a property owner in respect of harm committed by a third party may be described as a kind of default action. That is to say, it will generally only be pleaded as an alternative to nuisance, in circumstances in which, for some reason, an action in nuisance will not lie. This will usually be because the connection between the third party harm-doer and the defendant's land will be too transient to constitute a nuisance. Typically, there will have been no pre-existing relationship between the defendant and the third party, and the harm complained of will result from a single act on the part of the latter that just somehow happens to incorporate the defendant's property.[44] Indeed, most of the cases in this particular area follow a similar fact pattern in that they involve actions by property owners in respect of damage to their properties caused as a result of third party intruders gaining unlawful access to the defendant's neighbouring property.

[42] Bright, above n 20, at 312.

[43] [2000] QB 1 at 28.

[44] Although it is possible for an isolated incident to constitute a nuisance, this will only be in exceptional circumstances where it can be said to stem from an existing state of affairs on the defendant's property.

There is another reason why a nuisance argument may not be viable in these cases, one that relies on the authority of the *Hussain* decision. It is that the act of the third party causing the harm may not actually take place on the defendant's land. Furthermore, it could also be that the type of harm suffered by the claimant is not recoverable in nuisance, following the dicta of Lord Hoffmann in *Hunter v Canary Wharf*.[45] For he has suggested that, where personal injuries are concerned, the only appropriate cause of action is negligence and not nuisance.[46] On this point, however, it ought to be pointed out that all the third party negligence actions against landowners thus far have been in respect of either property damage or economic loss.

On the relationship between nuisance and negligence in this domain, the predominant view appears to be that there is really very little difference between the two.[47] Indeed, Lunney and Oliphant have commented that, at least as far as those cases involving property damage are concerned, 'any liability in nuisance mirrors that in negligence.'[48] This, however, is to overstate greatly the degree of overlap between them. It has already been pointed out that the reason an analogy is drawn between these two torts in this respect is that, by contrast to ordinary creation cases, liability for third party nuisance is determined principally by reference to the reasonableness of the defendant's conduct. But again as already stated, this fault test differs from the breach element of negligence in that it is subjective. Moreover, there are two other conditions of liability to be met in negligence that do not directly correspond to any element of nuisance liability. These are, of course, the existence of the common law duty of care and the requirement of a causal link between the negligence and the harm that is both factually direct and legally not too remote. And indeed, it is these latter elements of duty and causation that have proven to be the most problematic in the negligence cases in this field.

Taking first of all the duty issue, it is true that the concept is not unknown in nuisance, in that the responsibility of the property owner in cases of continuation is said to consist of a duty to abate. However, the very foundation of this duty marks it out as entirely distinct from the duty of care that arises in negligence. While the nuisance duty is a quasi-automatic one, stemming directly from the status of the defendant as occupier and subject only to the additional proviso that there be knowledge of the existence of the nuisance, the existence of the negligence duty is subject to a variety of preconditions and is essentially dependent upon factual circumstance. As such, the negligence duty is variable in nature and consequently much more difficult to establish than the nuisance duty.

Moreover, to complicate matters in negligence even further, it seems that the

45 [1997] 2 All ER 426.

46 *Ibid*, at 458.

47 See, eg, *Goldman v Hargrave* [1967] 1 AC 645, at 656, 657, and *Smith v Littlewoods Organisation Ltd* [1987] 1 AC 241 at 274 per Lord Goff, although it should be noted here that he is referring specifically to harm caused by fire.

48 *Tort Law: Text and Materials* (OUP, 2003), p 608.

courts do not have any clear or consistent ideas as to what these preconditions to the common law duty of care actually are, or indeed, what they should be. The problem is that the courts have not yet specifically addressed the issue of the nature and foundation of this type of third party duty. Instead, they have simply assumed that the relevant authority is the well-known third party liability case of *Home Office v Dorset Yacht*[49] and have consequently tried to construe the duty involved as being one to control the actions of the third party. This approach, however, is entirely inappropriate, given that the third party perpetrators in the relevant case law were all complete strangers to the defendants.[50] It ignores the fact that there are different types of affirmative duties at play in third party liability cases. It also explains, in part, why the cases in this particular category of third party liability, which are indeed among the most high-profile of all the third party liability cases generally,[51] are so acutely misunderstood. Part of the focus of the following discussion will therefore be to identify the true nature and foundation of the duty involved here.

Moving on to causation, there can be further identified from the case law a veritable judicial obsession with the notion of remoteness. For, when faced with the issue of the third party liability of property owners, the general tendency of the courts is to leap right in at the legal causation stage, and to analyse the whole case in terms of remoteness, to the exclusion of all other elements of negligence. Arguably, most of these cases should instead have been principally dealt with on the basis of duty. Of yet greater concern, however, is that the courts do not seem to recognise the difference between duty and remoteness issues in these cases. Often they purport to be talking in terms of duty, but actually concern themselves entirely with remoteness arguments. And to make matters worse, the remoteness rules that they apply are not even the correct ones in the circumstances. It is submitted that the confusion here has been caused, at least in part, by Lord Reid's misleading remoteness speech in *Dorset Yacht*.[52]

(ii) The Negligence Cases

In *P Perl (Exporters) Ltd v Camden London Borough Council*,[53] thieves had broken into the defendants' unsecured premises, knocked a hole through an interior dividing wall in order to gain access to the claimants' adjoining business premises, and from there had stolen a quantity of merchandise. In suing the

[49] [1970] AC 1004.

[50] Eg *P Perl (Exporters) v Camden London Borough Council* [1984] 1 QB 342 (thieves); *Ward v Cannock Chase District Council* [1985] 3 All ER 537 (vandals); *King v Liverpool City Council* [1986] 3 All ER 544 (vandals); *Smith v Littlewoods Organisation Ltd* [1987] 1 AC 241 (vandals).

[51] In academic circles, discussions of the general issue of third party liability in negligence tend to centre around these property cases. See, eg, D Howarth, 'My Brother's Keeper? Liability for the Acts of Third Parties' (1994) 14 LS 88, and GHL Fridman, 'Non-Vicarious Liability for the Acts of Others' (1997) 5 Tort LR 102.

[52] See ch 2, section I above.

[53] [1984] 1 QB 342.

defendants in negligence, the claimants put forward a number of reasons as to why a duty of care arose on the part of the defendants to secure their premises in order to protect their neighbours from property damage. First of all, the claimants actually leased their premises from the defendants, and consequently the defendants were aware that they had valuable goods stored there. Secondly, the defendants knew that unauthorised persons regularly entered their property, that vagrants had actually been camping out there at the relevant time, and indeed that frequent burglaries occurred there. Thirdly, numerous complaints had previously been made to the defendants about their total lack of security, but they had failed absolutely to do anything about it.

Clearly, the case put forward by the claimants was essentially based upon the extremely high degree of foreseeability that harm of the type complained of would be caused to the claimants. Taken in conjunction with the fact that, against this risk, the conduct of the defendants in failing even to have a lock fitted on their front door had been utterly unreasonable, it cannot be doubted that the claim was, at the very least, an entirely plausible one. Indeed, it succeeded at first instance. Before the Court of Appeal, however, it was rejected on the ground that it did not come within any of the recognised exceptions to the common law rule against holding one person liable for the acts of another. It is submitted that the main reason why the Court of Appeal dismissed the action was that it did not actually know how properly to assess it, and indeed ended up going about it in entirely the wrong way. For it is arguable that if it had proceeded on the correct basis then it might actually have approved the action.

The principal difficulty for the Court of Appeal in *P Perl* was the complete lack of direct precedent for the issues at stake. Unfortunately, Waller, Oliver and Goff LJJ did not actually appreciate this fact, for they neglected to consider in any detail at the outset what the exact issues were, and instead just jumped straight in to an assessment of what they presumed them to be. Most importantly, they failed to give any consideration at all to the question of the precise nature of the affirmative duty forming the crux of the claim and simply took the very broad and generalised view already adverted to that as the notion of 'third party liability' was involved, then *Dorset Yacht* applied and the relevant duty was one of control.[54] This consequently represented the first nail in the coffin for the claimants, for obviously no relationship of control could be said to exist in this case as the defendants and the third parties were total strangers. Indeed, the identity of the third parties was never even discovered. That a duty of this type could therefore not arise was, of course, then quickly pointed out by the court.[55]

[54] See, in particular, dicta of Waller LJ at 349 and of Oliver LJ at 355. It is noted that the judges did recognise that there were some other exceptional circumstances in which a third party duty could arise in the absence of any special relationship between the defendant and the third party tortfeasor, the prime example being a *Stansbie v Troman* ([1948] 2 KB 48) scenario. These circumstances, however, were included almost as afterthoughts and quickly dismissed as inapplicable in the present case – see, eg, at 357 per Oliver LJ and at 359 per Goff LJ.

[55] At 349 per Waller LJ and at 355 per Oliver LJ.

Clearly, however, at no point in the victims' statement of claim had it been suggested that the defendants had any responsibility to influence directly the behaviour of the particular individuals who broke into their premises, as indeed Goff LJ expressly acknowledged.[56] The duty actually alleged was rather one of protection owed to these particular claimants in respect of a particular type of harm caused in a particular manner. The focus of the court's attention should therefore have been on the justifications for this particular type of duty in the circumstances. What was the nature of the relationship between the defendants and the claimants? Could any specific reasons be advanced as to why these particular defendants should be obliged to act to the benefit of these particular claimants?

As has already been stated, the claimants' case in this respect was based upon the very high degree of foreseeability that harm of the type complained of would be caused to them as the proximate neighbours of the defendants. What the Court of Appeal should therefore have been asking was whether the notion of likelihood of harm could actually be used to found a duty of care. Moreover, close consideration should also have been given to the exact nature of the role played by the defendants in the commission of the tort. Rather than just labelling it as a mere omission, the court should have inquired into the causal relationship between the defendants' failings as regards security, and the actions of the third parties in causing the damage. For it is submitted that the defendants' failings were pivotal in the sense that they actively facilitated the third party conduct. Their role was indeed instrumental in this sense. What the court was dealing with then was not a pure omission, but rather positive contributory conduct of the type falling into the hybrid category between commissions and omissions. As discussed in chapter 1,[57] it is much easier to justify the imposition of a duty for this type of conduct than it is for a mere omission. Arguably, then, what the Court of Appeal should have been considering in this case was whether the high likelihood of harm taken in conjunction with the fact that the defendants had actively facilitated the commission of the tort sufficed to provide the necessary justification in this respect. It is submitted that, on the facts, this did indeed provide a very strong foundation for a duty of care.

In *P Perl*, Waller and Oliver LJJ did realise that the foreseeability factor was central to the claim, but failed to identify the element of negligence to which it was most relevant, for they dealt with it more or less exclusively in terms of remoteness.[58] This was because the claimants' arguments about the likelihood of the harm happened to correspond exactly with the remoteness aspect of Lord Reid's speech in *Dorset Yacht*, particularly the part at which he stated:

[56] [1984] 1 QB 342 at 359.
[57] See above p 11.
[58] Goff LJ dealt solely with the duty issue and, accordingly, his judgment was rather short.

> [W]here human action forms one of the links between the original wrongdoing of the defendant and the loss suffered by the plaintiff, that action must at least have been something very likely to happen if it is not to be regarded as a *novus actus interveniens* breaking the chain of causation.[59]

Concentrating on this remoteness issue, rather than on duty, perhaps because they realised that the *Dorset Yacht* formulation of duty did not work very well in this case, Waller and Oliver LJJ focused on what exactly Lord Reid meant by the above statement in terms of the specific degree of likelihood required. And while they were unable to reach any definite conclusions about this, they were confident that the degree of foreseeability in this case that the thieves would use the defendants' property to gain access to the claimants' storeroom[60] would not, in any event, be high enough to satisfy this test, whatever it turned out to be.

The same preoccupation with remoteness issues can also be seen in the next case to invoke the third party liability of a property owner, *Ward v Cannock Chase District Council*.[61] It is, however, to be distinguished from *P Perl* in three different respects: first, it is only a first instance decision; second, it has received much less academic attention; and third, and most importantly, it involves an action that was successful.

The claimant in *Ward* was the owner of a terraced house which became damaged when the adjoining property collapsed due to the complete failure of its owner, the defendant local council, to maintain it. The claimant's house was subsequently deemed unfit for habitation, with the result that the claimant and his family had to be rehoused. The council accepted its responsibilities to carry out the necessary repairs to the property, but then failed to do anything about it. Eventually a court order requiring the work to be done had to be issued against the council. Initially, it agreed to comply, but then, the very next day, vandals broke into the claimant's property and actually removed parts of the building, causing further substantial damage. The council then argued that, as the situation had changed since the mandatory order had been made, its obligations had also altered. In particular, it denied having any responsibility in respect of the additional damage caused by the vandals. It then refused to carry out any repairs at all. During this stand-off, the state of the property was allowed to deteriorate to the point that it became so unsafe it had to be demolished. The issue for the court to decide was therefore whether the council could be made liable for the additional costs involved in rebuilding the property, as opposed merely to carrying out the moderate repairs originally required.

Deciding the case, Scott J concentrated on the appropriate foreseeability test to be applied for the purposes of legal causation, in accordance with Lord Reid's speech from *Dorset Yacht*. By contrast to *P Perl*, however, it is submitted that, in this case, this was the correct approach for the court to have taken. This is

[59] [1970] AC 1004 at 1030.
[60] They rated such conduct only as a foreseeable possibility. See 357 per Oliver LJ.
[61] [1985] 3 All ER 537.

because the defendants had already inflicted an identifiable harm on the claimants even before the intervention of the third parties and, more importantly, accepted responsibility in court for this. The conduct of the third parties facilitated by the original act of negligence on the part of the defendants then caused additional harm to the claimants. The issue for the court, therefore, was not whether the defendants were actually liable at all, as it was in *P Perl,* since here the defendants were clearly liable for the original harm, at the very least, as they had already conceded. Rather it was whether the defendant could be made liable for the additional harm, and this is more clearly construed as a causation issue.[62]

Having gone through all the relevant authorities on the remoteness issue and considered all the different formulations of Lord Reid's 'likelihood' test, Scott J concluded that, in the end, they all amounted to the same thing – reasonable foreseeability – and that such a requirement was readily fulfilled in this case. Although he may have glossed over somewhat the dicta in support of a *high* likelihood test, the finding that in this case the harm was not too remote seems correct. Of crucial importance in this respect was the evidence before the court about the nature of the locality in which the properties in question were situated. The area, known as 'the Mossley', had a particularly bad reputation for crime, especially theft and vandalism, and this led Scott J to conclude that it was 'virtually certain'[63] that the claimant's property would succumb to the harm in question.

A further factor militating strongly in favour of liability was the high degree of fault clearly evident on the part of the defendants, for in addition to the fact that its failures to act were wholly unjustified, there was some suggestion that it had victimised the claimant. Indeed, Scott J, on at least two occasions, made pointed reference to the council's 'disgraceful treatment' of the claimant and his family.[64] He also commented specifically on the fact that the court order issued against the defendants had been framed in very strong terms, thus emphasising further the level of judicial disapproval of its conduct.

Overall, *Ward* would appear to have been correctly decided. That the next decision in this series, however, is to be characterised by the same judicial confusion between duty and remoteness that manifested itself in *P Perl* would suggest perhaps that the court's adoption of the correct approach to liability in *Ward* had more to do with chance than actual discernment of the issues at stake.

In *King v Liverpool City Council,*[65] it was once again the activities of vandals that lay at the centre of a negligence action against a property owner. In this case, the targeted property was an empty and unsecured council flat. Unidentified third parties broke into the flat and tampered with the water system on three separate occasions, and each time caused water to flood the claimant's flat

[62] For another case involving similar issues, see *Lamb v Camden London Borough Council* [1981] QB 625.
[63] [1985] 3 All ER 537 at 553.
[64] *Ibid,* at 542, 543.
[65] [1986] 3 All ER 544.

situated directly below. After the first break-in had been reported, the council had arranged for a plumber to come in to do some repair work, but he was unable to turn off the rising main supply of drinking water as this would have affected the other flat. Although it was standard practice for the council to arrange for vacant properties to be boarded up, for some reason this was not done in this case. There was evidence that boarding-up work had been carried out after the third break-in, but this was strongly disputed in court and, in any event, it was evident that even if any such work had been initiated, it had not been effectively done.

The thrust of the claimant's allegation against the council was that the evident vulnerability of the empty flat to acts of vandalism gave rise to a duty of care on the part of the council, as owner of the property, to ensure that it was adequately protected against such dangers, and that this duty had not been fulfilled because the steps it had taken to this effect had fallen far below the standard of reasonableness required.[66] The Court of Appeal disagreed. Indeed, it is clear from the negative tone of the main judgment, given by Purchas LJ, that the Court was of the opinion from the very beginning that the claim never had any chance of succeeding. Unfortunately, that was where its certainty ended, for it is also evident from Purchas LJ's judgment that the Court was entirely unclear as to the exact reasons why it was destined to fail. Most significantly, he vacillated between duty and remoteness issues without making any distinction between them, indeed seemingly without realising that there was any distinction to be made between them. One moment he was discussing the notion of a duty to control, the next he was citing remoteness arguments from *Dorset Yacht* and *P Perl*. In fact, his whole judgment contained very little analysis of how any of the points raised applied to the claim in *King* itself. Even more confusingly, he then appeared to suggest in his concluding remarks that the main reason the claim failed was either lack of fault or absence of factual causation, for he treated as determinative the (rather dubious) finding of the trial judge that there were no effective steps the defendants could have taken in the circumstances to defeat the activities of the vandals.[67] Of course, he did not present this as a breach or factual causation issue, instead stating that it could relate either to the question of the

[66] At first instance, the claimant also sought to argue nuisance, on grounds of continuation, but this was swiftly rejected by the trial judge as untenable on the facts. It is submitted, however, that his reasoning in this respect is subject to question. He held that, in calling the plumber, the council had taken reasonable, albeit ineffective, steps to abate the nuisance and thus had fulfilled its duty in this respect. But this is only convincing if the source of the nuisance could be said to have been the actual escape of the water. Realising this, the claimant tried to argue that it was rather the condition of the premises that constituted the nuisance, and that, in this respect, the action taken by the council had not been reasonable. Clearly, there is much force in this argument, for if the flat had been properly secured the vandals would not have been able to break in and cause the flooding in the first place. At the very least, the nuisance should have been regarded as a combination of both the lax security and the escape of the water. Indeed, in both *Sedleigh-Denfield* (above n 9) and *Leakey v National Trust* (above n 21), a similarly broad approach was taken to the question of what constituted the nuisance in those cases. The trial judge, however, simply rejected this argument outright as being 'of no significance'. Arguably, this was very ill considered on his part.

[67] [1986] 3 All ER 544 at 552.

ambit of the duty (breach?) or to legal causation. Then he went on to conclude that the claim failed for lack of duty!

Ultimately, it would appear that the principal motivation for the decision was a basic floodgates fear. For it was pointed out in court that vandalism was a particularly big problem at that time in the area concerned. And indeed, the defendant's status as a local authority undoubtedly further influenced the court in this respect. But if vandalism was such an obvious risk in the circumstances, should this not instead have been considered as a factor militating in favour of compelling the council to take precautionary measures? It is significant that the Court of Appeal entirely glossed over this point.

The next case in this series is arguably also the most important one. It has certainly received the most academic attention. *Smith v Littlewoods Organisation Ltd*[68] involved a derelict cinema that had fallen prey to repeated acts of vandalism. Its owners were unaware of this, and consequently made no attempt improve security on the premises. On one occasion, a fire was started in it which spread to adjoining properties and caused serious damage. The owners of these properties duly sued the owners of the cinema in negligence, alleging a breach of duty to prevent the entry of the intruders who had started the fire in the first place. The claim succeeded at first instance, but was then dismissed on appeal by both the Court of Appeal and the House of Lords.

That the claim ultimately failed comes as no great surprise at this point, in view of the attitude demonstrated by the courts towards this type of liability in the cases already discussed. Of more interest in the present context is the way in which the House of Lords arrived at its decision to reject the claim, for it is submitted that, for the first time, the correct approach to liability was *consciously* adopted by at least one member of the court. Unfortunately, the Law Lord in question, Lord Mackay, did not make his speech explicit enough in this respect and, as a result, the whole case has been wrongly interpreted on a number of fronts.

The standard view of *Smith* is that it stands as firm authority for the rule that there can be no duty at common law to control the actions of another. This view stems from a reading of the case which treats the speech of Lord Goff as the leading judgment. Taking a very straightforward and orthodox approach, Lord Goff avoided having to go into the substantive details of the case by basing his analysis solely in terms of the law on omissions and concluding that, as the claim did not fit within any of the established exceptions to the general rule against liability for omissions, it was bound to fail as having no legal foundation.

Writing separately, both Markesinis and Howarth, however, have suggested that an entirely different reading of the case can be taken, one which instead treats the speech of Lord Mackay as setting out the *ratio decidendi*, and that this actually casts a whole new perspective on this area of negligence law, perhaps

[68] [1987] 1 AC 241.

even opening up a novel category of liability.[69] The thrust of their argument is that, while Lord Goff abstractly denied the existence of a duty of care and this created, in effect, a blanket exclusion of liability extending to all cases in which property owners who fail to prevent third parties from gaining access to their property are blamed for harm that is subsequently caused to neighbouring properties, Lord Mackay, by contrast, based his decision to dismiss the claim on the facts of the case, thus theoretically leaving this avenue of third party liability open for future exploitation. They maintain that the reason Lord Mackay's speech is to be regarded as the leading judgment is that his is the one that received the support of the majority.[70] In asserting this, they argue that both Lord Griffiths and Lord Brandon framed their decisions in terms similar to those stated by Lord Mackay, with Lord Griffiths actually expressing himself to be in total agreement with Lord Mackay. While Lord Keith's position would seem impossible to categorise here since he, incomprehensibly, expressed himself to be in total agreement with both Lord Mackay and Lord Goff, he does not actually affect the balance in this respect, for even if he were to be discounted, or indeed placed on the side of Lord Goff, Lord Mackay would still hold the majority.

It is submitted that this reading of *Smith* is essentially correct. However, it is further submitted that Markesinis and Howarth erred in interpreting Lord Mackay's substantive analysis of the claim as being based primarily on issues of fault and causation. For a close reading of his Lordship's speech reveals that he actually formulates the ratio of the case in terms of duty and that his comments on breach and remoteness issues are merely to be regarded as obiter dicta. Admittedly, Lord Mackay did not help to clarify the matter by failing to explain, at the different stages of his speech, which element of negligence he was specifically referring to.

The first crucial point is that Lord Mackay treated the notion of the foreseeability of the conduct of the vandals as being determinative of the duty issue, for he stated:

> [U]nless Littlewoods were bound reasonably to anticipate and guard against the danger, they had no duty of care, relevant to this case, requiring them to inspect their premises. Unless, therefore, Littlewoods, on taking control of these premises without any knowledge of the subsequent history of the property after they assumed control, ought reasonably to have anticipated that they would be set on fire and thus or otherwise create a substantial risk of damage to neighbouring properties if they did not take precautions, the claims must fail.[71]

He thus implied that if the defendants had ever been informed about the previous acts of vandalism, then a duty to secure the premises would have been

[69] B Markesinis, 'Negligence, Nuisance and Affirmative Duties of Action' (1989) 105 LQR 104, D Howarth, 'My Brother's Keeper? Liability for the Acts of Third Parties' (1994) 14 LS 88.

[70] Indeed, Howarth even goes so far as to describe the speech of Lord Goff as akin to a dissenting judgment, 'Negligence After *Murphy*: Time to Rethink' [1991] CLJ 58 at 77.

[71] [1987] 1 AC 241, at 257–58.

imposed on them.[72] By making actual or constructive knowledge of the very high risk of harm a key factor, he thus enables a strong parallel to be drawn between this form of negligence liability and third party nuisance liability under the *Sedleigh-Denfield* principle.

For Lord Mackay, the entire claim was consequently dealt with on this basis.[73] However, he felt the need to go on and add his own 'observations'[74] about some of the other matters raised by the claim, notably breach and remoteness issues, expressly because of their 'general importance'.[75]

He addressed, first of all, the by now notorious question of how to interpret Lord Reid's 'likelihood' speech from *Dorset Yacht*, and concluded that the test for remoteness set out was that the harm caused by the intervention of the third party had to be reasonably foreseeable as probable rather than just possible.[76] He then turned to breach, but basically said in this respect that the ordinary test of the reasonable man would apply. One interesting point he did make here, however, was that there was a distinction to be drawn at this stage of the liability assessment between cases of fire involving third parties (that is, a *Smith* or *Goldman v Hargrave* scenario) and cases of theft involving third parties (a *P Perl* or *King* scenario). What he appeared to be suggesting here was that a higher standard of care would generally apply in relation to the former, the reasons for this being that fires are more inherently hazardous than acts of theft and that fires continue to represent sources of danger *on the defendant's property* until they are put out, whereas the use of the defendant's land by thieves would be transient, simply to gain access to the neighbouring properties. Lord Mackay also considered that victims would be able to take independent action to protect themselves against theft in a way that would not be possible with fire. As he was talking only at a general level, however, he did not attempt to consider how any of this would apply to *Smith* itself.

For present purposes, it is Lord Mackay's approach to the duty issue that is of most significance, for it is submitted that it comes close to establishing a logical and workable test for duty in this type of third party liability case. It may be recalled that Lord Mackay proceeded on the basis that a duty would be imposed if there were a high degree of foreseeability that the third party conduct causing the harm would take place. This makes sense, since it is clear that the reason why these particular defendants have been targeted is that they have been in a position to prevent a highly obvious risk. It is recognised that there is a general judicial hostility towards such all-embracing foreseeability tests,[77] with even the usually

[72] On this analysis then, he presumably would have recognised a duty of care in *P Perl*.

[73] [1987] 1 AC 241 at 259.

[74] *Ibid*.

[75] *Ibid*.

[76] *Ibid*, at p 261.

[77] Hence the demise of the two-stage test for duty established by Lord Wilberforce in *Anns v Merton London Borough Council* [1978] AC 728. According to this test, the existence of a relationship of neighbourhood between the harm-doer and the victim would give rise to a prima facie duty of care, and this duty would stand unless any good reasons were put forward for negativing or limiting it.

progressive Markesinis commenting that such a duty test would be dangerously expansive.[78] It is submitted, however, that such vehement distrust of the concept of foreseeability is unfounded. It stems from the misconception that foreseeability automatically equates with liability, a position that would clearly be dangerously expansive, when in fact it is being used only to determine whether the claim can pass through the first stage of the liability inquiry and go on to be substantively litigated. To concede a duty is not to concede automatic liability. In any event, it is not proposed to make the high degree of foreseeability requirement the sole basis for the duty in these cases, for it is recognised that with such an exceptional form of liability further justification is needed. Some other link between the particular defendant and the harm complained of needs to be made, something to correlate with the role carried out in ordinary personal negligence cases by the act of misfeasance on the part of the defendant.

It could be argued that the necessary link in this respect is provided by the fact of the defendant's control of the property in question, but it is thought that this is not reason enough to impose what may in some cases turn out to be rather onerous responsibilities. There needs to be a sense that the individual defendant personally deserves to be so obligated, which has to mean focusing on the defendant's conduct. If all the cases just discussed are looked at from this perspective, it can be seen that in each one there was some kind of initial failing on the part of the defendant which enabled the third party intervention to take place, and without which the third party intervention could probably not have taken place at all. Arguably, this fact of positive, direct and instrumental facilitation of the commission of the tort, taken in conjunction with the high degree of likelihood of the third party conduct taking place, would suffice to justify the duty to take reasonable care in all of the cases apart from *Smith*, where the degree of likelihood was not high enough. Indeed, this was the very idea canvassed earlier in relation to the *P Perl* case, and having examined the rest of the case law, it does seem to constitute, at the very least, a feasible approach to duty. If applied strictly, and alongside the standard *Caparo* tripartite test for duty,[79] or at least alongside the 'proximity' and 'fair, just and reasonable' stages of this test, as the foreseeability requirement is probably incorporated into the principles just discussed, then there is no reason why liability could not be tightly controlled and, consequently, there should be no real fear of opening the floodgates. A further point to be made is that if this approach were to be adopted then there would be no need to apply Lord Reid's likelihood test at the remoteness stage, since this will already have been dealt with in these cases under the rubric of duty. Indeed, it is submitted that it will only ever be appropriate to apply his remoteness test in cases involving a duty to control, as in *Dorset Yacht* itself.

A crucial consequence of basing a duty on a positive facilitation of the

[78] Above n 69, at 105.

[79] Derived from the House of Lords decision in *Caparo Industries plc v Dickman* [1990] 2 AC 605, the elements of the test are: (1) foreseeability; (2) proximity; and (3) the fairness, justice and reasonableness of imposing a duty of care.

commission of the tort, plus a high degree of likelihood of the third party intervention, is that there would be nothing to link it specifically to property owners, or indeed to property damage, so that it would have the potential to constitute a principle of general applicability. It is submitted, however, that this would not necessarily be a problem. In fact, it may even turn out to be a good thing, for such a general principle could be used to explain, in a consistent manner, many other related instances of third party liability that, at present, appear somewhat disparate.

Take, for instance, the well-known case of *Haynes v Harwood*,[80] which involved a claimant injured by some runaway horses. The defendant owner of the horses had left them unattended in a busy street, near to where children were playing, and the horses bolted when one of the children threw a stone at them. The claimant was injured while trying to stop the horses. The defendant was held liable, essentially on the ground that he should have anticipated that children in such close proximity would become engaged in some sort of mischievous enterprise: in other words, because it was highly foreseeable that the harm would occur. It is interesting that in *Smith*, Lord Goff categorises *Haynes* as a special case of third party liability based on the defendant's creation of a source of danger.[81] He obviously conceives of this category as being strictly limited, however, to dangers that are capable of being instantaneously 'sparked off', such as those represented by horses or fireworks, or the like. It is contended here, rather, that what should count should not be the actual source or nature of the danger, but the likelihood of its occurrence.

Another relevant case in this respect would be *Stansbie v Troman*,[82] in which a decorator who left the claimant's house unlocked was held liable for the actions of a thief who subsequently entered and stole property. Lord Goff treated this decision as being based upon an assumption of responsibility on the part of the decorator towards the claimant, arising from the contract between them.[83] Lord Mackay, on the other hand, regarded the decorator's liability as being based rather on the idea of the foreseeability of the unlawful intrusion.[84] It is submitted that this is by far the most convincing, and indeed common-sense, explanation of the case, not least because the contract between the parties relied on by Lord Goff related only to the defendant's conduct in decorating the house, and there was no representation, either express or implied, on the part of the defendant as to the security of the property.

The idea of a positive facilitation of the commission of the tort accompanied by a high degree of foreseeability of the third party intervention may also be applied to another mini-series of cases: those involving harm caused by stolen

[80] [1935] 1 KB 146.
[81] [1987] 1 AC 241 at 273.
[82] [1948] 2 KB 48.
[83] [1987] 1 AC 241 at 272.
[84] *Ibid* at 265.

motor vehicles (particularly buses).[85] The three cases making up this series were briefly chronicled by Fleming,[86] but apart from this, they have received little academic attention. Of course, the fact that only one of the decisions was actually reported will not have helped to raise their profile.

The first case is from 1982. In *Hayman v London Transport Executive*,[87] an unattended bus, which had been stolen from an area in which children frequently meddled with unattended buses, collided with the claimant's car. The Court of Appeal held the Transport Executive liable, more or less on the basis that it had taken wholly inadequate precautions against what was, in the circumstances, an obvious risk of harm. Then in 1986, in *Denton v United Counties Omnibus Co*,[88] a similar claim arose in respect of damage caused by another stolen bus. This time, however, the Court of Appeal refused to impose liability. Relegating *Hayman* to the status of a case based on its own special facts, it took a very orthodox approach to the duty issue, applied *P Perl* and held that the claim was duly defeated by the general rule against imposing duties to control the acts of another. Finally, in *Topp v London Country Bus (South West) Ltd*,[89] an unattended minibus was stolen, and this time the consequences were much more serious, the claimant's wife being knocked down and killed as a result of the thief's reckless driving. On the authority of *Denton* and *Smith v Littlewoods*,[90] the Court of Appeal once again denied that any duty of care was owed by the defendant bus company.

Arguably, in both *Denton* and *Topp*, the high degree of foreseeability that the buses would be stolen and that harm would consequently be caused to other road users actually provides a very strong foundation for the existence of a duty, given that the defendants in each case had contributed to the creation of the risk by leaving the vehicles unattended in the first place. This was particularly the case in *Topp*, in which the defendants admitted that it was their company's policy for drivers to leave buses unlocked with the keys in the ignition at changeover points, so that they could be collected by the next driver. On the occasion in question, the company had moreover been informed that the changeover driver for the bus at the centre of the incident had not turned up, and that meant that the bus was

85 Worthy of mention also in this context is Lord Denning's brief attempt to introduce into English law a special category of vicarious liability in relation to cars. Commonly referred to as 'the family car doctrine', it involved holding car owners liable for the negligence of their immediate family members in using the car: *Launchbury v Morgans* [1971] 2 QB 245. This doctrine was, however, quickly rejected by the House of Lords, which stated clearly that the liability of a car owner for the use of his or her car by another could only be established by evidence of 'casual delegation', ie by evidence that the car was being used with the owner's permission and at least partly in his interests: *Morgans v Launchbury* [1973] AC 127. For the Australian position, see *Soblusky v Egan* (1960) 103 CLR 215, but note also the more recent decision of the High Court of Australia in *Scott v Davis* (2000) 74 ALJR 1410, as noted by P Handford at (2001) 9 Tort LR 97.

86 JG Fleming, 'Injury caused by Stolen Motor Vehicles' (1994) 110 LQR 187.

87 Unreported, 4 March 1982 (CA).

88 Unreported, 1 May 1986 (CA).

89 [1993] 1 WLR 977.

90 Above n 68.

stranded, but they simply did nothing about it. In the end, the bus was left sitting for about nine hours before eventually being stolen.

There is one last, isolated, case that can be explained on the basis of the duty principles being advocated. It differs, however, from the others just discussed in that it is an example of when *not* to apply these principles, for in this case they were simply not supported by the facts. In *Paterson Zochonis v Merfarken Packaging Ltd*,[91] the defendants were printers who unwittingly supplied the packaging for tubes of counterfeit face cream. They were sued by the holders of the copyright for the cream on the grounds that their suspicions should have been aroused that the packaging was to be used for a wrongful purpose by a number of specified small details and that, consequently, they should have checked that the persons who had placed the order had had the necessary authority to do so. Clearly, in view of the entirely innocent role played by the defendants, these allegations were very tenuous. Not surprisingly, the Court of Appeal rejected the claim and, as such, it may be commented that, if nothing else, the *Paterson* decision at least demonstrates that it is possible to keep the foreseeability duty principle within definable limits.

III. CONCLUSION

In general, while the use of the law of nuisance to engage the third party liability of property owners has been too expansive, the use of the law of negligence in this respect has, arguably, been too restrictive.

In nuisance, the most worrying development has been the replacement of the requirement, in cases of continuation, that the third party conduct constituting the nuisance should actually take place on the defendant's land with the rather vague idea that the conduct needs now only to be construed as somehow 'emanating' from the defendant's land. It has been pointed out that the defendant's liability in these cases is based solely upon his status as a property owner, and that means that the only real link between the defendant and liability is the land. To remove this link is therefore to remove the legal foundation from the duty to abate.

In negligence, a misplaced fear of opening the floodgates appears to be all that guides the judicial approach to this branch of third party liability, as the case law has certainly demonstrated that it consists of very little in the way of principle. A new and radical approach to the duty issue has been suggested, one that predicates liability upon the defendant's positive facilitation of the commission of the tort against the background of a highly obvious risk. Not limited specifically to property owners, this new duty principle would, in effect, amount to a general principle of third party liability capable both of reconciling many existing

[91] [1986] 3 All ER 522.

isolated instances of such liability, and of setting out a consistent approach to future cases. It would explain, for example, why the oft-quoted scenarios of handing a loaded gun to a child or giving a set of car keys to a drunk should give rise to affirmative duties, situations in which it is accepted without question that third party liability should arise, but in relation to which the reasons for such liability have never actually been articulated in any principled manner.

It has also been pointed out that one further consequence of applying the new duty principles being advocated is that there would no longer be any need to apply Lord Reid's famous likelihood test at the remoteness stage, since this will already have been incorporated into the duty analysis. At the legal causation stage, therefore, it will be necessary to consider only the ordinary *Wagon Mound*[92] test of reasonable foreseeability of the type of harm and/or *novus actus* arguments concerning either the claimant's conduct or that of an outside party other than the third party perpetrator.[93]

One final point to be made is that it is envisaged that the ordinary test of the reasonable man would continue to apply at the breach stage.

[92] *Overseas Tankship (UK) Ltd v Morts Dock & Engineering Co Ltd, The Wagon Mound* [1961] AC 388.

[93] As pointed out in ch 2, Section I, to construe the third party perpetrator's conduct as a *novus actus* would obviously be to defeat the duty analysis.

4

Third Party Liability in Respect of the Intoxicated

OF THE VARIOUS new categories of third party liability, it is arguably that which arises in respect of the intoxicated that causes the most concern. While its development in English tort law is yet at an embryonic stage, this category of 'alcohol liability' has already taken strong root in a number of Commonwealth jurisdictions and is currently experiencing a period of rapid growth. Unfortunately, in the scramble to jump on this particular liability bandwagon in these jurisdictions, it appears that the basic principles of tort law have been all but trampled underfoot. For this extension of the boundaries of tortious liability has been effected for primarily socio-political purposes, but with little or no consideration of its wider legal ramifications.

Third parties may be held personally liable in respect of the intoxicated in two distinct ways: for harm by another to the intoxicated or for the tortious conduct of the intoxicated. The intoxicated person may therefore feature either as the victim or as the perpetrator of harm. In the first case, the defendant's duty of care will be one of protection owed to the intoxicated; in the second case, it will be one of control owed to others. It is important that these two scenarios are not dismissed as merely exemplifying different facets of the one duty, for that would constitute a dangerous oversimplification of the legal issues at stake: dangerous in the sense that the legal implications of each form of liability would not be fully explored. As will be seen presently, the Canadian experience of alcohol liability provides ample proof of this danger. Rather, the duties of a third party to protect the intoxicated from others and to protect others from the intoxicated must be recognised as two entirely separate legal duties, each governed by its own particular set of legal rules.

I. THE COMMONWEALTH POSITION

(i) Canada

Among Commonwealth jurisdictions, the notion of alcohol liability is most developed in Canadian tort law. Its origins trace back to the 1974 decision of the Supreme Court of Canada in *Jordan House Ltd v Menow*,[1] which saw a tavern owner held liable for the injuries sustained by a drunken patron, subsequent to his ejection from the establishment. The claimant in question was an habitual drunkard and a known troublemaker who had previously been banned from the defendant's hotel for anti-social behaviour. On the night in question, he was thrown out for being drunk and annoying other guests and, while making his way home, he was hit by a negligent motorist. In seeking to hold the company that owned the hotel (hereafter 'the hotel') jointly responsible for his injuries, the claimant's argument was that the hotel had breached its common law duty to protect him in his intoxicated state.

That the hotel owed the claimant a duty of care was not doubted by the Supreme Court. Its primary concern was rather the nature and scope of this duty. On this issue, two distinct views emerged. For Laskin J, everything more or less turned on the hotel's special knowledge of the claimant's particular susceptibility to alcohol and the effect it had on him.[2] This gave rise to a duty to take reasonable steps to ensure that he got home safely. The bar staff, in Laskin J's view, should either have arranged safe transport for him, called the police or even put him up for the night in the hotel. Given the magnitude of his expectations, it would seem clear that Laskin J regarded the duty of care involved as being of an exceptional nature, for he surely could not have thought it reasonable to oblige hoteliers to provide their overly intoxicated patrons regularly with the benefit of accommodation services normally reserved for paying guests. Indeed, he stressed that he was not imposing 'a duty on every tavern owner to act as a watch dog for all patrons who enter his place of business and drink to excess.'[3]

Richie J, on the other hand, imposed a much stricter test of liability. In his view, the defendant's duty was not merely to protect the claimant once he became intoxicated, but rather to *prevent* intoxication in the first place. For him, therefore, the duty of care arose at a much earlier point. Whereas, under Laskin J's formulation, the duty of care arose when the claimant became too drunk to look after himself, for Richie J, it presumably came into play when the hotel employees provided the claimant with his first drink. From the point of view of the claimant, the practical significance of framing the duty in such terms is that it makes it much easier to satisfy the fault element of negligence. If the defendant

[1] (1973) 38 DLR (3d) 105. For a comment on the decision, see H Silberberg, 'The Intoxicated Patron: A Re-appraisal of the Duty of Care' (1974) 20 McGill LJ 491.

[2] *Ibid*, at 113.

[3] *Ibid*.

has not taken reasonable care to prevent intoxication, that in itself operates to breach the duty, and nothing that is done afterwards to help the patron will suffice to undo that breach. Even providing a personal escort to take the claimant home would not make any difference, unless of course it had the effect of preventing the harm from occurring in the first place. However, such divergence of opinion within the court was, in the end, of little consequence in this case, for the defendant's conduct was such that it constituted a breach of both versions of the duty of care. Together with the negligent motorist, the hotel was held liable for two-thirds of the claimant's losses.

Arguably, the correct way to interpret the decision in *Jordan House* would be to simply regard it as limited to the very special facts of the case. Of course, that is not how it has been interpreted. Not only subsequently did courts unfortunately latch on to the test propounded by Richie J, rather more worryingly, they fashioned it to serve specific socio-political purposes, and thereby significantly widened its sphere of applicability. The potential of the *Jordan House* decision to be used as a weapon in the fight against drink-driving was quickly recognised. Thereafter, it was a slippery slope.

In *Canada Trust Co v Porter*,[4] the Ontario Court of Appeal accepted *Jordan House* as establishing a new general principle of liability based on the provision of alcohol and used it to authorise a claim in negligence against a tavern owner brought by the victims of a road accident caused by one of the tavern's intoxicated patrons. Suddenly, without any discussion of the matter, the duty of commercial alcohol providers to protect their intoxicated patrons had been transformed into an all-encompassing duty, notably entailing an additional obligation to control the actions of such patrons in order to protect third parties. In a further twist, this duty of care was made to extend to all patrons, irrespective of whether they had had any personal dealings with the defendant. The claimant in *Canada Trust* was effectively a stranger to the bar staff and had, moreover, been served from behind a partition, so that the staff were not in a position to keep track of how much he, or any other patron, was drinking or to monitor his conduct. According to the Court, it was the defendant's responsibility to establish serving and staffing practices to ensure that no one on the premises was served beyond the point of intoxication.

Allowing a duty of care to arise from the mere fact of serving alcohol, in the absence of any personal relationship between the claimant and the defendant, introduces a range of problems. For clearly, to remove that requirement for a personal relationship, which acted as an effective control mechanism, is to invite an influx of vexatious claims. It also raises practical difficulties of implementation, for there are various degrees of intoxication which depend to a large extent on the constitution and temperament of the particular individual concerned. How is a bartender to determine the time at which it becomes appropriate to intervene and stop serving?

4 Unreported, 28 April 1980 (Ont CA).

This point is aptly illustrated by the next major case on alcohol liability to arise in Canada . The facts of *Schmidt v Sharpe*[5] are as follows. Already intoxicated, the first defendant entered the second defendant's establishment whereupon he consumed three beers, then got into his car and promptly drove off the road, seriously injuring his passenger. Together, the two defendants were held liable for 70 per cent of the victim's losses: the first defendant for obvious reasons; and the second defendant for breaching its duty not to serve an intoxicated patron. In the light of the first defendant's blood alcohol level, the Court considered that the bar staff should have noticed his drunkenness. Given that the first defendant was not known to the bar staff, had not been showing any visible signs of intoxication when he arrived, and had consumed only a small proportion of his overall alcohol intake for the evening on the second defendant's premises, the judgment against the second defendant would appear unduly harsh.

Moreover, even though the victim had been drinking with the first defendant prior to accepting a lift from him, the Court refused to accept the defence argument that he had consented to the risk of injury. By deliberately construing the defence of *volenti non fit injuria* in a very narrow sense, the Court was able to dismiss it as inapplicable in the circumstances. It simply pointed out that the victim had not been aware that the first defendant had been drinking before they met, so that he could not be taken to have understood the true nature and extent of the risk he was taking. That the Court, nevertheless, expected such awareness of the bar staff is a clear illustration of its pro-victim stance.

With such rapid developments in this area of the law, it will have come as a surprise to no one when, in 1986, the principles governing provider liability, erstwhile limited to those supplying alcohol for commercial gain, were extended to include social hosts.[6] However, *Schmidt v Sharpe* probably represents the high point of alcohol provider liability in Canada. From subsequent case law there can be detected signs of a slight judicial retreat.

The facts of *Hague v Billings*[7] follow a familiar pattern – the victims of a road accident caused by a drunken driver brought a claim in negligence against the alcohol provider. A notable feature of this case, however, is that two licensed establishment that had provided the driver with alcohol were sued. The first bar had served him with just one drink before staff realised that he was already drunk and refused further service. He then made his way to the second bar, where he was served four more drinks. It was after leaving this bar that he drove into the claimants' car.

That the liability of the second bar was upheld comes as no great surprise in the light of the previous case law. Of greater interest, in the present context, is how the issue of the first bar's liability was dealt with. The Ontario High Court,

[5] (1983) 27 CCLT 1.

[6] *Baumeister v Drake* (1986) 38 CCLT 1. See also *Wince v Ball* (1996) 136 DLR (4th) 104 and, more recently, *Childs v Desormeaux* [2004] OJ No 2065.

[7] (1989) 68 OR (2d) 321.

and later the Ontario Court of Appeal,[8] decided that the staff of this bar could not be liable for serving the driver beyond the point of intoxication simply on the basis of the single drink they had provided, for, at that stage, they had not had time properly to ascertain his state of inebriation. While the first bar might not have been under a duty to prevent intoxication, however, the Court did consider that it was bound by a duty to prevent him from driving, and that this duty arose at the point at which the staff realised that he was drunk. Moreover, it found that the efforts of the proprietor to persuade the driver to hand over his car keys to one of his friends were insufficient to fulfil this duty. Actual control needed to be taken of the situation, and if the staff were not capable of doing this themselves, then they should have called in the police. On this analysis, therefore, the duty of care had been breached. Liability was, however, ultimately avoided on the basis of causation, as it was found that even if the police had been summoned, the accident would still have occurred.

The main point of significance to be drawn from *Hague v Billings* is that the judicial approach to the duty issue adopted in that case was more akin to that set out by Laskin J in *Jordan House* than to that of Richie J. As such, it marks a clear departure from the previous trend. That it represents the shape of things to come would appear to be confirmed by the most recent significant decision in this field: *Stewart v Pettie*.[9] Accompanied by his wife, sister and brother-in-law, Pettie spent the evening at a dinner theatre where he consumed between 10 and 14 measures of rum. He was served each time by the same waitress, who kept a running total of all alcohol ordered by the group. Upon leaving the theatre, a group decision was made to allow Pettie to drive them all home, even though both Pettie's wife and his sister were sober and were aware of how much he had had to drink. On that particular night, the roads were slippery and, although Pettie drove in a cautious and safe manner, he lost control of the vehicle. Pettie's sister was seriously injured in the crash that followed and, together with her husband, she brought an action in negligence against, inter alia, Pettie and the dinner theatre. On the issue of the theatre's liability, the trial judge's decision to dismiss the action was overturned by the Court of Appeal and then reinstated by the Supreme Court of Canada.

Given the particular importance of the Supreme Court's decision, as the highest-ranking judicial pronouncement on the subject of alcohol provider liability, it is to be regretted that the judgment handed down is not easy to analyse. Although the Supreme Court clearly considered that over-service would not, in itself, suffice as a basis for the liability of an alcohol provider, which is a clear endorsement of the more lenient approach adopted in *Hague v Billings*, it rather confusingly chose to explain its reasoning in terms of breach rather than duty. The essence of what the Supreme Court said was that, on the authority of *Jordan House*, there could be no doubt that commercial providers of alcohol owe

[8] (1993) 15 CCLT (2d) 264.

[9] (1995) 23 CCLT (2d) 89. See also *Wince v Ball* (1996) 136 DLR (4th) 104.

a duty of care to their own patrons and to third parties who might reasonably be expected to come into contact with an intoxicated patron, most obviously, users of the highway. Cast in such broad terms, it is not surprising that the court recognised a duty in this case. More problematic, in its view, was the issue of the standard of care required of the defendant theatre in order to discharge this duty. It was under this rubric that the Supreme Court went on to consider the kind of issues that previous courts, quite correctly, it is submitted,[10] had treated as relevant to the question of the existence of the duty in the first place. In particular, it was only at this point that the Supreme Court questioned whether the circumstances were such that the theatre was under an obligation to take positive steps to ensure that Pettie did not drive. It considered that positive steps would have been required only if there had been a foreseeable risk that Pettie would drive. The fact that he was accompanied by two sober adults negated the existence of the necessary risk factor. The theatre had met the standard of care required of it by simply 'remaining vigilant' in the circumstances, and so liability was avoided on the basis that the duty had not been breached. Alternatively, it was held that the action would also fail for lack of causation, for the inference drawn by the court was that, even if the theatre had intervened, the claimants would still have allowed Pettie to drive.

Apart from the fact that it makes difficult a neat summary of the current approach of the Canadian courts to alcohol provider liability, the confusion evidenced by the Supreme Court in *Pettie* as regards the nature of the distinction between the duty and breach elements of negligence is of little concern in the present context. A broad conclusion which can still be drawn is that those who provide alcohol in Canada to persons who subsequently become intoxicated risk incurring liability in tort if such provision takes place in circumstances in which there is a foreseeable risk that the intoxicated person will engage in a potentially harmful course of action. The cases may further suggest that it is only the risks associated with roads and road vehicles that would be deemed foreseeable enough in this respect. If so, then this would certainly constitute one way in which the principles of alcohol provider liability are self-limiting.

It is to be noted at this point, however, that it is not only by placing themselves in the position of providers that Canadian citizens run the risk of being sued in respect of alcohol-related injuries. There is a designated area of Canadian tort law known as alcohol liability, which boasts a number of established categories.[11] Of these, provider liability is simply the one that has received the most attention. The others include: alcohol-related occupiers' liability;[12] liability for sponsoring

[10] On this point, see the dicta of Evans LJ in *Barrett v Enfield London Borough Council* [1997] 2 FLR 167.

[11] See further, R Solomon and J Payne, 'Alcohol Liability in Canada and Australia: Sell, Serve and be Sued' (1996) 4 Tort LR 188.

[12] See, eg, *Niblock v Pacific National Exhibition* (1981) 30 BCLR 20; *Buehl v Polar Star Enterprises Inc* (1989) 72 OR (2d) 573; *McGinty v Cook* (1991) 79 DLR (4th) 95.

dangerous activities involving the intoxicated,[13] and liability for transporting the intoxicated.[14] Significantly, if the importance of each category were to be judged in accordance with the amount of litigation generated by it, alcohol-related occupiers' liability would actually rank much higher than provider liability. This is because in Canadian tort law the principles governing occupiers' liability are expansive, particularly in comparison with those existing in the UK. Such liability may arise not only in respect of the condition of the premises and activities taking place there, but also by reference to the conduct of entrants. There are a number of reasons why the provider liability cases have, nevertheless, attained the highest profile. First, these cases have reached the highest courts and have been officially reported, whereas the others, for the most part, have warranted a mention only in the regional or local press. Also, insurance companies are often quick to settle alcohol-related occupiers' liability claims at the outset, for it has become a fairly established area of liability, with the result that these suits do not get any publicity.

(ii) Australia

The development of alcohol liability in Australia, although along similar lines to that in Canada, has progressed at a much slower pace, Australian judges having tended to proceed with much greater caution than their Canadian counterparts.[15] As yet, it is only occupiers[16] and commercial alcohol providers[17] who may find themselves saddled with liability in respect of the intoxicated, with the courts using the notion of proximity and the requirement of a high degree of foreseeability as mechanisms of control. The Australian courts are also more likely than those in Canada to allow a *volenti* defence to be used against an intoxicated claimant.[18] Nevertheless, a significant body of jurisprudence on the subject now exists, and recent indications are that it is going to continue to expand.

[13] *Crocker v Sundance Northwest Resorts Ltd* (1988) 44 CCLT 225.

[14] *Dunn v Dominion Atlantic Railway Co* (1920) 60 SCR 310; *The Canadian Pacific Railway Co v Blain* (1904) 34 SCR 74.

[15] For a good example of Australian caution in this respect, see the recent decision of the High Court of Australia in *Cole v South Tweed Heads Rugby League Football Club Ltd* [2004] HCA 29.

[16] *Chordas v Bryant (Wellington) Pty Ltd* (1988) 92 FLR 401; *Wormald v Robertson* (1992) *Australian Torts Reports* 81-180; *Gorman v Williams* [1985] 2 NSWLR 662.

[17] *Johns v Cosgrove & Chevron Queensland Ltd* unreported, 12 December 1997 (Qld Sup Ct); *Rosser v Vintage Nominees Pty Ltd Licensee* unreported, 5 June 1998 (District Court of Western Australia). References taken from T Blyth, 'Hotelier and Social Host Liability for Alcohol-Related Injuries – A Review of The Law in Australia' (1999) E Law – Murdoch University Electronic Journal of Law, vol 6, no 3.

[18] R Solomon and J Payne, above n 11, p 120.

II. THE POSITION IN ENGLISH LAW

Writing in 1988 about the development of alcohol provider liability in the United States, Jeremy Horder concluded that it was unlikely, 'if not impossible',[19] that this kind of liability would ever find a place in English tort law. It is true that, as yet, this specific form of alcohol liability has not established itself in England and Wales.[20] However, diverse forms of alcohol liability are beginning to creep into the legal system, albeit in a rather haphazard fashion.

Our starting point is *Barrett v Ministry of Defence*,[21] in which the widow of a naval airman who died at an airbase after consuming an excessive quantity of alcohol sued the Ministry of Defence (MoD) for failing to prevent her husband's death. The deceased had been stationed at an isolated base in northern Norway at which seemingly unlimited quantities of low-priced alcohol were freely available. On the fatal night in question, the deceased, who had been celebrating both his thirtieth birthday and news of a promotion, drank himself into a stupor. When he became unconscious, the duty senior rating organised for him to be taken by stretcher to his bunk, where he was placed in the recovery position. No medical attention was sought, although the duty ratings did check on him a number of times. The deceased, nevertheless, suffocated on his own vomit. In holding the MoD liable, Phelan J explained that, although it was only in exceptional circumstances that a defendant could be fixed with a duty to take positive steps to protect an adult of full capacity from his own foibles, such exceptional circumstances existed in this case. The fact that the deceased was known to be a heavy drinker, combined with the free availability of alcohol and the very lax attitude of those in charge towards drunkenness, made it readily foreseeable that the deceased would become intoxicated. Of particular importance also was the capacity of the defendant to exercise control over the prevailing environment and to discourage drunkenness through the implementation of the existing codes of discipline. Instead, these were largely ignored. By the standards set out in the relevant Navy regulations and standing orders to cover the exact type of situation in question, the care provided to the deceased was wholly inadequate. Phelan J did recognise, however, that the deceased was at least partly to blame for his own fate, and made a finding of 25 per cent contributory negligence.

The MoD appealed against the decision, contending that the judge had been wrong to find that a duty of care existed in the circumstances, or that, alternatively, the finding of contributory negligence should have been fixed at, at least, 50 per cent. Beldam LJ, delivering the main judgment of the Court of Appeal, agreed with the defendant's arguments to the extent that the judge had erred in

[19] 'Tort and the Road to Temperance: A Different Kind of Offensive Against the Drinking Driver' (1988) 51 MLR 735 at 743.

[20] For an example of an early, unsuccessful, attempt to establish such liability in English law, see *Munro v Porthkerry Park Holiday Estates Ltd* (1984) 81 LSG 1368 (QBD).

[21] [1995] 1 WLR 1217 (CA).

his reasoning on the issues of duty and breach. In his view, the imposition on the defendant of a duty to control the actions of the deceased in order to prevent him from injuring himself would represent an unwarranted contravention of the principle of individual responsibility. He stated:

> I can see no reason why it should not be fair just and reasonable for the law to leave a responsible adult to assume responsibility for his own actions in consuming alcoholic drink. No one is better placed to judge the amount that he can safely consume or to exercise control in his own interest as well as in the interest of others. To dilute self-responsibility and to blame one adult for another's lack of self-control is neither just nor reasonable and in the development of the law of negligence an increment too far.[22]

He then went on to distinguish the Canadian decisions, *Jordan House*[23] and *Crocker v Sundance*,[24] stating that the duty of care in these cases was founded on factors additional to the mere provision of alcohol and the failure to enforce provisions against drunkenness.[25]

Crucially, however, although Beldam LJ concluded that the defendant was not under a duty to prevent the deceased from drinking so much that he fell unconscious, he held that, through its actions in putting the deceased into his bunk after he had collapsed, the defendant 'assumed responsibility' for the deceased and so placed itself under a continuing duty to exercise reasonable care to ensure his safety. Beldam LJ further held that, although the trial judge had been wrong to equate the Navy's regulations and standing orders with the legal standard of care required of the defendant, a breach of the duty of care could, nevertheless, still be established because, even by ordinary standards of reasonableness, the steps taken were wholly inadequate.

Beldam LJ therefore ultimately concurred with the judge's finding that liability should be imposed on the defendant. However, he chose to give effect to his view that individuals should be made to take primary responsibility for their own actions by varying the apportionment of liability, increasing the deceased's level of contributory negligence from one quarter to two thirds.

Interestingly, the issue of the liability of the MoD for harm suffered by intoxicated servicemen has arisen once again for consideration. The outcome does not bode well for the MoD. In *Jebson v MoD*,[26] the claimant was a soldier who had fallen from the back of an army lorry after climbing onto its tailgate in a fit of drunken high spirits. He was with a group of soldiers being transported back from a night out organised by the company commander. The thrust of his argument was that in arranging the outing with the knowledge that it would involve heavy drinking, and in supplying the transport, the defendants had placed

[22] *Ibid* at 1224.
[23] Above n 1.
[24] (1988) 44 CCLT 225.
[25] [1995] 1 WLR 1217 at 1225.
[26] [2000] 1 WLR 2055.

themselves under a duty to provide adequate supervision of the men while in the lorry and that they had failed to do this. The driver, who was the only sober member of the party, was unable to see into the back of the lorry from his front cab. Overturning the decision of the trial judge, the Court of Appeal found in favour of the claimant.

In a judgment that has clear echoes of Beldam LJ in *Barrett*, Potter LJ stated that, although ordinarily an adult could not rely on his drunkenness so as to impose a duty on others to exercise special care, this was not an invariable rule.[27] It did not apply in this case, because the defendants had impliedly undertaken an obligation of care towards the claimant. For Potter LJ, the fact that the defendants had provided the transport for the soldiers, knowing that they were all likely to become inebriated, was crucial to this conclusion.[28] He did, however, assess the claimant's contributory negligence at 75 per cent.

Jebson would thus appear to send out a clear message to the MoD that the courts do not intend to resile from the principle of third party liability in respect of the intoxicated set out in *Barrett*. Unfortunately, the Court of Appeal did not avail itself of the opportunity presented by this case to elaborate on the reasons why the MoD has been made a particular target for this kind of liability. It can only be assumed that it has to do with the nature of the relationship that exists between servicemen and their employers, with its emphasis on control, and perhaps with the strong alcohol-related culture that seems to pervade military life. It is noteworthy that Potter LJ did try to pre-empt the making of a direct link between the finding of liability and the military status of the defendants, but his attempt was so feeble as to be without meaning. His example of 'an appropriate analogy from civilian life'[29] was that of a works outing arranged by an employer, together with transport and a driver, for 'a group of young and boisterous employees'.[30] Not content with limiting the ambit of the ratio by reference to the characteristics of potential claimants, however, he went on to introduce the type of vehicle involved as a further qualifying factor, specifying that it be a lorry with a similarly positioned tailgate and a driver who is unable to see into the back of it. It is submitted that this would seldom apply to a non-military vehicle.

The next case of interest in this context is *Griffiths v Brown*,[31] which involved a claim in negligence against a taxi driver for injuries sustained by an inebriated passenger *after* he had alighted from the vehicle. The passenger in question had been dropped off by the taxi driver across the road from the specific destination he had requested. While crossing the road, he was hit by a car and seriously injured. He sued the taxi driver, alleging that the latter was under a duty of care not to set him down at any point at which it was foreseeable that, because of his intoxication, he would be at a greater risk of injury than a sober person. He

27 *Ibid* at 2066.
28 *Ibid.*
29 *Ibid* at 2065.
30 *Ibid.*
31 (1998) *The Times*, October 23.

argued that the taxi driver had breached this duty by obliging him to cross the road to get to his destination.

The claim failed. Jones J opined that the defendant was under no duty of care to the claimant, other than to take reasonable care to carry him safely during his journey and to set him down at a place where he could safely alight. In this, his duty was no different to that which would be owed to a sober passenger. He distinguished the Canadian authorities in much the same way as Beldam LJ did in *Barrett*, stating that the particular circumstances that gave rise to the duties in those cases were not present in the case at hand. However, in a move that had the effect of seriously undermining the conclusiveness of this pronouncement on duty, Jones J went on to consider the question of breach, making it clear that his purpose in doing so was to guard against the possibility that a duty did actually exist in the circumstances. In doing this, he also further elaborated on the kind of situation in which, in his view, it would be feasible for a duty of care to exist. For him, the degree of intoxication was determinative, for he considered that such a duty could exist only where a passenger had reached such a state of intoxication as to be plainly incapable of taking care of his or her own safety. It followed that this was also the only circumstance in which the duty could be breached. In this case, the claimant had consumed somewhere in the region of 12 to 13 pints of strong lager and was obviously very drunk. But the fact that he was able to walk without staggering and give instructions to the defendant as to his destination was taken as evidence that he still retained some degree of control over himself. This, in consequence, meant that a breach of duty could not be established.

The natural conclusion is that had the claimant been in a worse state, a duty of care could have been both owed and breached by the taxi driver.[32] Interpreted in this way, the decision is entirely reconcilable with *Barrett*. The principle to emerge is that an undertaking to provide a service to, or in some way to come to the aid of, an individual who is so intoxicated as to be incapable of taking care for his or her own safety will be held to amount to an 'assumption of responsibility' for that person and so give rise to a duty of protection. That this notion of there being an 'assumption of responsibility' is judicially recognised as constituting a legitimate ground on which to base a duty to rescue the intoxicated is supported by other dicta of Jones J in *Griffiths*.

When discussing the kinds of situation in which a duty of care would arise on the part of the taxi driver, Jones J put forward the example of a young child or a mentally impaired person travelling alone in a taxi. He opined that, due to the inability of such passengers to take proper care for their own safety, they would be carried only by virtue of some special arrangement under which the taxi driver would assume some 'added responsibility' towards them. He cited also the example of an individual intending to become intoxicated on a night out and ordering a taxi in advance to take him or her home safely. If these drinking intentions were made known to the driver then Jones J considered that a duty would

[32] Such is the interpretation of the decision given by R Lawson at (1998) 142 SJ 1064.

arise 'because of what had been agreed or arranged and the express or implied assumption of added responsibility by the driver'. Arguably, this latter example could be seen as an extension into the 'civilian' world of the principle of liability set out in *Jebson.*

Of course, identifying the concept of an 'assumption of responsibility' as forming the basis of the duty to protect the intoxicated is the easy part. The more difficult task lies in determining what actually constitutes such an assumption, for, other than the fact that it stems from an 'undertaking', which may be either express or implied, the judgments considered above provide little guidance. Clearly, where there is an express undertaking there can be no problem. The difficulty lies with knowing how to identify an implied undertaking to assume responsibility. It becomes necessary to take our analysis further afield.

An obvious starting point would be the House of Lords decision in *Hedley Byrne & Co Ltd v Heller & Partners Ltd*,[33] which famously established a limited exception to the rule against recovery in tort for negligently inflicted economic loss. This case sets out that a duty to take reasonable care not to cause pure economic loss will arise where a special relationship exists between the claimant and the defendant, such relationship being based upon two reciprocating factors: a voluntary assumption of responsibility on the part of the defendant, and reasonable reliance on this assumption on the part of the claimant. Although the *Hedley Byrne* principle was originally confined to cases of economic loss arising from negligent misstatements, it was later extended to include instances of such loss caused through the provision of services,[34] and it is this latter category that would appear to be of most relevance to the issue at hand. However, it takes only a brief excursion into this area of the law to realise that this line of inquiry is unlikely to lead anywhere. For although the *Hedley Byrne* concept of 'assumption of responsibility' is now into its fourth decade of existence, there is still much debate surrounding such fundamental issues as its true meaning,[35] purpose or, indeed, utility. It has been severely criticised in judicial quarters as being more of a label than a substantive test,[36] for it gives no indication of the criteria that underpin it. Nor has it even been applied in a consistent manner by the courts. As Janet O'Sullivan points out,[37] in some cases it has been used to label a genuine exercise of choice by the defendant in question to act on behalf of the particular claimant;[38] in others, to denote a situation in which the defendant ought to have decided to act on behalf of the claimant, whether or not he or she actually did.[39]

[33] [1964] AC 465.

[34] *Henderson v Merrett Syndicates Ltd* [1994] 3 All ER 506.

[35] The current predominant view seems to be that it refers to relationships that are 'equivalent to contract'. See D Howarth, *Textbook on Tort* (Butterworths, 1995), p 276.

[36] See, eg, dicta of Lord Griffiths in *Smith v Eric Bush* [1989] 2 All ER 514 at 536, and of Lords Roskill and Oliver in *Caparo Industries Plc v Dickman* [1990] 2 AC 605 at 628 and 637. See also K Barker, 'Unreliable Assumptions in the Modern Law of Negligence' (1993) 109 LQR 461.

[37] 'Negligence Liability of Auditors to Third Parties and the Role of Assumption of Responsibility' (1998) 14 PN 195 at 198–99.

[38] See, eg, *Henderson v Merrett Syndicates Ltd* [1994] 3 All ER 506.

[39] An example of this may be found in *White v Jones* [1993] 3 All ER 481.

Used in this latter way, it is a legal fiction which constitutes little more than a watered-down proximity test, for it may be based on merely the fact that there is a close relationship between the claimant and the defendant, even in the absence of any personal dealings between them.

Moreover, due to the fact that it applies exclusively to cases of economic loss, and that these cases straddle the boundary between tort and contract, the *Hedley Byrne* concept of assumption of responsibility has strong contractual affinities. In the context of the present discussion on alcohol liability, the principles of contract law have no application at all. The need for a concomitant reliance on the part of the claimant also further distinguishes the *Hedley Byrne* notion from that used in relation to alcohol liability, for it cannot realistically be suggested that the reason why individuals actively seek to become intoxicated, knowing that the attainment of such a state carries with it certain risks, is that they rely on others, especially strangers, to protect them from such risks. If they give any thought at all to the risks, they either see them as highly unlikely to materialise, or as simply outweighed by the benefits. Even if such reliance did exist, it could hardly be deemed reasonable.

If the courts have not set out any guiding principles for determining the existence of an assumption of responsibility, then the natural conclusion to be drawn is that they do not have in mind any specific principles, but simply approach the question in individual cases on an ad hoc basis. In the context of alcohol liability, the attribution of this kind of an assumption would seem to be made on the basis that the particular defendant could easily prevent the injury through low-cost measures, and it is considered appropriate in the circumstances that he or she should render such protection. This could be construed as the introduction into our legal system of a duty of easy rescue, such as that advocated by Weinrib almost three decades ago.[40] Quite apart from the fact that it would be effecting a complete reversal of well-entrenched law without any overt discussion of the issue, the recognition of an affirmative duty of action on such terms would appear to be entirely unjustified in the context of harm suffered as a result of voluntary intoxication. None of the factors underlying the other established third party duties to protect that have been discussed so far in this book are present here. In particular, there is no relationship of authority and control between the parties, such as that existing between parents and children or referees and rugby players,[41] and the victims involved in these intoxication cases cannot be regarded as inherently vulnerable, in the sense that they do not have to depend almost entirely on the defendant to safeguard them in certain situations. Indeed, the fact that any risks to which they may be exposed will be ones that they have created for themselves, and indeed have positively embraced, should, arguably, by itself prevent them from invoking the responsibility of anyone other than themselves in the event of the actual materialisation of the risks.

[40] EJ Weinrib, 'The Case for a Duty to Rescue' (1980) 90 Yale LJ 247.

[41] See ch 5.

The third and final decision for discussion in the present context is that of the Court of Appeal in *Brannon v Airtours Plc.*[42] Its significance in the present context lies primarily in what it reveals about the court's attitude to the issue of the intoxicated victim's contributory negligence. Illustrating the diverse contexts in which the principles of alcohol liability in English tort law have been applied, the defendant in this particular case was a tour operator, responsible for organising an evening of entertainment at which the claimant was injured. The festivities in question took place at a holiday resort in Tunisia, where the claimant was staying as part of a package deal organised by the defendants, and consisted of the usual mixture of food, music and copious quantities of alcohol. Long tables with benches had been arranged to seat the party-goers, and at the end of these were placed electric fans. A general warning had been issued at the start of the evening by an Airtours representative about the dangers of walking on the tables because of the presence of the fans. However, as the night wore on, and inhibitions became loosened by alcohol, the claimant, like many others, began to walk across the tables anyway. Predictably, he ended up injuring himself on one of the fans.

At trial, the judge held Airtours liable for the claimant's injuries on the grounds that it had knowingly introduced him into a dangerous setting and intentionally put him into a party mood by providing him, free of charge, with unlimited quantities of alcohol. Moreover, Airtours had known the fans to be a danger since another holidaymaker had previously been injured by one, yet its representatives had issued only one warning about this on the night in question and made no attempt to prevent the party-goers, including the claimant, from climbing onto the tables. Recognising, however, that the claimant was primarily to blame for his own injuries, in that he had walked into a readily visible fan, the court made a finding of 75 per cent contributory negligence. It is against this finding that the claimant successfully appealed.[43] Giving the judgment of the Court of Appeal, Auld LJ accepted the claimant's argument that the figure had been set too high and duly reduced the figure to 50 per cent.

III. CONCLUSION

As yet, the development in English law of a set of principles of liability in respect of the intoxicated has taken place at a fairly restrained pace, particularly by comparison with other Commonwealth jurisdictions. Such liability has not yet extended beyond the factual scenario of the intoxicated as the victim, as opposed to the perpetrator, of harm. As a result of its foundation upon the entirely nebulous concept of 'an assumption of responsibility', however, concerns must already

[42] (1999) *The Times*, February 1.

[43] Significantly, no cross-appeal was made by the defendants against the finding of negligence.

be voiced about the legitimacy of such a form of third party liability, and moreover, about the potential for the scope of such liability to expand even further. Indeed, it is entirely conceivable that future ill-considered and equally loose applications of this 'assumption of responsibility' notion could result in the extension of the law on liability for the acts of others beyond all defensible limits. For this reason, the response to the existence in English law of any form of alcohol liability on this basis has to be one of hostility.

5

Third Party Liability in Sport

A FURTHER IDENTIFIABLE category of third party liability involving private law defendants concerns the world of organised competitive sport. One of the more recent additions to the field, it is most notable perhaps for its singularity. That is to say, the sporting arena does not form the most obvious backdrop to actions of this nature and seems to share little in common with the contextual settings of the other established categories. In particular, there is typically no issue of vulnerability arising. However, one need only consider the combination of fast-paced activity and competitive spirit, the high degree of physical contact and elevated risk of injury, together with the existence of an often large number of intermediaries who will be involved in a directional capacity, to see that the sporting arena can be fertile ground indeed for the formation of claims invoking the liability of third parties.

I. THIRD PARTY LIABILITY ACTIONS AGAINST REFEREES

In England, the issue of third party liability in sport first came before the courts in the case of *Smoldon v Whitworth*,[1] in which the referee of a colts rugby match was sued by one of the players in respect of the serious injuries he sustained when a scrum collapsed.[2] The basis of the claim against the referee was that he had been negligent in failing to implement specific safety measures designed to prevent collapses. The safety rules were said to be contained in the Laws of the Game issued by the sport's governing body, the International Rugby Football Board. In recognition of the increased physical vulnerability to injury of players under the age of 19, the Laws contained special provisions relating to colts games. The claimant relied, in particular, on Law 20, which set out that, for safety purposes, a routine known as the 'phased sequence of engagement' was to be followed in all colts matches. There was ample evidence to demonstrate that the defendant did not even understand the purpose of this particular provision, let

1 [1997] PIQR 133.

2 The claimant also sued one of the opposing players, but the claim was dismissed at first instance and no appeal was made against that decision.

alone enforce it, and the abnormally high number of collapsed scrums that had taken place during the game in question was particularly prejudicial to his case in this respect. It followed that if the claimant could just establish a duty to implement the rule then the breach element would more or less establish itself.

At trial, Curtis J did not treat the claim as being in any way exceptional. He did not advert to the fact that it was predicated upon the concept of liability for the acts of another and simply dealt with the duty issue by way of a straightforward application of the *Caparo* three-stage test.[3] In particular, he saw no reason why it would be unfair or unjust to impose a duty of care on the defendant and went on to find that liability in negligence could be easily established.

The defendant appealed on the basis that the standard of care applied by the judge was not appropriate to the circumstances of the case, and that the finding of fault was therefore insupportable. That he did not contest the finding of a duty of care is of crucial importance in the context of the present discussion, for not only does this imply an unquestioning acceptance of the admissibility of the principles of third party liability into this particular field, which in turn suggests a possible softening of the traditionally hostile judicial approach to this type of liability, it also constitutes a significant expansion of the grounds upon which such liability can be founded. In *Smoldon*, the duty was based seemingly entirely upon the defendant's position of authority and consequent power to exert active control over the conduct of the players, without any real concomitant reliance on the part of the potential victims. The duty of care owed by a referee can thus be described as the amalgamation of both a duty to control and a duty to protect. It is distinctive, however, in that the class of persons that the referee is bound to control corresponds exactly with the class that he is bound to protect. That is, the potential third party perpetrators and the potential victims are one and the same.

That a special pre-tort relationship can consequently be established between the referee and both of the other parties involved in the tort action is what makes the imposition of a duty of care justifiable in this type of third party liability case, not least because it imports a significant restriction on the scope of the duty. It is submitted that the potential third party liability does not therefore extend beyond injuries as inflicted between players on the actual playing field. Notably, it would not cover harm caused by players to spectators or officials, or vice versa. The existence of two concurrent special relationships, that is, one between the referee and the claimant and another between the referee and the third party harm-doer, is thus to be regarded as an essential prerequisite to the existence of the referee's affirmative duty of action.

While the defendant in *Smoldon* did not rely on the exceptional nature of the liability issue at stake to contest the duty of care, he did introduce it as a remoteness argument. Relying on dicta of Lord Mackay in *Smith v Littlewoods Organisation Ltd*,[4] he asserted that where it is sought to hold one person liable for

[3] From *Caparo Industries plc v Dickman* [1990] 2 AC 605, the elements of the test are: (1) foreseeability; (2) proximity; and (3) fair, just and reasonableness.

[4] [1987] AC 241 at 261.

the acts of another, it must be shown that the kind of injury suffered by the claimant was a highly probable consequence of the defendant's breach of duty. In other words, in this type of case, the ordinary *Wagon Mound*[5] test of reasonable foreseeability is replaced with a much more stringent 'high likelihood' requirement. It is submitted that, in the circumstances, this was an entirely valid point for, as discussed in chapter 3, while a 'high likelihood' test for remoteness may not be appropriate in the type of scenario found in *Smith*, it probably does apply in third party liability actions based upon a duty to control.[6] However, the Court of Appeal in *Smoldon* rejected this argument outright, holding that it was sufficient that the harm complained of could be shown to be a foreseeable result of the defendant's failure to prevent the scrum collapsing, and that this was so even though, statistically speaking, it was a result that was very unlikely to eventuate.[7]

The issue that most preoccupied the Court of Appeal, and indeed that upon which the finding of liability ultimately rested, was the applicable standard of care. As already stated, this constituted the main basis of the defendant's appeal. Relying on *Wooldridge v Sumner*,[8] the defendant's argument was that nothing short of a reckless disregard of the claimant's safety would suffice to establish a breach of duty. The claimant, on the other hand, put forward the authority of *Condon v Basi*[9] and contended that the defendant's duty was to exercise such a degree of care as was appropriate in the circumstances. Like the trial judge, the Court of Appeal agreed with the claimant on this issue also. Bingham LCJ stated that, although sporting competitors in a vigorous and fast-moving contest may be entitled to be all but oblivious of those around them, so that any conduct falling short of recklessness could be more or less excused, the same could not be said of referees.[10] Their position is different precisely because one of their main functions is to ensure the safety of players. The standard of care to be expected of them is, therefore, much higher. The only concession to be made on their part is that in a fast-moving game, the referee would not ordinarily be held liable for a mere error of judgment. On this analysis, a breach of duty was easily established in the present case, for there was a very clear failure on the part of the defendant to enforce the relevant safety rules.

In giving judgment against the defendant, Bingham LCJ made clear his concern lest the decision be seen as leading referees into a downward spiral of litigation. He thus took great care to emphasise the special nature of the circumstances involved and how this placed clear limitations on the ratio of the

[5] *Overseas Tankship (UK) Ltd v Morts Dock & Engineering Co Ltd, The Wagon Mound* [1961] AC 388.

[6] See above pp 52–61.

[7] [1997] PIQR 133 at 139, 140.

[8] [1963] 2 QB 43.

[9] [1985] 2 All ER 453.

[10] [1997] PIQR 133 at 139.

decision.[11] In this context, the fact that it had been a colts match was of crucial importance, since the safety rules in question applied only to this type of game. Moreover, the failure on the part of the defendant to enforce these rules had been particularly blatant. From this latter point, it could be deduced that if the fault of the defendant had been less serious or less clear, the court might have been less inclined to impose liability.

Nevertheless, it was somewhat predictable that the decision in *Smoldon* should trigger a highly publicised backlash of opinion.[12] Indeed, the National Union of Teachers even threatened to boycott after-school sports unless commitments were made to ensure that teachers involved in these activities would be adequately covered by insurance. It would be easy now, with the benefit of hindsight, to dismiss such furore as an overreaction, for the anticipated barrage of similar actions would not appear to have materialised. The only significant subsequent case that seems to have been founded directly on *Smoldon* is that of *Vowles v Evans*,[13] in which, on a remarkably similar set of facts, an amateur referee was again held liable in negligence for serious spinal injuries caused as a result of a collapsed scrum. Of course, the absence of reported cases in this context does not mean that *Smoldon* has not had a great legal impact, for it is entirely possible that any claims being brought on this basis are simply being settled out of court and thus not being publicised. It will certainly also have had obvious insurance implications for clubs and referees, so that the main consequences of the decision are being felt behind the lines, as it were. In any event, what is important for present purposes is the fact that *Smoldon* has created a whole new strand of third party liability, and that its ratio could clearly be applied to any sport in which the risk of injury is high. Obvious examples would be football, hockey, judo, karate, and boxing, to name just a few. Any failure to enforce recognised safety provisions could be cited as negligence, and the main hurdles would be to establish that the defendant's fault was sufficiently serious and that there was an adequate causal link between this fault and the harm complained of.

In the meantime, however, the law on sports liability has developed in a different direction, for it is rather the sports administrative bodies responsible for rule-making that have been targeted in recent years. It is more attractive to pursue governing bodies as defendants because, in comparison with the position of the referee as in *Smoldon*, their potential liability is much more far-reaching. It was in Australia that this type of action was first mounted.

[11] *Ibid*, at 139 and 147.

[12] See, eg, 'Teachers May Refuse to Take Up Whistle', *Daily Telegraph*, 18 December 1996, and 'Teachers Threaten to Boycott Sport', *The Guardian*, 20 May 1996. See also S Greenfield and G Osborn, 'The referee's fear of a penalty' (1996) 12 PN 63.

[13] [2003] EWCA Civ 318.

II. THIRD PARTY LIABILITY ACTIONS AGAINST SPORTS GOVERNING BODIES

In two separate incidents in Australia in the mid-1980s, two rugby players suffered similar catastrophic injuries in scrumming accidents. Determined to obtain compensation through the tort system, but unable to point to anyone as being immediately and directly responsible for the harm,[14] they adopted an innovative approach to establishing liability and targeted numerous third party defendants in a series of legal actions spanning more than a decade. Focusing their attentions on the way in which the rugby matches in question had been generally conducted and, in particular, on how the formal rules of the game had been applied, the claimants brought negligence actions against, among others, the opposing clubs, the referees, the referees' association, the Australian Rugby Football Union, the New South Wales Rugby Union and the Sydney Rugby Union.

The allegations against the defendants related, in part, to a failure to properly enforce the rules of the game, although in the circumstances, this argument was not, in itself, strong enough to sustain the claim. The claimants recognised that, as far as the actual infliction of their injuries was concerned, the real problem had been that the rules themselves had been inadequate in that they did not make adequate provision for safety regarding scrummages.[15] Thus, in a rather audacious move, the claimants further contended that these defendants had been negligent also in failing to have the rules modified so as to allow for scrummaging to take place safely. They were, thus, in effect, reproaching the defendants, on the one hand, for failing to apply certain rules and, on the other hand, for actually applying others. It was clear, however, that this latter argument was fatally flawed in that the parties pursued were not responsible for making the rules, this being rather the sole domain of the sport's governing body, the International Rugby Football Board (IRFB). It would therefore have been open to these defendants to have met this allegation with the argument that they had no discretion on the matter and simply had to apply the rules as promulgated by this body. In anticipation of this, the claimants sought to join the IRFB as co-defendant. While, in theory, this may have sounded like a straightforward solution, in practice, it turned out to be a particularly problematic task that was to launch them into a whole new saga of litigation and ultimately take them all the way to the High Court of Australia.

The first hurdle the claimants encountered was that, as an unincorporated association, the IRFB was not a legal entity and so could not be sued as such.[16] To

[14] No allegations of negligence could be made against any of the opposing players.

[15] It is important to note, however, that at no point was it suggested by the claimants that the rules of the game were, in themselves, legally dispositive.

[16] See *Luke Douglas Hyde v Australian Rugby Football Union Ltd as representative of the International Rugby Football Board*, unreported, 10 February 1994 (NSW Supt Ct).

get around this, the claimants instead joined the actual Member Unions of which the IRFB was made up and the representatives of the Member Unions who had attended the relevant meetings, that is, those meetings taking place before the claimants' injuries were occasioned and at which the rules of the game could have been modified. It is of interest to note that the principal amendment to the rules that the claimants argued should have been made was the introduction of the 'crouch-touch-pause-engage' sequence, or 'phased sequence of engagement' procedure, as a compulsory requirement. It was the non-enforcement of this specific requirement which formed the basis of the referee's liability in *Smoldon* a few years later, it having been officially incorporated into the rules by the IRFB in 1988.

Having overcome this initial hurdle, however, the claimants still had to convince the court, in accordance with the New South Wales Supreme Court Rules 1970, that they had a 'good arguable case' against these IRFB defendants, otherwise leave to proceed against them could not be granted. At first instance, they were unsuccessful.[17] For Grove J, the sheer physical distance between the parties was more or less fatal to the existence of a duty of care, for it meant that the requirement of proximity could not be meaningfully satisfied. The individual IRFB defendants were, after all, from different parts of the world and connected to each other only by their attendance at various meetings held in Europe, while the claimants were just two unknown rugby players from Australia. To be taken in conjunction with this also was the voluntary nature of the rules concerned. The IRFB was a voluntary association, and the claimants were adults who had made the choice to participate in the sport and who had thereby implied their acceptance of the rules laid down by this governing body. Moreover, given that there existed no precedent for this particular duty, a very strong and compelling case for its current recognition would have to have been made out, and this simply had not been done in this instance.

The claimants appealed successfully to the Court of Appeal of New South Wales.[18] Without expressing any definite opinion as to whether or not a duty of care was owed by the IRFB in the circumstances, Spigelman CJ, Mason P, and Stein JA were sufficiently persuaded by the claimants' arguments of the theoretical possibility of its existence to allow the matter to proceed to full trial. Crucial to this decision was 'evidence of assumption of control by the members of the IRFB and tenable allegations of reliance by the players of the sport',[19] the relationship of rule-maker and those bound by the rules creating the necessary relationship of proximity. The geographical distance between the parties was considered to be of little consequence. Thus, while the Supreme Court had required evidence of real and effective control by the defendants of the circumstances and, by extension, of a de facto control of all the players on the field, to

[17] *Hyde v AE Agar; Worsley v Australian Rugby Football Union*, unreported, 22 July 1996 (NSW Supt Ct).

[18] *Hyde v Agar; Worsley v Australian Rugby Football Union Ltd* (1998) 45 NSWLR 487.

[19] *Ibid* at 512.

satisfy the proximity element of the *Caparo* three-stage test for duty, the Court of Appeal was prepared to accept that a mere notional control of the general situation would suffice. Given that the high incidence of spinal cord injuries to rugby players had been well documented for many years, it was also arguable that the defendants should reasonably have foreseen that their failure to amend the rules to make better provision for safety would result in harm of this nature being sustained by the claimants. Furthermore, it could not be concluded at this stage that an argument that it would be unfair, unjust or unreasonable to impose a duty on the IRFB would necessarily defeat the claim. The defendants duly appealed.[20]

In the High Court of Australia, the principal focus of attention was on the issue of control and, in particular, on the circumstance in which the exercise of a power to control could be said to give rise to an 'assumption of responsibility', for this was treated by Gleeson CJ, Gaudron, McHugh, Gummow, Hayne, and Callinan JJ as being more or less determinative of the duty issue. They disagreed with much that had been said on the matter in the Court of Appeal, aligning themselves much more closely with the reasoning of Grove J in the Supreme Court. In their opinions, there were a number of factors that clearly negated the existence of any real control on the part of the IRFB defendants. First of all, there was the lack of any prior personal contact between the parties:

> To speak of persons who were sent once a year to London as representatives of national unions, as controlling a game of football played in a Sydney suburb, or a country town, by reason of their collective capacity to alter the international rules, is to speak of a remote form of control.[21]

Second, there was the fact that the various IRFB defendants did not have the power as individuals, and therefore in the capacity in which they were being sued, to change the laws of the game, since any proposed amendments had to be approved by a majority of at least three quarters of those present at the relevant meeting.[22] Finally, the victims in question were adults who had participated in the sport of their own free will.[23]

The High Court judgments were permeated by a marked fear lest the floodgates be opened up. Gleeson CJ stated that the extent of the potential liability of the defendants would be limited only by the number of persons who chose to play this sport anywhere in the world.[24] It is clear that this fear greatly influenced the judges' ultimate decision and, in their eagerness to present their denial of liability as categorically as possible, they put forward as many justifications for it

[20] [2000] HCA 41 (3 August 2000).
[21] *Ibid* at para 16 per Gleeson CJ.
[22] *Ibid* at para 74.
[23] *Ibid* at para 13.
[24] *Ibid* at para 19.

as they could muster. Unfortunately, some of the arguments advanced are not capable of withstanding much scrutiny. Gleeson CJ, for instance, claimed that one reason militating against the existence of a legal duty was '[t]he high degree of subjectivity of an assessment as to what level of risk inherent in the sport as played according to a certain set of rules, is unnecessary.'[25] However, that amounts to saying that difficult, though not impossible, tasks should not be attempted by the courts at all, as though the courts' convenience is more important than the issue of the validity of the claimant's right to compensation. The courts are confronted by such difficulties all the time and should be quite competent at dealing with them. It was also said that, in order to determine the issue of reliance, factors such as the attitudes, capacities and propensities of individual players would have to be taken into account, and that these were beyond the influence of the defendants.[26] However, this would not be a problem if reliance were simply construed as an objective concept.

These criticisms aside, the grounds given by the High Court for its dismissal of the action do, in general, have sound basis in established legal principle.[27] As such, the decision has to be regarded as constructing a bar to future claims by injured sportspersons against the individual members of distant supranational rule-making bodies for making inadequate provision for safety in the rules of the game. It is submitted, however, that if it had not been for the status of the IRFB as an unincorporated association, then the outcome might have been entirely different. For, arguably, if it had not been necessary to single out the individual members of the body, the High Court would not have been so insistent that some kind of personal contact or personal dealings be established between the parties to the action as a prerequisite to legal proximity. If so, it follows that the *Hyde* litigation may still provide the theoretical basis for other negligence actions against sports governing bodies that can be sued in their own right. The proximity requirement would probably take on a more abstract form and be more easily satisfied in consequence. Further actions of this nature involving any sport in which the risk of injury is known to be high would then have to be anticipated. That such an action has already been successfully brought in the UK, in the context of professional boxing, lends much support to this proposition. Although not strictly a third party liability action, in that the negligence of the defendant regulatory body in this instance related to its failure to remedy the consequences of harm occasioned through the medium of a third party, rather than to failings relating specifically to the actual harm-causing conduct as such, the case in question is nevertheless instructive in this context in that the legal approach it demonstrates to the general issue of

[25] *Ibid* at para 18.
[26] *Ibid* at para 21.
[27] For a contrary view, see S Yeo, 'The Infallibility of Rule-Making Sporting Bodies' (2001) 9 Tort LR 104.

liability for inadequate safety provision would also extend to factual situations involving rules relating to conduct.

Watson v British Boxing Board of Control[28] involved a negligence action by the former super-middleweight boxer Michael Watson against the British Boxing Board of Control (BBBC), a limited company, for the injuries he received during his famous world title fight against Chris Eubank in 1991. During the contest, Watson sustained a head injury resulting in a condition which, according to the weight of medical opinion, would have been largely remediable had appropriate medical treatment been promptly received. Unfortunately, the necessary resuscitation facilities were not available on the premises in question, the doctor attending at the ringside did not have the knowledge of the required resuscitation procedure, and the ambulance in attendance did not have the necessary resuscitation equipment. By the time Watson was taken to hospital and treated there, the condition had become irremediable and he suffered serious and permanent brain damage.

In the High Court, Kennedy J upheld Watson's claim, deciding that the BBBC was under a duty of care to its members and that this consisted of an obligation to alter its rules and regulations concerning safety to provide for resuscitation facilities, including the presence of a doctor with the relevant expertise, at the ringside for every one of its fights. An appeal by the BBBC was roundly dismissed by the Court of Appeal.[29] Giving the judgment of the court, Lord Philips MR specifically based the Board's positive duty to Watson on evidence of an assumption of responsibility with concomitant reliance. Fortunately, in this instance, and by contrast to the alcohol liability cases, the factors underlying this application of assumption of responsibility reasoning as the basis of liability were clearly spelt out.[30]

Of foremost importance was the absolute control exercised by the BBBC over professional boxing in the United Kingdom, to the extent that anyone wishing to play a role in this sport had to become one of its members and abide by its rules. The Board was also said to have encouraged and supported its members in the pursuit of an activity which involved inevitable physical injury and the need for

28 [2001] QB 1134.

29 Unfortunately for the Board, it is likely that the particular timing of the appeal will have done much to reinforce, in the eyes of the appellate court, the correctness of the first instance decision. For, in a strange coincidence, just several days prior to the hearing, another boxer suffered a similar injury in the ring to that sustained by Watson in 1991, and the incident was the subject of much media attention. See, eg, 'Sport Left Holding its Breath as Ingle Pays the Price of his Courage' (2000) *The Times*, 18 December; 'MP Calls for Inquiry After Boxer Left in Coma', (2000) *The Guardian*, 19 December; 'Sport Must Pay Heed to Lessons from Watson Verdict' (2000) *The Times*, December 20. This particular boxer, however, was fortunate enough to benefit from the tighter ringside safeguards that had been introduced in response to the Watson incident, and as a result, he was said to have made a much better recovery: 'Ingle Making Good Progress' (2000) *The Times*, December 28. Watson could not have asked for any greater vindication of the basic arguments underlying his claim.

30 [2001] QB 1134 at 1162, 1163

medical precautions. And not only had it publicly professed its concern for safety, it actually determined the measures taken to protect and promote the health and safety of boxers. Taken in conjunction with the fact that its safety stipulations were known to be readily obeyed by the various promoters and organisers of boxing matches, the evidence that the Board had held itself out as taking responsibility for safety in boxing was clearly very strong. In the circumstances, Watson's reliance on the Board to make adequate provision for safety was also entirely reasonable.[31] That the Board was a national governing body, rather than an international one like the IRFB, will presumably also have operated in Watson's favour, for it meant that the boundaries of its liability could be limited to a smaller and more readily definable class. There was thus not the same fear of indeterminate liability in this case as had been in evidence in *Hyde*.

In comparison with *Smoldon*, the duty of care in this case was clearly framed in more abstract terms. There was no physical contact between the defendant and the claimant, and the defendant did not exercise any de facto control over the actual match in question. Rather, its responsibility was linked to its more general position of authority and its indirect, but nonetheless effective, capacity to control the circumstances. Thus, while the liability of the referee under *Smoldon* is limited to what takes place on the sports field while he is there acting as an adjudicator, the liability of the rule-making body under *Watson* is potentially much wider and of a much more general nature. Nevertheless, it is submitted that the imposition of a duty of care on the defendant body in this instance was justifiable on the basis of its specific undertaking to its members. The duty is again limited by the existence of two, identical, special relationships of close proximity: one as between the defendant and the third party harm-doer and another as between the defendant and the victim.

Concerning breach and causation, Lord Philips MR merely endorsed the findings of Kennedy J. As regards breach, Kennedy J had applied a simple cost–benefit analysis and concluded that the Board had acted unreasonably. Crucial to this finding was the fact that the effectiveness of the particular resuscitation procedure in question in treating head injuries of the type sustained by Watson had been widely recognised since at least 1980. Moreover, the Board had failed to put forward any convincing reasons as to why it had not introduced this procedure as a standard response, which had led Kennedy J to the conclusion that the matter had simply not been given any consideration at all. While not referred to by Lord Philips MR, Kennedy J had also been critical of the fact that the doctors who had been recruited to attend the matches had not been chosen on account of their particular skills or experience, but had been selected rather because they had

[31] Not surprisingly, the Court of Appeal distanced itself from Kennedy J's rather sweeping and completely unsubstantiated statement at the trial that 'the pool from which professional boxers tend to be recruited is unlikely to be one with an innate or well-informed concern about safety' [2000] ECC 141 at 153.

been friends of existing doctors or had merely had an interest in the sport.[32] Overall, the evidence suggested that the level of fault was high.

On the issue of causation, although there was no conclusive evidence to show that Watson would have made a better recovery had he received timely resuscitation, there was enough to satisfy the balance of probabilities.[33]

Given that, as a direct result of the Watson case, the BBBC has now remedied its various failings concerning safety, it is unlikely that any further claims of this particular nature could be successfully brought against the Board in the future. Nevertheless, the decision is likely to have profound consequences for the sporting world generally. For not only is it apt to encourage similar actions against the governing bodies of other dangerous sports, it is also likely, given the extensive media coverage it has received, to bring the whole idea of suing in respect of sports injuries back to the forefront of public attention. It may thus inspire the formation of negligence actions on other grounds, with referees or other adjudicators becoming the obvious targets in this respect.[34]

That is not to suggest, however, that such claims would necessarily succeed, for both *Watson* and *Smoldon* would appear to set the fault requirement at a very high level. Potential claimants would thus need to be able to furnish very clear proof of unreasonable conduct, and this may be difficult to do in practice.[35] Moreover, it would seem that in relation to claims against rule-making bodies, the status of the body will also be of crucial importance, with international unincorporated associations being the most difficult to sue. The primary legal significance of the cases just discussed is that they establish that the matter is at least justiciable.

III. CONCLUSION

In conclusion, there are at least two grounds upon which a common law duty to prevent harm in sport may be based: (1) the occupation of a position of immediate authority with a resultant power of immediate and effective control; and (2) the occupation of a position of general authority and indirect control in which there has been an express assumption of responsibility with concomitant reliance. In both cases, the duty will be further subject to the existence of two special relationships of close proximity. Given that the potential scope of liability based

[32] *Ibid* at 154.

[33] Kennedy J's rejection of a defence of *volenti non fit injuria* on the grounds that Watson had not been aware of the Board's lax rule-drafting and that he could not therefore be taken to have consented to the dangers that this raised was not challenged by the Board on appeal.

[34] *Vowles v Evans* [2003] EWCA Civ 318 may indeed be said to constitute early evidence of this.

[35] See also J George, '*Watson v British Boxing Board of Control:* Negligent Rule-Making in the Court of Appeal' (2002) 65 MLR 106 at 116.

upon the second ground is clearly very wide, the additional requirement of an express undertaking on the part of the defendant to ensure the safety of the claimant carries out an essential limitative function. On either ground, however, the duty owed can be generally classified as one of protection arising out of a power of control over circumstances.

6

Third Party Liability Actions Involving Public Authority Defendants

PUBLIC AUTHORITY LIABILITY is a complex and confused area of the law. Given such a problematic starting point, it comes as no surprise to discover that, in cases where the allegations invoking that liability take the form of third party liability arguments, the law is confounded to the point of obscurity. To date, third party liability actions against public authorities in respect of the exercise of public law functions have all been founded in negligence, and so it is the law of negligence that will form the primary focus of this chapter. However, it is necessary to consider also the impact of the Human Rights Act 1998.

I. LIABILITY UNDER THE HUMAN RIGHTS ACT 1998

The Human Rights Act 1998 (hereafter HRA), which came into force on 2 October 2000, is designed to give 'further effect' to the European Convention for the Protection of Human Rights and Fundamental Freedoms (ECHR). Section 6(1) of the HRA imposes a duty on public authorities to act compatibly with Convention rights. Where a public authority, in breach of this provision, contravenes an individual's protected rights, section 7 provides that proceedings may be brought against the authority, and section 8 confers upon the court the power to provide the claimant with a remedy. Under section 8(4), the remedy may take the form of an award of damages. For those who have been harmed by a public authority, the HRA may thus provide an alternative route to compensation.

Until very recently, it was thought that the HRA would more or less subsume negligence actions against public authorities, particularly after the ruling of European Court of Human Rights (ECtHR) in *Z v UK*[1] and its endorsement of the policy arguments employed by the House of Lords in *X & ors v Bedfordshire County Council & ors*[2] to negative the existence of a common law duty of care on

[1] [2001] 2 FLR 612.
[2] [1995] 3 All ER 353.

the part of a local authority to take vulnerable children into care. However, as a result of the Court of Appeal decision in *JD & ors v East Berkshire Community Health & ors*[3] the legal landscape has changed dramatically and the negligence route to some forms of public authority liability has been completely opened up.[4] *JD & ors* involved negligence actions against child welfare professions in respect of psychiatric harm[5] suffered by three sets of parents who had been wrongfully accused of abusing their own children, and by one child who had been wrongfully removed from the family home as a result of false allegations of parental abuse. Distinguishing between the position of the parents and that of the child, the Court of Appeal decided that, as regards child claimants, the decision in *X v Bedfordshire* could not survive the HRA. In arriving at its decision, the Court was persuaded that the policy reasons cited in *X v Bedfordshire* had become discredited. Central also to its reasoning was the fact that an action under section 7 of the HRA was not open to the child victim in this case on the basis that the harm in question had occurred before 2 October 2000. Rather than allow the time factor to deprive her of a remedy, therefore, the Court decided to develop the common law in order to plug the gap. In the words of Lord Philips: 'the absence of an alternative remedy for children who were victims of abuse before October 2000 militates in favour of the recognition of a common law duty of care once the policy reasons against this have lost their force.'[6] The court thus decided that it would no longer be legitimate to rule that a common law duty of care was not owed to a child in the investigation of suspected child abuse and the initiation and pursuit of care proceedings.[7]

As regards the parents, however, the court considered that there remained cogent reasons of policy for denying the existence of a duty of care. Of foremost significance was the potential conflict of interest between parent and child, in that it would always be in the interests of the parent not to have the child removed. Moreover, this denial of a duty to the parents has since been upheld by the House of Lords.[8]

Where claimants have a choice between an action for negligence and a claim under section 7 of the HRA, it is likely that they will opt for the former, for not only does the HRA have a limitation period of just one year,[9] more importantly, if the Strasbourg model is indeed to be followed, the level of damages awarded is likely to be much more modest than under the tort system.[10] From a third party liability perspective, a further indicator that the HRA will not prove particularly

[3] [2003] EWCA Civ 1151.

[4] It must be noted, however, that, as a result of the (highly questionable) House of Lords decision in *Brooks v Commissioner of Police for the Metropolis* [2005] UKHL 24, an immunity from negligence liability had effectively been conferred upon the police. See p 118 below.

[5] In one of the cases, *MAK and RK v Dewsbury Health Care NHS Trust and Kirklees Metropolitan Council*, damages for financial loss were also sought.

[6] Above n 3, at para 83.

[7] *Ibid*, at para 84.

[8] *JD & ors v East Berkshire Community Health Trust & ors* [2005] UKHL 24.

[9] Section 7(6).

[10] See J Wright, *Tort Law and Human Rights* (Hart Publishing, 2001), p 44.

advantageous for claimants is provided by the Strasbourg jurisprudence on positive obligations. In short, both the initial existence and subsequent breach of a positive obligation relating to the harm-causing conduct of another are likely to be extremely difficult to establish under the HRA.

Under the ECHR, Articles 2 (right to life), 3 (prohibition of torture) and 8 (respect for private and family life) are capable of giving rise to positive obligations in respect of third party conduct. The relevant established duty arising under Article 2 is described by Mowbray as the obligation to provide protective policing measures,[11] and it was first set out by the ECtHR in *Osman v UK*.[12] As this case is discussed in detail in the following section on negligence, it suffices at this point to explain that it involved a complaint against the police for failing to protect a young boy and his family from the actions of an obsessed schoolteacher. In holding that the obligation arising on the state under Article 2 did extend to the taking of preventive operational measures to protect an individual whose life is at risk from the criminal acts of another individual, the ECtHR stated that such positive steps would be required only in circumstances where it could be established that 'the authorities knew or ought to have known at the time of the existence of a real and immediate risk to the life of an identified individual or individuals.'[13] In setting the threshold requirement for the existence of the duty at such a high level, the court was concerned not to impose an impossible or disproportionate burden on the authorities, bearing in mind 'the difficulties involved in policing modern societies, the unpredictability of human conduct and the operation choices which have to be made in terms of priorities and resources ....'[14] Given the highly extraordinary nature of the facts of *Osman*, as will be seen presently, the conclusion of the ECtHR that such an obligation did not arise on the part of the police authority in this case on the grounds that the necessary degree of knowledge had not been established provides very clear evidence that claims on this basis are unlikely ever to succeed.

Where Article 3 is concerned, the relevant duty is simply referred to by Mowbray as the obligation to take protective measures,[15] and it covers situations where an individual is at risk of serious mistreatment at the hands of another. The applicants in *Z v UK* successfully argued before the ECtHR that the failure of their local authority to take them away from their abusive parents amounted to a violation of Article 3. There can be no doubt, however, that the shocking nature of the facts in this case was central to the court's findings. Not only had the authorities known about the appalling neglect and abuse suffered by the applicants, they had allowed it to continue for almost five years before taking any

[11] A Mowbray, *The Development of Positive Obligations Under the European Convention on Human Rights by the European Court of Human Rights* (Hart Publishing, 2004), p 15. Although there are a number of other positive obligations under Art 2, the responsibility to provide protective policing measures is arguably the only one that is capable of giving rise to a form of third party liability.

[12] [1999] 1 FLR 193.

[13] *Ibid*, at para 116.

[14] *Ibid*.

[15] Mowbray, above n 11, p 43.

decisive action. As with Article 2, it would appear that the positive obligation of protection under Article 3 is subject to a requirement of actual or constructive knowledge of the risk of harm. Moreover, it will also be necessary to show that the mistreatment is severe enough to constitute inhuman and degrading treatment.[16] As Bailey-Harris and Harris comment, while it is fortunate that not every child abuse case is as extreme as *Z v UK*, this threshold of seriousness will necessarily prevent some victims from obtaining a remedy under the HRA for breach of Article 3.[17]

While positive obligations arising under Article 8 to prevent third parties from interfering with Convention rights are also readily applicable to situations of physical or sexual abuse, in the cases brought so far at least, they have related only to the efficacy of the domestic legal measures in place for providing victims of such abuse with an appropriate means of redress, and as such, they do not give rise to true third party liability. For example, in *X and Y v The Netherlands*,[18] a young mentally impaired woman who had been sexually assaulted complained that her attacker had been able to escape criminal prosecution because of the fact that, due to the complainant's disabilities, she had been unable to meet the Dutch law requirement that all victims over the age of 16 personally file a complaint to the police. The ECtHR held that this gap in the Dutch criminal law violated the young woman's right to respect for private life.[19] In addition, it is also necessary to take into account Article 8(2), which sets out the circumstances in which it is permissible to interfere with the right to private life, as well as the fact that states tend to enjoy a wide margin of discretion in this context in determining what steps are necessary to ensure compliance with the Convention.

For all of these reasons, but particularly because of the influence of the HRA on the development of the common law, it is likely that third party actions against public authority defendants will continue to be founded on the law of negligence.

II. LIABILITY IN NEGLIGENCE

In basic terms, the reason why public authority defendants pose such difficulties for the law of negligence generally is that they are regarded as having special status, warranting the application of exceptional rules designed to restrict liability. For the most part, these rules relate to the duty of care issue. Unfortunately, the fundamental questions of what exactly these rules are, and how and

[16] Bailey-Harris and Harris draw an analogy here with the notion of 'significant harm' found in s 31(2) of the Children Act 1989: R Bailey-Harris and M Harris, 'Local Authorities and Child Protection – The Mosaic of Accountability' [2002] CFLQ 117.

[17] *Ibid.*

[18] (1985) 8 EHRR 235.

[19] See also, *Stubbings and Others v UK* (1996) 23 EHRR 213.

when they are to be applied, have not yet been fully resolved. The uncertainty to which this has given rise has then, in turn, engendered a litany of misapprehensions, misconceptions and misinterpretations.

Addressing first of all the issue of why public authorities are accorded such special treatment in the law of negligence, the general tenor of the justifications traditionally advanced is that to impose such liability on them operates to the detriment of society and the common good. This stems from the fact that, unlike private persons, the sole purpose of these bodies is to serve the community. Indeed, they have been created specifically to carry out functions designed to benefit the community. And to this end, they are financed out of the public purse, or to put it another way, are paid for by the taxpayer. The first objection then to making public authorities liable is that any compensation must come from their allocated public funds. This then reduces the amount of money available for the performance of the authorities' relevant public functions which, if argued to its logical extreme, means that for the benefit of one aggrieved individual, the whole community has to suffer. A related 'floodgates' concern is that, in our increasingly litigious society, the perceived 'deep-pocket' status of public authorities will make them vulnerable targets for wily claimants.

The other main argument in favour of shielding public authorities from the full rigour of negligence law is the 'defensive practice' argument. Its thrust is simple: the ever-looming threat of liability may cause public servants to adopt excessively cautious approaches to their work, which would lead not only to an inefficient use of both time and resources, but also to the sacrifice of innovation. Moreover, the task of actually defending claims will typically involve a further diversion of resources.

These general public interest concerns about public authority liability, taken in conjunction with other, more context-specific ones which will be encountered presently,[20] tend to be referred to collectively under the umbrella term 'public policy considerations'. Although they are clearly of some force, such that they undoubtedly justify the limitation of public authority liability *in some instances*, in the past the courts tended to attribute to them far too much significance and to use them in a sweeping and indiscriminate manner to establish broad areas of complete public authority immunity from negligence liability. So blatant was this tendency that, as well as being the subject of some particularly vociferous and widely expressed academic criticism,[21] it eventually received stark reproof from the ECtHR in *Osman v UK*.[22] More recently, the tendency has been to the other extreme. In the immediate aftermath of *Osman*, the courts became reluctant to use policy considerations to strike out any negligence action against a public

[20] See pp 112, 113 below.

[21] See, eg, SH Bailey and MJ Bowman, 'Public Authority Negligence Revisited' (2000) 59 CLJ 85 and B Markesinis, J-B Auby, D Coester-Waltjen, and S Deakin, *The Tortious Liability of Statutory Bodies: A Comparative and Economic Analysis of Five English Cases* (Hart Publishing, 1999).

[22] 1999] 1 FLR 193.

authority,[23] and this has culminated most recently in the Court of Appeal's very bold decision in *JD v East Berkshire Community Health* to remove the established immunity of child welfare professionals altogether. The approach of the English courts to the public policy issue may thus be criticised as highly reactionary. What is required of them is a more pragmatic and measured response to each separate liability scenario they are presented with. Specific focus needs to be placed on the actual significance of each individual public policy consideration, in terms of its capacity to override the claimant's corrective justice entitlement to compensation and, in particular, how this may vary from context to context. For instance, it is argued that, contrary to the current state of affairs, the recognition of a policy-based quasi-immunity on the part of child welfare professionals is actually entirely justifiable, while the conferral of such an immunity on the police[24] is highly dubious.

Aside from the public policy issues, there is another major complicating aspect of public authority liability, and it is this that most obviously justifies the application of a different set of rules from that which applies in ordinary negligence cases. The typical negligence allegation against a public body will be framed in singular terms, in that it will relate to the exercise or non-exercise of statutory functions and thus straddle the boundary between private law and public law. This raises the problem of how to deal with public law issues in a private law context. Of most concern are those instances in which the statute conferring the function on the public body in question also confers upon it an element of discretion as regards the actual exercise of the function. Where the particulars of a negligence claim involve the court in an assessment of a public body's use of its statutory discretion, issues of a constitutional nature come into play. The very essence of an award of discretion is that it confers a certain freedom of decision. If the use of this freedom is to be monitored, then this necessarily detracts from the very purpose of having the discretion in the first place. Such monitoring could be seen to amount to a usurpation of competence by the court. Given that the discretion has been bestowed by Parliament, such judicial interference with obvious parliamentary intention could be viewed as an infringement of the separation of powers principle.

The much-maligned policy/operational distinction, in various guises, has been the principal tool used by the courts to address these constitutional competency issues. To date, this approach has been far from successful. It is argued, however, that this has been due mainly to a lack of clarity as to how the distinction is actually supposed to work, and to several key terminological problems. From the point of view of enabling the courts to identify those areas that are

[23] As evidenced most notably by the decisions in *Barrett v Enfield London Borough Council* [1999] 3 All ER 193 and *Phelps v Hillingdon London Borough Council* [2000] 3 WLR 776, and as recognised by the ECtHR in *Z v UK* (2002) 34 EHRR 3. See also *S v Gloucestershire County Council* [2001] 2 WLR 909.

[24] See *Brooks v Commissioner of Police for the Metropolis* [2005] UKHL 24, and C McIvor, 'Police immunity and the legacy of Hill v Chief Constable of West Yorkshire' (2005) 21 PN 201.

within their competency and those that are not, it is the essence of the policy/operation distinction that arguably provides the best guidance. To this end, an attempt will be made to provide the clarifications required in order to make the distinction workable.

Lastly, there are various difficulties associated with the omissions issue in a public authority context. Many of the negligence actions against public authorities take the form of omissions actions, and it is difficult to work out just what the significance of the omissions issue is in the various contexts. This has much to do also with the point made above about certain negligence claims against these bodies being framed in unique terms, for one of the most common allegations made against a public body is that it has been negligent in failing to exercise a discretionary function. Clearly, the fact that reference may be made to the statute as evidence that the defendant public body targeted had either a public law power or a duty to act is what fuels the claimant's argument that it also had a duty of care to act at common law for the purposes of a negligence action. While it is obvious to any tort lawyer that to reason so simplistically is to misunderstand entirely the function of the duty of care concept in negligence, there are, nevertheless, some conceptual difficulties with denying a duty in this scenario simply on the basis of it being a case of nonfeasance. Indeed, none of the traditional arguments in support of the non-liability for omissions rule actually apply in respect of statutory bodies.[25] In particular, there is no 'why-pick-on-me' argument – the body is targeted specifically because of its publicly advertised responsibilities in the domain in question. That is not to suggest that the omissions rule should not then have any significance in a public authority context – clearly, imposing omissions liability on public bodies will be highly undesirable in certain circumstances for other reasons. It is a case of having to work out what these reasons are and what kind of variables they will be affected by. At a general level, however, it is submitted that there can be identified at the outset two factors of crucial importance affecting the relevance of the omissions argument: the nature of the negligence allegation at stake, particularly in terms of the modified policy/operational distinction mentioned above, and the nature of the particular public body involved, in terms of its main functions and responsibilities. In respect of certain functions, some public bodies will be more easily targeted by omissions claims than others.

Only after addressing all of these issues in relation to the general negligence liability of public authorities is it possible to analyse coherently the sub-category of public authority liability that is the actual focus of this chapter, namely third party liability. It is submitted, however, that even at this initial stage, it is clear that the most important factor regarding the success or failure of third party liability claims in this context is going to be the categorisation of the main functions of the public authority defendant in question, some functions being more

[25] As Lord Hoffmann recognised in *Stovin v Wise* [1996] 3 All ER 801 at 821.

conducive to the imposition of typical third party duties of control or protection than others.

(i) The Case Law

The starting point for any analysis of the modern negligence liability of public authorities has to be the seminal House of Lords decision in the five consolidated appeals collectively referred to as *X (a minor) and Others v Bedfordshire County Council and Others.*[26] Of the five appeals, two involved allegations of negligence against local authorities in respect of the performance of their child protection functions, and three concerned allegations of negligence against education authorities in respect of their specific statutory duties towards children with special educational needs. In the actual judgments, they are thus referred to, respectively, as 'the abuse cases' and 'the education cases', and the decision is split accordingly.

In the first abuse case, *X v Bedfordshire County Council*, five siblings suffering from severe parental neglect and abuse sued the local authority for failing to protect them from their parents by not taking them into care soon enough. The local authority had indeed been notified by various persons, including relatives, neighbours, the police, the family's GP, a head teacher, the NSPCC, a social worker and a health visitor, that the children were at risk while living with their parents and that their living conditions were appalling, but it waited for almost five years before even placing them on the Child Protection Register. Inevitably, by the time they had finally been taken into care, irreparable physical and psychological damage had already been sustained.

In the second abuse case, *M v Newham London Borough Council*, the allegation of negligence was actually to the opposite effect, namely that the defendant local authority had acted too quickly in removing a child from the parental home in an attempt to protect her from suspected sexual abuse. This action followed an interview which had taken place between the child and a psychiatrist and a social worker in which the child had given the name of her abuser. The psychiatrist and social worker wrongly assumed that this was the mother's boyfriend who was living with them at the time and who had the same first name, even though there was no other evidence implicating him. The mistake was only discovered some time later, when the mother was granted access to the transcript of the interview and realised that the child had actually been referring to a cousin of the same name who had previously lived with them. Although the local authority admitted its mistake and took steps to rehabilitate mother and child, by this time they had already been separated for a year. Both brought negligence actions against the local authority, the psychiatrist and the social worker for harm in the form of anxiety neurosis.

[26] [1995] 3 All ER 353.

In the first education case, *E v Dorset County Council*, the defendant local authority was sued, in its capacity as education authority, first for failing to identify that the claimant was suffering from a learning disorder requiring special educational provision and then, after later acknowledging his special needs, for deciding that the school he was attending at that time was appropriate to meet his needs. His claim was for damage in the form of pure economic loss, relating principally to the expense incurred by his parents in placing him at a special school.

In the second education case, *Christmas v Hampshire County Council*, the claimant's vicarious liability action against the local education authority (LEA) was based upon the failure of his primary school headmaster to refer him for formal assessment of his learning difficulties, and the failure of the teachers' advisory centre to which he was later sent to identify his specific learning difficulties. The resultant harm was said to consist of a severe limitation of his educational attainment and prospects of employment.

The final education case is *Keating v Bromley London Borough Council*, in which the central allegation once again related to the failure of an LEA to make adequate provision for special educational needs. This time, however, part of the complaint was that the defendant LEA had, on two occasions, placed the claimant in special schools when he did not have any *serious* disability and should have been educated in an ordinary school, and that, at other times, it failed to provide him with a place in any school at all. He claimed damages in respect of the impairment of his personal and intellectual development and for the limitation of his prospects of employment.

In the House of Lords, the main judgment in respect of these claims was delivered by Lord Browne-Wilkinson. As tends to be the case with very important decisions, the judgment is not easy to analyse. Indeed, that even Peter Cane has confessed to having had some difficulty with it should give some indication of the degree of complexity involved.[27] Without a doubt, this is due almost entirely to the complexity of the legal issues at stake. However, it is suggested that, at times, his Lordship is not as clear as he could be on certain points. And it is further suggested that this masks the fact that he is not entirely certain about the exact legal significance of some of the matters he elaborates on. This, however, should not be regarded as too strong a criticism for, overall, it is clear that he does have a very keen appreciation of the pertinent issues at stake, but that he has just not entirely worked his way through the very complicated task of deciding how they actually relate to each other.

In addressing, at a general level, the crux of the issue common to all five claims, namely whether the performance of a statutory *duty*[28] can give rise to a

[27] 'Suing Public Authorities in Tort' (1996) 112 LQR 13.

[28] It is clear that his Lordship intends to refer, at all times, to statutory functions in the form of duties rather than powers, because those are the only kinds of functions in issue in the cases at hand. Unfortunately, he is not very strict in his use of terminology in this respect, and occasionally refers to statutory powers instead, which can be rather confusing: see, eg, [1995] 3 All ER 353 at 369 and 370.

common law duty of care so as to found an action in negligence, Lord Browne-Wilkinson begins by drawing a broad distinction between: (a) cases in which it is alleged that the authority owes a duty of care in the manner in which it exercises a statutory discretion; and (b) cases in which a duty of care is alleged to arise from the manner in which the statutory duty has been implemented in practice.[29] Therein lies the first major difficulty. What exactly is the essence of this distinction? Helpfully, his Lordship does go on to elaborate a bit further, giving an example of each limb. Thus, a decision whether or not to exercise a statutory discretion to close a school would fall under category (a), while matters relating to the actual running of the school would fall under category (b). But even taken in conjunction with the above description of the distinction, this illustration reveals very little about the determinative features of each category, arguably because the example provided for category (b) is far too broad. There are innumerable matters relevant to the actual running of a school of which many will involve the exercise of statutorily conferred discretion. Does this not mean that these particular matters should then fall under (a)? If not, what is it about the decision whether or not to close a school, in terms of the exercise of statutory discretion, that makes it so different from all of the matters relating to the running of the school, including those of a discretionary nature? The most obvious deduction would be that it has something to do with the nature of the discretion involved. This would seem to be supported by the further elaboration that it is the difference between, on the one hand, taking care in exercising a statutory discretion whether or not to take an action and, on the other, having decided to do that act, taking care in the manner in which you do it.[30] On this basis, it would seem that the distinction is actually between decision making and the mechanics of decision implementation. If this is correct, then it is submitted that the main source of confusion arising from his Lordship's original description of the distinction lies in his unqualified reference to the concept of statutory discretion in relation to the first limb.

Alternatively, it could be thought that what he is actually referring to is the notorious policy/operational distinction, introduced into English law by Lord Wilberforce in *Anns v Merton London Borough Council*.[31] Indeed, this was how Peter Cane interpreted the distinction, in a case-note written just after the report of the *X v Bedfordshire* decision was published.[32] It would appear, however, that such an interpretation is not supported by the rest of the speech. Lord Browne-Wilkinson makes separate reference to Lord Wilberforce's discussion of the policy/operational dichotomy in *Anns* and does not try to relate it directly to his own distinction. Moreover, it is clear that under Lord Wilberforce's test, the

[29] [1995] 3 All ER 353 at 368.

[30] Furthermore, the use of the term 'manner' in (a) would appear to be incongruent with the school closure example given. As an instance of strategic decision making, this example would clearly go to the 'nature' of the discretion, rather than to the manner of its exercise.

[31] [1978] AC 728.

[32] Cane, above n 27, at 16.

policy limb of the distinction is to be equated directly with the concept of discretion,[33] while Lord Browne-Wilkinson seems to treat them as two separate issues.[34] That said, the similarities between the two approaches are too striking to ignore. It may be that what Lord Browne-Wilkinson is actually doing here is putting forward his own version of the policy/operational test, which takes into account the main criticisms levied at the traditional version. Significantly in this respect, he makes explicit reference to the controversy surrounding the traditional version of the distinction, mentioning in particular the well-known dicta of Lord Keith in *Rowling v Takaro Properties*,[35] criticising the popular misconception that the dichotomy can serve in itself as a basis for determining issues of liability, when it is clear that it has a solely exclusionary function. Indeed, it is submitted that the main problem with Lord Wilberforce's formulation, and the main reason why the policy/operational test has not worked very successfully in the past, is the description of policy as discretion. This is much too loose and imprecise, and, consequently, it is also misleading. Not all instances of discretion are to be equated with policy, as it is intended to be understood for the purposes of the dichotomy. Given its ordinary meaning, 'discretion' is actually a very broad term, and elements of ordinary discretion can obviously also arise in respect of operational activities, as indeed both Lord Wilberforce and Lord Browne-Wilkinson expressly recognise.[36] Clearly, it is only certain types of statutory discretion that fall under the policy limb. Bearing in mind that the policy/operational test serves only an exclusionary role, in that it is designed solely to identify those particular areas of public authority activity that are unsuitable for judicial scrutiny for reasons of constitutional competency, then it is obviously only those exercises of statutory discretion that involve a consideration of certain types of high-level policy matters that can carry the 'policy', as opposed to 'operational', label. Lord Browne-Wilkinson himself gives examples of such non-justiciable policy matters, ranging from matters of social policy to those involving the allocation of finite financial resources between the different calls being made upon authorities, and the balance between pursuing desirable aims as against the risk to the public inherent in doing so.[37]

It is entirely possible that, recognising the utility of the basic policy/operational distinction, Lord Browne-Wilkinson was trying to emulate it, but discreetly so, in order to avoid the criticisms commonly associated with it. Certainly, he does recognise that the whole purpose of the distinction is to determine issues of justiciability, and even more importantly, he does not try to equate policy directly with discretion. Unfortunately, however, by failing to expressly

[33] 'Most, indeed probably all, statutes relating to public authorities or public bodies, contain in them a large element of policy. The courts call this "discretion", meaning that the decision is one for the authority or body to make and not for the courts': [1978] AC 728 at 754.

[34] As indeed Lunney and Oliphant also point out in *Tort Law: Texts and Materials* (OUP, 2003), at p 470.

[35] [1988] AC 473 at 501.

[36] See, respectively, [1978] AC 728 at 754 and [1995] 3 All ER 353 at 369.

[37] [1995] 3 All ER 353 at 370.

qualify his own references to the term 'discretion' in this respect, it may be said that he simply succeeds in introducing another level of confusion to this area.

Ultimately, however, it is submitted that, in initially drawing his own very broad distinction between (a) cases in which it is alleged that the authority owes a duty of care in the manner in which it exercises a statutory discretion, and (b) those in which a duty of care is alleged to arise rather from the manner in which the statutory duty has been implemented in practice, his Lordship was simply trying to make the general point that, as a guiding rule of thumb, duties of care are going to be much more difficult to establish in cases falling under the first limb than in cases falling under the second limb. For he then goes on to discuss the legal position in detail under the separate headings of discretion, justiciability, and the policy/operational test, and does not attempt to relate any of this back to his initial distinction. This would then mean that the distinction, which has been the subject of much academic attention, is actually of very little significance, and that it is the rest of his discussion which should actually be focused on.

Dealing with discretion first of all, which his Lordship treats as being an automatically relevant factor, on the assumption, it seems, that the vast majority of statutory duties will contain some discretionary element, he makes the point that any local authority decisions falling within the ambit of the conferred statutory discretion cannot be actionable at common law. As already mentioned, the reasoning behind this is that the courts must not be seen to interfere with Parliamentary intention. This begs the question, however, of what actually counts as 'falling within the ambit of the discretion', and it would seem that the answer lies in the concept of unreasonableness. According to Lord Reid in *Home Office v Dorset Yacht*,[38] mere errors of judgment are protected, while decisions that are made so carelessly or unreasonably that there cannot be said to be any real exercise of the discretion at all, will fall outside the ambit of the discretionary immunity. Lord Browne-Wilkinson interprets this part of Lord Reid's speech as establishing a requirement that, in any negligence action in respect of the exercise of a statutory discretion, it must first be shown that the decision in question was outside the ambit of the discretion altogether, failing which the action cannot proceed any further. This has subsequently been interpreted as the application of a test of *Wednesbury* unreasonableness.[39] Although the basis for this additional duty hurdle in negligence actions against public authorities would appear to be Lord Reid's speech in *Dorset Yacht*, made some 25 years earlier, it is notable that *X v Bedfordshire* was the first case to recognise it formally as an actual legal requirement in such actions, as it did not even form part of the ratio of *Dorset Yacht*. Indeed, Cane comments that its imposition of a duty requirement of *Wednesbury*

[38] [1970] AC 1004 at 1031.

[39] *Associated Provincial Picture Houses Ltd v Wednesbury Corporation* [1948] 1 KB 223. See, eg, M Andenas and D Fairgrieve, 'Sufficiently Serious? Judicial Restraint in Tortious Liability of Public Authorities and the European Influence', in M Andenas (ed), *English Public Law and the Common Law of Europe* (Key Haven Publications, 1998).

unreasonableness is one of just two ways in which *X v Bedfordshire* actually breaks fresh ground.[40]

Lord Browne-Wilkinson then goes on to deal with non-justiciable policy matters. He first makes the point that in deciding whether or not the requirement of unreasonableness is satisfied, the court will have to assess the relevant factors taken into account by the defendant authority, and then goes on to say that if these relevant factors include policy matters, giving the examples quoted above of social policy and resource allocation, then the court must terminate its inquiry immediately. He mentions Lord Wilberforce's policy/operational dichotomy ostensibly as a potential method of identifying whether or not a particular decision is a non-justiciable policy decision. To this end, however, his discussion lacks content. He merely quotes Lord Wilberforce's description of the distinction alongside Lord Keith's well-known dicta, mentioned earlier, from *Rowling v Takaro Properties Ltd*.[41] This gives no guidance whatsoever as to what can actually constitute a non-justiciable policy matter.

He then moves swiftly on to make the point that in those cases in which the allegation of negligence relates to how an act has been performed, as opposed to the actual taking of a discretionary decision to do some act, the ordinary *Caparo* tripartite test will apply. This is clearly a reference back to his own distinction, and coming in at this stage it does not make sense at all. What he appears to mean here is that, after overcoming the two duty hurdles just discussed, namely the unreasonableness hurdle and the policy hurdle, the claimant will still have to satisfy the ordinary *Caparo* test for duty. Indeed, this is clear from the sub-heading he uses: 'If justiciable, the ordinary principles of negligence apply'.[42] Overall, the impression created is one of organised disorder. Lord Browne-Wilkinson elaborates on all of the above issues, knowing that they are all ultimately relevant, but he is not entirely clear as to how exactly they all relate to each other.

The final point he makes at this stage, however, is clearly relevant to all negligence actions against public authorities and it is that the statutory framework surrounding the acts complained of must always be taken into account in deciding whether a common law duty of care can exist in the circumstances. In

40 The other being the introduction of a novel distinction between liability for breach of direct duties of care and vicarious liability: Cane, above n 27, at 22.

41 See above n 35.

42 However, by relating his point specifically to cases falling under the second limb of his distinction, what he implies is that these are the only type of cases that will ever be actionable at all, when the purpose of the preceding discussion was that *any* claim against a public authority will be actionable as long as the additional hurdles discussed are overcome. Presumably, his train of thought here was that it is only in relation to the type of allegation falling under the first limb that matters of policy are likely to arise, so that under the second limb it would usually be possible to go straight to the *Caparo* test, although even here he would seem to contradict himself somewhat as regards the existence of some element of discretion in relation to purely implementational matters. Does the requirement of unreasonableness not apply to these exercises of discretion also? It would seem that his Lordship just wanted to bring in his own distinction at some point in order to accord it some significance, perhaps to justify to himself having made it in the first place.

his Lordship's own words: 'a common law duty of care cannot be imposed on a statutory duty if the observance of such a common law duty of care would be inconsistent with, or have a tendency to discourage, the due performance by the local authority of its statutory duties.'[43] Cane duly refers to this latter requirement as 'the compatibility issue'.[44]

So, to summarise this first part of Lord Browne-Wilkinson's speech, where the statutory duty that is alleged to have been negligently performed involves some discretionary element, it must initially be shown that the defendant authority acted outside the ambit of the discretion by satisfying a test of *Wednesbury* unreasonableness. If, however, in the course of this particular exercise, certain policy matters that the courts are not fit to comment on arise for consideration, then the claim is automatically rendered non-justiciable. Having satisfied the *Wednesbury* test, the next stage is the *Caparo* tripartite test. Put like this, it seems much simpler than a first reading of the full discussion would suggest.

In practice, the policy issue will fall to be considered before anything else, for it is only after having eliminated this concern that there can be any point in addressing the unreasonableness question. Thus, the policy/operational test is typically the first stumbling block to be encountered. Given the notoriety of this test, it does not serve as a good starting point psychologically and this can tend to taint the whole exercise. As already mentioned, however, most of the difficulties associated with the distinction stem from a flawed understanding of its nature and purpose. The tendency is to focus too much on labels, that is on trying to categorise a given decision or activity as either a policy issue or an operational issue, as though the attribution of one of these labels would be directly determinative of whether or not a duty of care arises. Moreover, this is often done without even a clear understanding of what exactly constitutes a policy matter or an operational matter, and much effort is then commonly wasted in debating the difference between the two. Since the actual purpose of the test is to exclude those matters that are not suitable for judicial assessment, referred to for convenience purposes as non-justiciable policy issues, clearly it is only the identification of these particular matters that can be of any interest. Would it not be much simpler to abandon the policy/operational terminology, and pose instead the question whether or not the claim involves a consideration of matters that the courts are not actually fit to pronounce upon, be it because they lack the necessary knowledge of the affairs at stake or because their interference would be regarded as constitutionally inappropriate? Indeed, such a suggestion has also been put forward by Paul Craig.[45] If, however, the distinction is to be retained, then effort must be made to ensure that its role is clearly understood. It must be emphasised that it can serve only as a guide to the main issue at stake, which is that of justiciability, in that non-justiciable policy issues are only really likely to arise in respect of matters falling under the first limb of the distinction, that is matters

[43] [1995] 3 All ER 353 at 371.
[44] 'Suing Public Authorities in Tort' (1996) 112 LQR 13 at 15.
[45] *Administrative Law* (Sweet & Maxwell, 2003), at p 897.

relating to the exercise of discretionary decision-making functions. As long as it is understood that not all matters falling under this policy limb of the distinction will necessarily be non-justiciable, and that policy is not be equated with bare discretion, this approach should work perfectly well.

As *X v Bedfordshire* itself, and indeed all of the other major decisions to date on the negligence liability of public authorities, show, the courts are very reluctant to dismiss claims on the basis of non-justiciability alone. Undoubtedly, this has had much to do with the fact that the vast majority of such claims have come before the courts as strike-out actions,[46] and consequently without a full presentation of the facts. It is submitted, however, that as the other methods commonly used by the courts to try and avoid the liability of public authorities can increasingly be called into doubt due to numerous dubious applications, a revival of interest in the justiciability issue would be a welcome development in the law. As long as the more focused approach outlined above is taken, it would certainly constitute a much more defensible basis for an outright denial of liability in applicable cases.

After discussing justiciability, Lord Browne-Wilkinson goes on to address the difference between the allegations before him that invoke the direct liability of the local authority defendants and those that invoke their vicarious liability for the acts of their employees. It is clear from the rest of his speech that his Lordship regards the distinction between direct and vicarious liability as being of great significance in this particular context. Not only does he make his whole discussion of the *Caparo* test, and in particular the 'fair, just and reasonable' requirement, subject to it, but he also bases his final conclusions around it. In view of this, it is perhaps somewhat surprising that he spends very little time elaborating on the significance of the distinction itself. That the distinction has since been carried on into later decisions, most notably *Phelps v Hillingdon London Borough Council* makes his brevity here all the more unfortunate. All that he actually says is that the two forms of liability are not mutually exclusive, and that the extent of the duties owed to the claimant under each may differ.

Given that public bodies, as legal entities rather than natural persons, can act only through their employees, the concept of direct liability on their part takes on a unique meaning that, moreover, would appear to overlap significantly with that of vicarious liability. There is also an apparent link with the concept of third party liability, but it is one that is not at all easy to pinpoint. In short, the distinction is apt to confuse and thus warrants a detailed explanation. According to Lord Browne-Wilkinson, it is really only as regards the attribution of the duty of care that the direct liability of the defendant authorities will differ from their vicarious liability for the acts of their employees, for otherwise, under both forms of liability, he envisages the breach requirement will always be determined by

[46] *Stovin v Wise* [1996] 3 All ER 801 and *Phelps v Hillingdon London Borough Council* [2000] 4 All ER 504 are the only ones so far to have involved full trials.

reference to the acts of individual employees.[47] Thus, with direct liability, the focus will be on the defendant body as regards the duty and on the employees as regards breach, whereas with vicarious liability, the focus will be on the employees as regards both. Consequently, both would appear to be forms of no-fault liability. Indeed, Peter Cane has commented that Lord Browne-Wilkinson's formulation of direct liability in this instance appears to resemble the 'long-abandoned' master's tort theory of vicarious liability.[48] Depending on the basis for the authority's direct duty, however, the scope of liability may vary significantly between the two approaches. As is clear from his speech, Lord Browne-Wilkinson would regard the foundation for the direct duty as being the status of local authorities as providers of public services. He draws an analogy with the direct liability of hospitals, but unfortunately does not elaborate upon it to any useful degree. His most glaring omission here is an explanation of the particular *nature* of the direct duties that may be owed by hospitals, for there are several. From the authorities he provides, however, it would seem evident that the type of direct duty that he is referring to specifically is what is known as the 'non-delegable' duty of hospitals to ensure that reasonable care is taken of their patients,[49] for this is the only direct duty owed by hospitals that may actually be breached by individual staff members. What is surprising about this is that, at the time of Lord Browne-Wilkinson's judgment, the existence of the non-delegable duty was a matter of some controversy.[50] A much more obvious type of direct duty to have referred to would have been the direct duty of a hospital to provide a safe health-care environment, which encompasses not just the provision of adequate equipment and facilities, including sufficient and competent staff, but also the idea of having in operation safe systems of care and communication.[51] The significance of this latter type of duty is that it can be breached even in situations where no individual can be shown to be at fault. This is because it is rather some kind of organisational or administrative failure on the part of the hospital that is required to establish breach. Taken in conjunction with the non-delegable duty, this makes the potential primary liability of the hospital very wide indeed. By implication, if local authorities were to be regarded as in a similar position, then from the perspective of claimants the direct liability route would appear to be very attractive indeed. Moreover, it may even be arguable that this would enable claimants to sidestep the *Bolam* defence.

By contrast, in the vicarious liability claims in *X v Bedfordshire*, the existence of a duty of care on the part of the individual employees was held to be

[47] [1995] 3 All ER 353 at 372.

[48] Cane, above n 27, at 21.

[49] As Grubb would also agree, *Principles of Medical Law* (OUP, 2004), p 516.

[50] The matter has since been settled in favour of the existence of such a duty: *M v Calderdale and Kirklees Health Authority* [1998] 4 Lloyd's Rep Med 157, as qualified by *A (a child) v Ministry of Defence* [2004] EWCA Civ 641.

[51] See, eg, *Bull v Devon Area Health Authority* [1993] 4 Med LR 117 and *Robertson v Nottingham Health Authority* [1997] 8 Med LR 1.

dependent upon evidence of specific assumptions of responsibility[52] on their part towards the particular claimants. The scope of any consequent vicarious liability arising on the part of the local authorities is thus much narrower and more tightly constrained.

(ii) The Significance of the Direct Liability/Vicarious Liability Distinction from a Third Party Liability Perspective

Given that public bodies can act only through their employees, it may be thought that every instance of direct public authority liability is a form of third party liability. This however is true only in a very loose sense. For the purposes of this book, the only type of third party liability that is of any real interest is that which involves one party being held liable, on a personal fault basis, for harm that has been actively inflicted by another. Clearly, public authority employees cannot constitute separate and independent parties from their employers for this purpose. Thus, to be relevant in the present context, there needs to be at least one additional party involved in the commission of the harm. Consequently, it is only where the direct liability of the public body is said to relate either to the failure of its employees, on the basis of a non-delegable duty argument, to prevent a third party from causing harm, or to some failure at organisational level to prevent a third party from causing harm, that a true third party liability issue arises.

As regards vicarious liability actions, these are of interest from a third party liability perspective only in instances where the personal liability of the employee triggering the vicarious liability of the authority relates again to a failure to prevent an independent third party from causing harm, as in *Home Office v Dorset Yacht*.[53] So here we are concerned only with the third party liability of individual public servants.

Applying this to the five claims involved in the *X* litigation, it may be seen that only one may actually be designated as a third party liability action, and that is the eponymous *X v Bedfordshire County Council*. It may be recalled that, in this case, the defendant local authority was being sued in the context of its social welfare functions for failing to remove sufficiently promptly the child plaintiffs from their abusive parents. The harm said to have been suffered by the children had clearly been inflicted by an independent third party in this instance, namely the parents. Significantly, however, given that the defendant had not been expected to act at the very outset to prevent the abuse, but only to intervene at the point at which it became aware that the children were at risk, it was not sought to make the authority liable for all of the harm resulting from the abuse,

[52] Although this particular phrase is not used, it is clear, from the authorities cited, that his Lordship was intending to refer to the application of *Hedley Byrne* principles: see [1995] 3 All ER 353 at 383, citing *Henderson v Merrett Syndicates Ltd* [1994] 3 All ER 506 and *White v Jones* [1995] 1 All ER 691.

[53] [1970] AC 1004.

but rather only for the additional consequences suffered by the children after the time by which they should reasonably have been removed.

It is to be noted that the other abuse case, *M v Newham London Borough Council*, involved an entirely different kind of allegation, namely that the defendant local authority had been negligent in removing the child plaintiff from the parental home. The type of liability issue at stake was one of ordinary personal fault-based liability for the positive infliction of fresh harm, for it was sought to hold the authority liable for psychological harm caused by the parent–child separation, and not for any kind of harm related to the abuse itself.

Nevertheless, it is still worth examining all of the decisions in the *X* litigation, for what they reveal about the general negligence liability of public authorities will be of obvious direct relevance to third party liability issues.

(iii) The Decisions in the Abuse Cases

As regards the abuse cases, Lord Browne-Wilkinson concluded that both the direct duty arguments and the vicarious duty arguments would fail but, significantly, for different reasons.

(a) The Direct Duty Arguments

The direct duty arguments failed on the basis that they were outweighed by five particular public policy arguments, and that, consequently, the 'fair, just, and reasonable' requirement of the *Caparo* test could not be satisfied. The five arguments are:

(1) that a common law duty of care would cut across the whole statutory system set up for the protection of children at risk;
(2) that the task of the local authority in dealing with such children is 'extraordinarily delicate';
(3) that the spectre of liability would perhaps cause local authorities to adopt a more cautious and defensive approach to their duties;
(4) that the uneasy relationship between the social worker and the child's parents would become a breeding-ground for ill feeling and hopeless litigation; and
(5) that there were alternative remedies available in the form of the statutory complaints procedures or an investigation by the local government ombudsman.[54]

It is important that these broad-based public policy considerations be distinguished from the types of policy issues discussed earlier which can arise in the course of the inquiry into the exercise of statutory discretion. Whereas those policy matters relating to the exercise of statutory discretion are essentially

[54] A further argument put forward that did not relate to public-policy was the absence of any analogous duty from existing case law.

concerned with the question of whether or not the courts are fit to pronounce on the issues at stake, the function of the broad public policy considerations detailed above is to determine whether, from the point of view of the impact upon society, there are any other general reasons why the imposition of liability would not be a good idea. In short, the first set of policy considerations is all about justiciability, while the second set is all about immunity.[55]

As mentioned briefly earlier, the application of the public policy arguments to immunise the local authority defendants in the abuse cases has been one of the most controversial aspects of the *X* litigation. A number of critical analyses of each of the five arguments have been undertaken[56] and the general consensus is that they are not convincing enough to justify immunity from negligence liability. Indeed, it was in being able to draw on these widespread criticisms and to thereby conclude that the policy arguments in *X* no longer had any force that the Court of Appeal felt empowered in *JD & ors v East Berkshire Community Health Trust & ors*[57] to ignore the doctrine of precedent and to purport to overrule *X*.[58]

However, it is argued that the problem with these policy arguments was not so much their application to the abuse cases in *X*, but rather other attempts to apply them, without modification, in entirely different and unsuitable circumstances. Central to the *X* policy arguments is a concern about defensive practice. It is submitted that the defensive practice argument does carry significant weight in the child protection context, and this is because of the severity of the potential consequences of the child welfare professional delaying intervention in cases of suspected abuse, for the greatest potential victim of the professional's hesitation will always be the vulnerable child. By contrast, an example of a situation where the defensive practice argument carries very little weight, and certainly does not justify the conferral of an immunity in negligence, is provided by the facts of *Osman v Ferguson*.[59] The negligence claim in this case was against the police for failing to prevent an identified individual from inflicting serious harm on members of a family against whom he was known to pose a significant threat. While only a detailed exposition of the facts of the case could convey the extraordinary nature of the circumstances giving rise to this claim, a brief synopsis is unfortunately all that can be accommodated here. The individual in question was a secondary school teacher who developed an unhealthy obsession for one of his young male pupils. Following a number of instances of highly inappropriate

[55] On this point see R A Buckley, 'Negligence in the Public Sphere: Is Clarity Possible?' (2000) 51 NILQ 25.

[56] See, most notably, SH Bailey and MJ Bowman, 'Public Authority Negligence Revisited' (2000) 59 CLJ 85, and B Markesinis, J-B Auby, D Coester-Waltjen, and S Deakin, *The Tortious Liability of Statutory Bodies: A Comparative and Economic Analysis of Five English Cases* (Hart Publishing, 1999).

[57] [2003] EWCA Civ 1151.

[58] On the propriety of the Court of Appeal decision in this respect, see J Wright, '"Immunity" no more: Child abuse cases and public authority liability in negligence after *D v East Berkshire Community Health NHS Trust*' (2004) 20 PN 58.

[59] [1993] 4 All ER 344.

behaviour on his part, complaints about him were made to members of the school's senior management team, and these were subsequently borne out in their entirety by the school's internal inquiry into the matter. Reports were duly passed on to the LEA and to the police. There followed a catalogue of sinister incidents involving the teacher, including a change of name by deed poll on his part to that of the schoolboy in question. In addition, numerous acts of vandalism were perpetrated on the boy's family home. An attempt was made by the police to arrest the teacher, but it was unsuccessful because on the day that they turned up at his house to do so he was out working at another school. Three months later, he went to the claimants' house, shot the boy and his father and then continued on to the home of one of the deputy headteachers, whereupon he shot him alongside his son. On being arrested the next morning, he reportedly stated: '"Why didn't you stop me before I did it, I gave you all the warning signs?'

In dismissing the claim for lack of duty, the Court of Appeal relied on the House of Lords decision in *Hill v Chief Constable of West Yorkshire Police.*[60] As is well known, this case involved an action against the police brought by the mother of the Yorkshire Ripper's last victim, alleging negligence on their part in failing to catch the serial killer before he had the chance to kill her daughter. The claim failed, first on the basis that the proximity requirement of the *Caparo* test could not be satisfied. There existed no special relationship between the police and the victim such as would have placed them under a duty to protect her specifically. She had not been known to them personally, and had not presented as being at any greater risk than the rest of the ordinary female population in the area at that time. Second, it was held that public policy militated against the imposition of liability against the police in respect of their activities relating to the investigation and suppression of crime. To the fore was the 'defensive practice' concern.

While *Osman* was clearly to be distinguished from *Hill* in the sense that the proximity requirement was evidently satisfied in this case, there even being some suggestion that individual members of the police had given personal assurances of protection to the Osman family, the Court of Appeal in *Osman* nevertheless held that the negligence claim failed on the alternative ground that, for reasons of public policy, the 'fair, just, and reasonable' requirement could not be satisfied.

Having been denied leave to appeal to the House of Lords, the Osmans took their case straight to the ECtHR, alleging a breach of Articles 2, 6, 8 and 13 of the ECHR.[61] Although the ECtHR held that there had been no violation of Articles 2 or 8, and that given the overall findings, no separate issue arose under Article 13, it is of crucial significance that they did conclude that there had been a violation of Article 6. The crux of the claimants' argument under Article 6, which concerns the right of access to a court and the right to a fair trial, was that the Court of Appeal's dismissal of their negligence action on grounds of public policy amounted to a restriction on their right of access to a court, because in practice it

[60] [1989] AC 53.
[61] *Osman v UK* [1999] 1 FLR 193.

conferred an immunity upon the police. That the ECtHR found that Article 6 was even applicable in the first place has outraged many black-letter judges and academics.[62] This is because the right of access had traditionally been interpreted as a purely procedural right, which required proof of a pre-existing substantive right on the part of the claimant to activate it, and the Osmans are said to have had no such substantive right host, as it were, for it was found in the Court of Appeal that not all of the constituent legal elements required for a negligence claim could be made out. Specifically, the 'fair, just and reasonable' requirement for the duty of care could not be satisfied. Thus, one of the main arguments put forward by the UK government at Strasbourg was that the application of Article 6 in such circumstances would result in 'the impermissible creation by the Convention institutions of a substantive right where none in fact existed in the domestic law of the respondent state.'[63]

The soundness of this criticism is open to question, for arguably the presentation of a tenable legal argument is all that is required to trigger the right of access to an adjudication. Given that the legal merits of the *Osman* case were particularly strong, this would surely mean that the Court of Appeal's dismissal of it on the basis of what were essentially untested presumptions dressed up as bona fide socio-legal considerations would have to be regarded as an access to justice issue. In any event, what is important in the current context is that Article 6 was held to be applicable.

Moving on from the applicability issue, in holding that Article 6 had indeed also been breached, the ECtHR incurred further domestic wrath. This is because the decision has been interpreted in some quarters as vetoing the conferral of public policy-based immunities altogether, and in some cases, by implication, as vetoing the use of the strike-out procedure. However, a careful reading of the decision reveals that the disapproval of the Court was directed not at the existence of the exclusionary rule, but rather at the particular application of the rule in the individual circumstances of the *Osman* case.[64] In this respect, it need only be pointed out that the restriction on the right of access here was held to constitute a violation of Article 6, not on the basis of one of the possible overarching grounds (that is, either that it was legally uncertain or that it pursued illegitimate aims), but rather on the individual fact-based ground that it was disproportionate. It was disproportionate because the court was able to identify other public interest considerations which pulled in the opposite direction to the application of the exclusionary rule, and which had not been weighed up by the Court of Appeal. Most importantly in this respect was the fact that, unlike the claimant

[62] See, in particular: Lord Browne-Wilkinson's speech in *Barrett v Enfield London Borough Council* [1999] 3 All ER 193 at 198; C Gearty, 'Unravelling *Osman*' (2001) 64 MLR 159; and C Gearty, '*Osman* Unravels' (2002) 65 MLR 87. See also Lord Hoffmann, 'Human Rights and the House of Lords' (1999) 62 MLR 159.

[63] (1998) 29 EHRR 245 at para 133.

[64] See L Hoyano, 'Policing Flawed Police Investigations: Unravelling the Blanket' (1999) 62 MLR 912.

in *Hill*, the Osmans were able to satisfy the proximity test, which the court described as 'a threshold requirement which is sufficiently rigid to narrow considerably the number of negligence actions against the police which can proceed to trial.'[65] It was also relevant that the allegation in this case was one of gross negligence rather than merely minor acts of incompetence, that the harm sustained was of the most serious nature, and that there had possibly been a specific assumption of responsibility on the part of the police to ensure the safety of the applicants.[66]

That the ECtHR was merely sounding a warning to the English courts to ensure that, in future, public policy-based immunities would be bestowed only after an assessment of the individual facts in issue had been carried out and it had been determined that a denial of liability on that basis was warranted, has arguably been confirmed by its decision in *Z v UK*.[67] The applicants in this case were the child claimants from *X v Bedfordshire County Council*, seeking to challenge that decision of the House of Lords to strike out their negligence action. Although they alleged violations of several articles of the ECHR, it is the findings of the ECtHR in respect of Article 6 that are of specific interest in the current context. In putting forward their case in relation to Article 6, to the effect that the denial of a duty of care on the part of the local authority on the basis of public policy considerations amounted to an exclusionary rule which deprived them of access to the court, the applicants relied heavily on the decision in *Osman v UK*. Implicitly distinguishing *Osman*, the ECtHR held that the there had been no violation of Article 6 in this case. Not only had the case been litigated up to the House of Lords, and had legal aid moreover been provided for that purpose, but the House of Lords had conferred the immunity in this instance only after carefully weighing in the balance the competing public policy considerations.[68] It did not therefore present itself as a blanket immunity such as to effect a true and disproportionate restriction on the right of access.

Key factors influencing this decision on the part of the ECtHR were the recent English jurisprudence in this area, and the impact of the exclusionary rule in terms of the multi-functional status of local authorities. As regards the recent jurisprudence, the court referred in particular to *W and Others v Essex County Council*,[69] in which the Court of Appeal refused to strike out a negligence action against a local authority for harm caused by a foster child to members of the foster family in which he had been placed, and *Barrett v Enfield London Borough Council*,[70] in which the House of Lords refused to strike out a negligence action in respect of inadequate care received by a child while in local authority care. As

[65] (1998) 29 EHRR 245 at para 151.
[66] *Ibid.*
[67] (2002) 34 EHRR 3.
[68] Wright would dispute this point: see J Wright, *Tort Law and Human Rights* (Hart Publishing, 2001), at p xxix.
[69] [1998] 3 All ER 111.
[70] [1999] 3 All ER 193.

deliberate attempts by the English courts to demonstrate to the ECtHR that they were heeding the warning set out in *Osman*, both decisions clearly had the desired effect. However, in view of the decision in *Z v UK* itself, issue may be taken with the decision in *Barrett*, for, as it involved the exercise of child protection functions on the part of the defendant local authority, arguably an immunity based on similar policy considerations to those set out in *X & ors v Bedfordshire & ors* could have been conferred.[71] While attempts were made at the time to distinguish the two decisions on the basis that *X* involved the issue of whether to take children into care, which brought into play the most delicate of policy concerns, whereas *Barrett* involved the supposedly less sensitive matter of the management of children once they are actually in care, the distinction would appear to be rather artificial and unconvincing. As Atkin and McLay[72] have cogently argued, policy should be regarded as a very great factor militating against the imposition of a duty of care in *all* child welfare cases, because the imposition of tortious liability would appear to conflict with the family law values and principles that predominate in this area. Certainly, more direct attention needs to be given to the matter of the interaction of tort and family law in this field. As regards *W v Essex County Council*, the exceptional circumstances pertaining to that case, in the form of the specific assumption of responsibility on the part of the defendant authority not to place anyone with a history of abusing children with the claimant family, and their reciprocal reliance on this undertaking, set this case apart and independently justified the imposition of a duty. This point will be returned to presently.

In respect of the multi-functional status of the defendant local authority in *Z v UK*, the ECtHR apparently considered it significant that the application of the immunity in this instance concerned only one aspect of the authority's powers and duties, and therefore it did not amount to 'an arbitrary removal of the court's jurisdiction to determine a whole range of civil claims.'[73] Thus, the conferral of the child protection function immunity was not all that drastic because there were still plenty of other things that local authorities could be sued for. This was to be contrasted with the position of the defendant police authority in *Osman* whose main function is the investigation and suppression of crime. The conferral of an immunity in this respect would consequently have had a much greater impact, for it would have effectively removed the police from the clutches of negligence law more or less completely.

Unfortunately, the courts have failed to engage with this entirely logical and workable interpretation of *Z v UK*, and in consequence, they have moved in

[71] For similar reasons, doubt may be expressed about the decision of the Court of Appeal in *S v Gloucestershire County Council* [2001] 2 WLR 909 to allow an action against a local authority in respect of sexual abuse committed by a foster carer to proceed to full trial. In contrast to *W v Essex County Council*, it is argued that the facts of this case were simply not exceptional enough to warrant a departure from the ratio of *X v Bedfordshire*.

[72] B Atkin and G McLay, 'Suing Child Welfare Agencies – A Comparative View from New Zealand' [2001] CFLQ 287.

[73] (2002) 34 EHRR 3 at para 98.

completely the opposite direction, effectively inversing the ECtHR's recommendations. For not only did the Court of Appeal in *JD v East Berkshire Community Health* remove the immunity of child welfare professionals, but more recently, in *Brooks v Commissioner of Police for the Metropolis*,[74] the House of Lords has reaffirmed the existence of an immunity for the police. The claim in *Brooks* related to the notorious Stephen Lawrence murder. Duwayne Brooks, who was with Stephen Lawrence on the night that he was fatally stabbed by five white youths, sued the police in negligence in respect of their mistreatment of him as a witness and as a victim. Central to Mr Brooks' allegations were the findings of the public inquiry led by Sir William Macpherson into the attack. Exposing a litany of failures in the police investigation, the Macpherson Report concluded that Mr Brooks had indeed been seriously mistreated and, damningly, that the cause of this mistreatment was collective racism in the police force. Nevertheless, the House of Lords dismissed the claim on the basis of the policy considerations set out in *Hill v Chief Constable.* Quite astoundingly, their Lordships completely ignored the ECtHR decision in *Osman v UK*, and appeared to interpret *Z v UK* as effecting no more than a mere terminological change to *Hill*, in that it was simply to be reformulated in terms of the absence of a duty of care rather than a blanket immunity. In blatant disregard of the proportionality principle, they concluded that the defensive practice argument alone militated in favour of a police immunity. And, crucially, they blankly refused to engage the fact that, insofar as it was based on straightforward allegations of misfeasance resulting in personal injury, the nature of the claim in *Brooks* was to be clearly distinguished from that in *Hill*.[75]

Consequently, it is argued that the current law on public authority negligence liability is misdirected.

(b) The Vicarious Liability Arguments

Addressing the conduct of the psychiatrist and the social worker in *M v Newham LBC*, the House of Lords concluded that the particular nature of the relationships existing between them and the individual victims was not such as to give rise to a duty of care based on an assumption of responsibility and reasonable reliance. Since the psychiatrist and the social worker had been retained by the local authority for the specific purpose of advising the authority and not the claimants, it followed that any duties they owed were solely to the authority. In support of this reasoning, an analogy was drawn with the position of a doctor instructed by an insurance company to examine an applicant for life insurance, whereby it was said that, apart from the duty to the applicant not to damage him in the course of the examination, the doctor's duties were owed only to the insurance company.

[74] [2005] UKHL 24.

[75] See further, C McIvor, above n 5.

Crucially, however, this was an application of the *Hedley Byrne* principles[76] as they stood prior to the decision in *Spring v Guardian Assurance*,[77] which effected an extension of these principles to third party beneficiaries in certain circumstances. The factual situation in *Spring* concerned an employer providing a reference about an employee to a prospective employer. The reference was provided carelessly and, as a direct consequence, the employee did not get the job. Liability was imposed on the basis that the employer had assumed responsibility towards the employee to provide the reference with reasonable care. Significantly, it has also since been held that a doctor carrying out a pre-employment medical assessment on a prospective employee owes a duty to the employee as well as to the company not to provide negligent advice.[78] Clearly, the abuse cases involve the same type of factual scenario, whereby A makes a statement to B about C, which B then acts upon to the detriment of C, which would presumably make them conducive to the same legal reasoning. However, it is acknowledged that the fact that the *Spring* principle appears to be limited to information that has been provided for a very specific purpose, in the sense that it concerned a reference in respect of a specific post, could significantly reduce the scope of any such analogies. In any event, it has to be noted that in *X v Bedfordshire*, Lord Browne-Wilkinson covers the eventuality that he is wrong about the social worker and the psychiatrist not assuming any responsibility towards the claimants by stating that individual duties on their part would always be avoided anyway on the basis of the same policy considerations precluding the existence of a direct duty on the part of the local authority.

(iv) The Decisions in the Education Cases

(a) The Direct Duty Arguments

In the education cases, two separate direct duties of care were argued. The first was based upon specific provisions of the Education Acts, and the second was said to arise from the provision of a psychology service.

Unsurprisingly, in light of the preceding discussion, the first direct duty argument failed. Interestingly, one of the reasons put forward by his Lordship in this respect was essentially that the existence of such a duty was unnecessary because in most cases parents would be able to proceed by way of a vicarious liability

76 Stemming from the House of Lords decision in *Hedley Byrne & Co Ltd v Heller & Partners* [1964] AC 465, these principles set out that a duty of care in respect of negligently-inflicted pure economic loss will arise where there is a special relationship between the defendant and the claimant, consisting of an assumption of responsibility and reciprocal reasonable reliance.

77 [1995] 2 AC 296.

78 *Baker v Kaye* [1997] IRLR 219. While there has been a more recent decision to the contrary, *Kapfunde v Abbey National plc* [1999] Lloyd's Rep Med 48, it can be distinguished for present purposes on the basis that it did not involve any personal dealings between the defendant and the claimant.

argument anyway.[79] Moreover, it was thought that recourse to the ombudsman was the most appropriate remedy of all. And, falling back on some actual law, there could be identified no analogous situations in which a similar type of duty had already been recognised.

His Lordship did, however, find the second duty argument persuasive, on the basis that, in holding itself out as offering a service, a statutory body was in principle in the same position as any private individual or organisation holding itself out as offering a service. By opening its doors to the general public to take advantage of the service, an authority offering a psychology service was in much the same position as a hospital, and this meant that it came under a duty to all those using the service to exercise care in its conduct.

Very significantly, however, Lord Browne-Wilkinson later retracts this statement in the course of his speech in *Barrett v Enfield London Borough Council.*[80] The evident impetus for the retraction was the finding of the Court of Appeal in *Phelps v Hillingdon London Borough Council*[81] that a psychology service was not provided as an open service at all, so that a local authority providing such a service could not be regarded in any way as being in a similar position to a hospital. A psychology service was established rather to advise the local authority as to the performance of its functions as an education authority. As such, the children could not be construed as patients of the service. It is likely that the underlying reason for this change of position was a realisation on Lord Browne-Wilkinson's part of the consequences of recognising a duty of such a general nature on the part of a public body, as discussed earlier. In view of the availability to claimants of the vicarious liability route, the continued existence of this direct route would moreover have been seen as entirely unnecessary.

(b) The Vicarious Liability Arguments

In contrast to the position of the psychiatrist and the social worker in the abuse cases, the employees of the education authority did have the necessary kind of relationships with the claimants to give rise to an assumption of responsibility on their part. In particular, there were no potential conflicts between their duties to the claimants and those that they owed to the education authority.[82]

A final note to be made here is that, contrary to popular belief,[83] there is no problem with allowing recovery for pure economic loss in these cases, given that they have all been subject to the application of the standard *Hedley Byrne* principles.

[79] [1995] 3 All ER 353 at 392.
[80] [1999] 3 All ER 193.
[81] [1999] 1 All ER 421.
[82] See also, more recently, *Carty v Croydon London Borough Council* [2005] EWCA Civ 19.
[83] See A Mullis, '*Barrett v Enfield London Borough Council.* A Compensation-Seeker's Charter?' [2000] CFLQ 185.

III. THE SIGNIFICANCE OF THE *X* LITIGATION FROM A THIRD PARTY LIABILITY PERSPECTIVE

Before its demise, *X & ors v Bedfordshire County Council & ors* was usually interpreted as establishing general principles of public authority liability in negligence. More specifically, it was read as establishing that, for reasons of public policy, negligence actions against public authorities would generally not succeed. It is submitted that this erroneous interpretation of *X* was the main cause of its downfall. Read properly, it is clear that the decision did not purport to set out general principles relevant to all public bodies. Its ratio was strictly limited, not just to local authorities, but to local authorities acting either in the context of their child protection functions or in their capacity as education authorities. Indeed, it was the particular nature of the functions in question that largely determined the outcomes to the claims. Strictly confined to this particular context, it is argued that the decision in *X* was entirely justifiable.

On this reading of the decision, the main consequence of *X* was that in certain social welfare contexts, notably those concerning delicate child protection issues, the majority of basic negligence actions against local authorities were destined to fail on the basis of policy. Moreover, this conclusion appeared to apply regardless of whether the action related to an omission or to a commission. This is illustrated by the decision in *M v Newham London Borough Council*, which clearly involved positive conduct on the part of the defendant authority. Moreover, it is highly significant in this respect that in pursuing their claim before the ECtHR, the claimants in *M* changed the basis of their negligence allegations altogether, from the authority's hasty decision to remove the child from the parental home to its withholding of the video evidence from the mother.[84] It is submitted that this was most likely due to a realisation that the policy card would inevitably be used to trump the child protection argument. And if policy concerns could make even the omission/commission distinction irrelevant in this domain, then it followed that the fact that the harm in question had been caused by a third party would have no impact at all on eventual outcomes. As an exception to this general position, the Court of Appeal decision in *W v Essex County Council*[85] appeared to demonstrate that, where there had been a specific undertaking on the part of a defendant authority such as to amount to an assumption of responsibility on their part towards the claimants, this would have been enough to override the policy issues and make a local authority liable not just for an omission, but even for an omission in respect of harm caused by a third party. In *W v Essex County Council*, the claimant family agreed to act as foster carers, but only upon the express condition that they would not be allocated anyone with a history of abusing children. Despite having accepted this condition, the local

[84] *TP and KM v UK* [2001] 2 FLR 549.

[85] [1998] 3 All ER 111. For an insightful commentary on the decision, see J Wightman, 'The Limits of the Rules on Recovery for Psychiatric Damage in the United Kingdom' (2000) 8 Tort LR 169.

authority went ahead and placed with them a teenage boy who was a known sexual abuser, and who subsequently abused the children in the family. The family sued the local authority in negligence. Upholding the claims of the children,[86] the Court of Appeal relied particularly on the fact that the parents had been given oral assurances by the defendant authority that a known or suspected abuser would not be placed with them, and that they had indeed even made specific inquiries to this effect about the boy in question, but had been wrongly told that he had no such history. It is submitted that, during the *X v Bedfordshire* era, it would always have taken circumstances as exceptional as this to justify a duty in this category of case.

Of course, where child claimants are concerned, all of this had now changed as a result of the Court of Appeal decision in *JD v East Berkshire Community Health.* The current situation is that, regardless of whether the negligence allegation relates to misfeasance or nonfeasance, child welfare professionals will more or less automatically owe a duty of care to children in the care system.

Outside the delicate policy-laden areas of public authority activity, however, it seems that that the legal position remains slightly different. Most significantly, the omission/commission distinction would appear to regain its significance, in the sense that claims framed in terms of a commission will be much more easily argued in terms of duty than those based on an omission. As regards omissions, the one thing that is abundantly clear from the case law is that an affirmative duty cannot be based upon the existence of statutory obligations alone. If no other convincing and independent reasons can be advanced in support of the duty, then the broad public policy considerations militating against the imposition of liability will hold sway. Thus, a bare claim against a public authority based on its failure to exercise a statutory function, whether it be a duty or a mere power, will fail outright for lack of duty. An illustration of this would be *Stovin v Wise.*[87] In this case, a highway authority was sued for failing to remove a hazard to a highway. The hazard in question was a mound of earth on a piece of land adjacent to the highway that obscured the view of motorists using a junction and checking for oncoming traffic. The claimant was injured in a crash caused by a motorist emerging from this junction and pulling out in front of her. She sued the motorist in negligence, and he in turn joined the highway authority as co-defendant on the basis that it had a statutory power conferred by the Highways Act 1980 to remove the hazard. Indeed, prior to the accident, the authority, which was well aware of the existence of the hazard, had actually taken steps to effect its removal but then had simply failed to follow the matter up. It even conceded that its conduct had been faulty, so that if a duty were held to exist then it certainly would have been breached. However, the authority contested the existence of a duty, and a bare majority of the House of Lords found in its favour.

[86] The claims brought by the parents were for psychiatric harm, and they were struck out on the basis that the special duty requirements governing such harm could not be met. This decision has, however, since been reversed by the House of Lords: *W v Essex County Council* [2000] 2 All ER 237.

[87] [1996] 3 All ER 801.

There were no exceptional circumstances present in the case to justify a duty. Lord Hoffmann did, however, indicate that one possible justification for a duty in claims based upon a failure to exercise a statutory function would be the doctrine of general reliance, although it did not apply to the case at hand. The doctrine of general reliance is said to apply when sections of the public rely on a public body to exercise a power or duty to confer upon them a benefit that they are unable to procure for themselves. In *Stovin*, Lord Hoffmann qualified the doctrine further by suggesting that it also had to be shown that the authority had arbitrarily denied to the claimant a benefit that was routinely provided to others. He considered that the improvement of road junctions was not a uniform service, and that the claimant in this case was moreover in the same position as all other road users.[88] More recently, however, Lord Hoffmann has distanced himself from this general reliance argument, and indeed in *Gorringe v Calderdale Metropolitan Borough Council*,[89] he went so far as to say that he now found it 'difficult to imagine a case in which a common law duty of care [could] be founded simply upon the failure (however irrational) to provide some benefit which a public authority has power (or a public law duty) to provide.'[90]

That the harm for which it was sought to make the authority liable in *Stovin* had been wholly inflicted by a third party was not actually discussed in court. This is interesting because it suggests that the third party issue was simply subsumed by the general omissions issue. In other words, it mattered not through what medium the harm had actually been caused, only that it had not been caused by the defendant. If this is the case, does it then mean that, in this area, third party liability cannot be regarded as a separate and identifiable category of liability in its own right? It is submitted that this would be a rash conclusion to draw. The problem with the claim in *Stovin* was that it was very weak from all sides. On the assumption that Lord Hoffmann was right to reject the general reliance argument, and in the absence of any other kind of special connection between the parties involved, the kind of liability being advocated and, more importantly, for which the case would have been setting a precedent, was simply much too wide and general. Thus, the basic misfeasance point was enough to dispense with the claim without even having to advert to the third party issue.

It is submitted that there is another reason why the third party liability claim did not work in *Stovin*, one that is indeed more pertinent to the theme of the present discussion. It is, quite simply, that the targeted functions of the defendant local authority in question were just not conducive to the idea of third party liability. It is argued that only those public duties that can be said directly to relate either to the protection of the public from harm caused specifically by third parties, or to the control of dangerous or irresponsible individuals posing risks to others, can, in themselves, defensibly give rise to the kinds of affirmative

88 Significantly, in his dissenting speech in *Stovin*, Lord Nicholls evidently considered that there was a strong basis for arguing reliance in that case: *ibid*, at 814–15.

89 [2004] UKHL 15.

90 *Ibid*, at para 32.

common law duties of care necessary to support a third party liability argument. Statutory obligations in respect of highway maintenance certainly do not fit either bill. In their case, additional exceptional circumstances independently justifying an affirmative duty in respect of third party harm would be needed, such as evidence of an explicit assumption of responsibility on the part of the authority.[91]

Planning authorities would also be in a similar position, in that their functions are not conducive to third party liability arguments. In their case, the relevant type of negligence allegation will typically relate to a grant of planning permission in respect of a dangerous structure that will later be the setting for an accident involving one party injuring another. It is to be noted immediately, however, that this type of scenario differs from the paradigm scenario in relation to highway authorities in *Stovin v Wise* in that it involves a degree of positive conduct on the part of the defendant authority which contributes to the creation of the circumstances giving rise to the harm. Thus, the nature of the allegation will differ in that it will take the form of a hybrid argument, rather than a pure omissions one. This should make it easier to establish an affirmative duty of action. The point is, however, that any liability that may ultimately arise will not be a form of true third party liability, even though the actual harm in question has actually been inflicted by a third party, because it will not be directed specifically to the harm-causing third party conduct. The fact that the harm has been inflicted by a third party will be entirely incidental and, by all accounts, entirely irrelevant to the liability issue. The planning authority's legal responsibility will be directed rather at its positive role in creating the dangerous situation which led to the infliction of the harm by the third party. The only live issue for the court will therefore be the ordinary omissions question rather than a specific third party liability one.

A good illustration of these points is provided by the case of *Kane v New Forest District Council*.[92] The defendant planning authority in question had granted planning permission for a development which required the developer to construct a footpath before commencing development works. It was realised that the footpath would end on the inside of a bend in a road with impaired visibility to oncoming drivers, which would compromise the safety of pedestrians wishing to cross at that point to the footpath on the opposite side of the road. Communications thus ensued with the local highway authority responsible for the roadway about improving the sightlines at the footpath exit. Before the proposed improvements were actually carried out by the highway authority, however, the

[91] The position of the various emergency services may be instructively considered in this context also. Their primary functions do not relate specifically to the prevention of harm caused by third parties either, any role played by third parties being strictly incidental. Indeed, this can be clearly illustrated by reference to the stage at which these public services typically intervene in the harm-causing situation, namely, after the event. In other words, their duties relate to controlling the consequences of harm, rather than to preventing the infliction of the harm in the first place. Thus, third party liability actions will generally not arise against the emergency services either.

[92] [2002] 1 WLR 312.

footpath was opened to the public. Unfortunately for the claimant, the foreseeable risk materialised when he was struck by a car while trying to cross the road at the end of the footpath. He alleged negligence on the part of the planning authority in failing, when granting the planning permission, to impose a condition forbidding the opening of the footpath to the public until the danger had been removed. In reversing the judge's decision to dismiss the action on the ground that it had no real prospect of success given the authority of *Stovin v Wise*, the Court of Appeal relied heavily on the fact that the defendant had actually created the source of the danger in the first place.[93] It was thus able easily to distinguish *Stovin* on the basis of the misfeasance/nonfeasance distinction.

As in *Stovin*, the fact that the harm for which it was sought to make the defendant responsible had actually been inflicted by an independent third party was not even mentioned in court. It is submitted that, in this case, a key reason why the Court of Appeal was able to go much further and actually impose liability without adverting to the role of the third party harm-doer is that the third party harm-causing conduct in question was entirely unintentional in nature, rather than an 'act of conscious volition', as referred to by Lord Reid in *Dorset Yacht*.[94] In terms of notions of moral responsibility, the main reason why the idea of making one person liable for harm intentionally inflicted by another is so instinctively objectionable and controversial is that the person being held liable is not the one most obviously responsible for the harm. With harm that has been caused accidentally and non-negligently,[95] on the other hand, it seems only natural to cast a wider net of responsibility. It is all about attributing responsibility to the highest degree of fault.

It may also be questioned at this point whether some kind of indirect link exists between the idea that only certain public functions are innately susceptible to third party liability arguments and the purely factual matter of the particular form of the negligence allegations constituting the basis of a claim, specifically in terms of whether or not the allegations relate to a failure to exercise certain discretionary statutory functions. To put it simply, it seems that where claimants have to point to specific statutory provisions setting out the precise functions of the defendant body as the main basis of their duty arguments, the functions in question tend not to be very susceptible to third party liability claims. This is

93 It is necessary to contrast *Kane* with the scenario occurring in *P Perl (Exporters) Ltd v Camden London Borough Council* [1984] 1 QB 342, as discussed in ch 3, in respect of which it was argued that a positive duty to control another party could be founded upon the defendant's active creation of the situation of danger in conjunction with a high degree of foreseeability of the harm occurring. For in *P Perl*, the defendant's positive contributory conduct directly affected the third party perpetrator's conduct, whereas in *Kane*, the grant of the planning permission instead affected only the victim's conduct and only in an entirely negative sense. Moreover, it cannot be said that the planning authority in *Kane* actively created the situation of danger. Rather, more remotely, it just contributed to the circumstances facilitating the commission of the tort.

94 [1970] AC 1004 at 1031.

95 The claimant in *Kane* did not place any blame at all on the motorist who actually struck him, believing that he had had no chance of avoiding him, and therefore did not bring any legal proceedings against him.

because claimants only need to resort to the statute in cases where the functions of the body are not obvious or commonly known, and third party arguments are going to work only in respect of clear-cut public duties to control or to protect.

Applying this reasoning, and notwithstanding the House of Lords decision in *Brooks*,[96] it is suggested that the most obvious candidate for a third party liability claim would be a police authority, given that its primary function is to protect the public from the harmful activities of third parties.[97] Indeed, to this end, the police are specifically empowered to control the conduct of risk-producing third parties. That is not to suggest, however, that the mere existence of this public function of protection and control should ever be thought to constitute, in itself, sufficient basis for an affirmative duty in respect of third party harm. This would certainly open up the police to a barrage of claims which, for the public policy reasons discussed earlier, would not be to the ultimate benefit of society. To say that the policing function is conducive to third party liability arguments is merely to imply that such arguments would at least have a logical foundation in this context, not that they should necessarily always succeed. Further requirements designed to control liability are necessary and desirable. Fortunately, a perfectly adequate control mechanism already exists in the law in this respect in the form of the, by now familiar, requirement that two special relationships of close proximity be established by the claimant: one as between the defendant and the third party perpetrator, and another as between the defendant and the victim. Notably, such a requirement would appear to apply to all third party actions against public bodies that are based on the existence of public duties to control and protect, as will be seen presently.

As regards police authorities, no better example of the kind of factual scenario required to found an actionable third party liability claim can be found than the background to the claim in *Osman v Ferguson*. The police in this case had undeniably close links with both the Osmans and the teacher who caused the harm. They had had numerous personal dealings with both parties and were indeed fully aware of the risk posed by the latter to the former. It is precisely because the case for a duty in this instance was so overwhelmingly strong that the decision to strike out the claim on specific duty grounds caused the uproar that it did. It is also highly ironic that by being so reactionary and adopting such a restrictive approach to public authority liability, thus inviting European intervention, the English courts ended up by actually widening the scope of liability beyond the necessary boundaries. What is meant by this is that, although a duty was clearly owed by the police in *Osman*, it is unlikely that the claimants would actually have been able to establish a breach on the facts, so that liability could ultimately have been avoided on this entirely legitimate basis. In support of this, reference need

[96] Above n 74.

[97] On this link between functions and liability, it is interesting to note also at this point the case of *Hardaker v Newcastle Health Authority and the Chief Constable of Northumbria* [2001] Lloyd's Rep Med 512, in which a negligence action against the police in the respect of its provision of certain medical facilities failed primarily on the ground that this did not constitute one of its main functions.

only be made to the fact that the ECtHR more or less exonerated the police for their investigation and decision making, finding that the evidence presented did not support the allegations directed specifically at their conduct under Articles 2 and 8. The ECtHR emphasised that, although it had found that there had been a violation of Article 6 in this case, this was not tantamount to saying that the Osmans would necessarily have won in the domestic courts. It meant merely that they had an arguable claim and that, consequently, they were 'entitled to have the police account for their acts and omissions in adversarial proceedings.'[98] Hoyano would regard this as a clear illustration of how the fault requirement may be used as an effective control mechanism.[99]

That there has already been a notable shift of emphasis from duty to breach, as effected principally by the House of Lords decision in *Barrett*,[100] is for the most part to be welcomed. Indeed, in academic circles, there is strong support for the adoption of a fault-led approach to public authority liability.[101] Concern is expressed, however, about what this kind of approach will actually entail for the duty concept. What will its future role be? For while it has inevitably been tainted by previous instances of judicial misuse, it ought not to be forgotten that the duty concept does function as an invaluable vetting tool, in terms of assessing at the outset the basic legal tenability of claims, and dismissing those that would represent a waste of time and money to pursue.[102] If the concept were to be sacrificed in the interests of allowing a detailed fault assessment to be carried out at full trial, by being reduced to a mere formality in the majority of cases, then the consequences could only be negative. Unfortunately, some of the recent case law on the matter would appear to indicate that this is already happening to some extent. The proper approach must surely be to clarify for all those concerned the precise role to be played by the duty concept, and to ensure that it is, in future, properly applied in practice. This duty requirement could then operate in conjunction with the breach requirement to ensure not only a fair and just approach to liability, but also a workable one.

Bearing all of this in mind, it is proposed to look individually at some of the main public authorities whose functions are susceptible to third party liability claims. It is envisaged that such public authority liability would generally be invoked vicariously in respect of the personal negligence of individual employees. It seems appropriate to begin with police authorities and to accompany an

98 (1998) 29 EHRR 245 at para 153.

99 L Hoyano, 'Policing Flawed Police Investigations: Unravelling the Blanket' (1999) 62 MLR 912 at 925.

100 See further, P Craig and D Fairgrieve, '*Barrett*, Negligence and Discretionary Powers' (1999) PL 626.

101 See, in particular, M Andenas and D Fairgrieve, 'Sufficiently Serious? Judicial Restraint in Tortious Liability of Public Authorities and the European Influence', in M Andenas (ed), *English Public Law and the Common Law of Europe* (Key Haven Publications, 1998). See also S Bailey, 'Beyond the Call of Duty' (1987) 50 MLR 956 at 963.

102 Jane Stapleton would appear to hold a similar view about the duty function: 'Duty of Care: Peripheral Parties and Alternative Opportunities for Deterrence' (1995) 111 LQR 301.

elaboration of the points already made in this respect with a detailed exposé of the relevant case law.

(i) Police Authorities

Swinney v Chief Constable of Northumbria Police[103] provides a further example of the type of situation in which the third party liability of the police might arise. The claim in this case arose out of the theft, by persons unknown, of a folder of information from an unattended police car. The information in question, which related to the activities of a violent individual, had been supplied by an informant whose personal details were also contained in the folder. The folder eventually made its way into the hands of the individual concerned, who proceeded to issue threats against the informant and her husband. Suing the police for the psychiatric harm she claimed to have suffered as a result of receiving the threats, the informant alleged negligence on their part in failing to keep the information secure in the first place. Thus it was sought to make the police liable for two separate instances of third party misconduct: the initial act of theft by the persons unknown, as well as the issuing of the threats by the named individual, for it was from this latter conduct that the harm complained was actually said to stem. Refusing to strike out the claim, the Court of Appeal held that there was a sufficient degree of proximity between the claimant and the police to place upon them a duty to take reasonable care to keep secure the information she had supplied to them.[104] Reference was also made to the strong public policy argument in favour of allowing liability in this instance, to the effect of encouraging informants to supply to the police information that can be used to fight crime. This alone outweighed all the *Hill* immunity arguments.

On the third party liability issue, it is to be noted that the duty of care in this instance was founded upon the existence of just one special relationship of close proximity, for this would appear to fly in the face of what has been said above about the need for two special relationships to be established. The facts of *Swinney*, however, are to be entirely distinguished from *Hill* and *Osman*. Indeed, the claim in *Swinney* cannot even be accurately described as a true third party liability one. The allegations of negligence were directed exclusively at the actions of the defendants in leaving the folder in the car. There was no further suggestion that they should have in some way attempted positively to control the conduct of the third party harm-doers. Nor indeed was such a suggestion even necessary, for the misfeasance on their part was clearly enough in itself to support all of the

[103] [1996] 3 All ER 449.

[104] The claim was ultimately unsuccessful at full trial, as the police were found not to have been in breach of their duty of care: *Swinney v Chief Constable of Northumbria Police (No 2)* (1999) 11 Admin LR 811. This serves as yet another reminder that to recognise the basic tenability of a claim through the imposition of a duty is not necessarily to open the floodgates to further claims, for at the next stage the fault requirement can then be employed as an equally effective, and ostensibly more legitimate, control mechanism.

relevant duty, breach and causation arguments. Thus, it was only a very weak, and essentially uncontroversial, form of third party liability that was in issue, in the sense that it was liability for an act of personal wrongdoing, but in respect of harm actually inflicted by a third party, with the link between the two being entirely indirect. The conclusion to be drawn from this has to be that the duty requirement that two special relationships of close proximity be established is limited to situations in which the duty is to control or in some other way actively to influence the conduct of the third party.

Whilst, in the majority of cases, this requirement of two special relationships is likely to constitute a significant obstacle to establishing liability against the police for failing to prevent crime, thus making it a very effective control mechanism, there is one category of claimants for whom it will pose no problem at all, and that is individual police officers themselves. Case law clearly dictates that police officers have a duty to come to the aid of fellow officers being attacked by third parties. In *Costello v Chief Constable of Northumbria Police*,[105] a female police officer was attacked and injured by a prisoner in a cell while one of her senior colleagues simply stood back and watched. In finding that the colleague had been under a duty to intervene and help to restrain the attacker, the Court of Appeal relied on the closeness of the relationship between the defendant and the claimant as fellow officers and on the close physical proximity of the defendant to the incident. It was also relevant that the defendant had been positioned close by for the specific purpose of lending assistance if required. The necessary special relationship between the defendant and the third party perpetrator would appear to have been satisfied in this instance by the fact that the latter was a prisoner in custody at the time and, perhaps more significantly, by the actual physical proximity between the two at the time of the attack. This latter factor is thought to be more significant because it would arguably have been sufficient in itself to satisfy the required relationship of close proximity. Given that the whole purpose of the special proximity requirements in these cases is to limit liability to the most exceptionally deserving cases, applying the duty to intervene to situations in which the defendant is actually present would seem perfectly defensible. Interestingly, in addition to being singled out as exceptional for the purposes of a duty to rescue, the relationship between police officers has also been made the subject of much wider duties of protection. Where these much broader third party liability issues are concerned, however, it seems that the relevant affirmative duties will be limited strictly to the most senior officers. In *Waters v Commissioner of Police of the Metropolis*,[106] the House of Lords refused to strike out a policewoman's claim that the defendant commissioner had been negligent in failing to protect her from victimisation by fellow officers. That the victimisation appeared to have been linked to the fact that the claimant had previously reported one of her fellow officers for sexual assault, and was thus seen by her colleagues to have

[105] [1999] 1 All ER 550.
[106] [2000] 4 All ER 934.

broken the team rules, was regarded by the House as relevant to the duty issue. This is significant in that it would appear to distinguish this employment relationship from other employment relationships, in terms of the nature of the internal politics involved, and would thus limit the ratio accordingly.

Aside from their main function in relation to the investigation and suppression of crime, there is one other aspect of the role of the police which may expose them to third party liability claims, and it is that which relates to the retention of persons in custody. By taking persons into custody, and thus purporting to exercise total control over their whole environment, custodial officers place themselves under a legal duty to ensure the general safety of their charges. An interesting third party perspective to this duty that has emerged from the case law in recent years is that, in certain circumstances, it may extend to an obligation to protect the detainees from themselves, in terms of the commission of acts of self-harm. Of the relevant cases in point, of which there are three, the acts of self-harm concerned have all been of the most extreme form, that is, suicide attempts. In both moral and legal terms, the idea of making a person liable for harm that another has deliberately inflicted upon himself or herself is instinctively even more objectionable than the ordinary third party claim, where the perpetrator and the victim are two separate parties, not just because the victim has, for want of a better description, actually desired the harm in question, but also because in these cases, the party most directly responsible for the harm is fully within the remit of the court's judgment. It is thus entirely possible for the court to attribute full legal responsibility to this party by actually denying them the right to sue in the first place. When a duty to prevent self-harm was first recognised on the part of the police, in the case of *Kirkham v Chief Constable of the Greater Manchester Police*,[107] controversy was for the most part avoided on the grounds that the detainee in question had been mentally ill. It was thus possible to justify the decision on the basis that the victim had not been capable of taking responsibility for his own actions. When the issue came before the courts again, however, in *Reeves v Commissioner of Police of the Metropolis*,[108] and the House of Lords imposed a similar duty on the police, this time in respect of a detainee 'of sound mind', the uncomfortable reality that simple knowledge of a detainee's suicidal tendencies would be enough to give rise to the custodial obligation to prevent self-harm had to be faced. This position has recently been confirmed in *Orange v Chief Constable of West Yorkshire Police*.[109] Moreover, because of the very specific nature of the duty in question in these cases, to prevent acts of suicide, the courts have refused to accept arguments that the actual commission of such acts can then be said to either amount to a *novus actus interveniens* or to permit a defence of *volenti non fit injuria*.

[107] [1990] 2 QB 283.
[108] [1999] 3 All ER 897.
[109] [2001] 3 WLR 736 (no duty because no actual knowledge of particular suicide risk).

By the same logic, the police should also have a similar third party duty, while acting in a custodial capacity, to protect detainees from each other. While the issue does not appear to have arisen directly for consideration in an action against the police, it has done so on numerous occasions against prison authorities. The prison authority is the more likely target for such third party actions, given that its custodial functions tend to relate to long-term periods of detention and allow for greater contact between detainees.

(ii) Prison Authorities

It was established as far back as 1953, by the Court of Appeal decision in *Ellis v Home Office*,[110] that a prison authority could be liable for harm inflicted by one of its prisoners upon another within the confines of the prison. A duty to protect prisoners from such harm seems to form an intrinsic part of the wider duty owed by prison authorities to ensure the general safety of their prisoners.[111] The justification for imposing an affirmative duty of this nature is obviously the legal authority and physical power of control exercised by the prison authority over both of the parties involved; or in other words, the existence of two special relationships of close proximity. While the duty may be easily established, however, the task of demonstrating that it has actually been breached is likely to pose considerable problems for claimants, for in what would appear to be a concerted attempt to control liability, the courts have tended to set the relevant standards of care in these cases at exceptionally low levels. A good illustration of this point is provided by Livingston and Owen. They refer to the finding of the Court of Appeal in *Palmer v Home Office*[112] that the actions of a prison authority in allowing a highly dangerous and violent prisoner to work in a tailor's workshop where he had access to scissors, which he then used to stab a fellow prisoner, could not be regarded as negligent. It was the opinion of Neill LJ that 'those responsible for prisons cannot keep prisoners permanently locked up or segregated from other prisoners. In addition, it is necessary, or certainly desirable whenever possible, to provide suitable employment for individual prisoners.'[113]

More complicated is the question of the third party liability of prison authorities in respect of harm caused to members of the public by escaped prisoners. In terms of duty, the main problem will be in establishing the necessary relationship of proximity between the defendant and the claimant. The principal point of

110 [1953] 2 All ER 149.

111 See further, S Livingstone and T Owen, *Prison Law* (OUP, 1999).

112 (1988) *The Guardian*, March 31.

113 Further cases involving similar third party liability actions against the prison service are: *D'Arcy v Prison Commissioners* (1955) *The Times*, November 17; *Egerton v Home Office* [1978] Crim LR 494; *Porterfield v Home Office* (1988) *The Independent*, March 9; *Steele v NIO* (1988) 12 NIJB 1; *H v Home Office* (1992) *The Independent*, May 6; *Hartshorn v Home Office* unreported, 21 January 1999 (CA), noted by S Foster (1999) NLJ 799.

reference here is obviously the seminal decision in *Home Office v Dorset Yacht.*[114] Given that the Law Lords all went to great lengths to emphasise the special facts of this case, in particular the highly significant geographical detail that the incident in question had taken place on an island, which had the effect not only of giving the victims the status of particularly foreseeable claimants but also of establishing a very clear and neat boundary to the scope of liability, the decision would appear to lend support only to claims brought by victims living in the *immediate* vicinity of the prison.

Claimants in this context must also ensure that in formulating their claims they do not fall foul of the rule against challenging policy decisions. By way of example, a decision to place a prisoner with a record of previous escape attempts in an open prison, from which it would obviously be very easy for him to abscond, would probably be regarded as falling into the policy bracket and would thus be non-justiciable for this reason.[115] Similarly, it was made clear by the Law Lords in *Dorset Yacht* that if the allegations in that case had been directed at the decision to run an open borstal, with all the risks that that obviously entailed, or presumably even to the decision to bring the boys in question onto Brownsea island in the first place for the purposes of their reformation, the claim would have automatically failed. Claimants must be able to point to some particular instance of individual faulty conduct, such as inadequate supervision, to have any chance of succeeding.

(iii) Health Authorities

It will be through their relationships with risk-producing patients that health professionals may expose themselves to third party liability actions. While those working in the mental health field will obviously be the most susceptible to such litigation, there are a number of situations in which it is foreseeable that the third party liability of ordinary doctors could arise.[116] Thus, in treating an infectious disease, a doctor may come under a duty to protect those likely to come into contact with the patient in question. Such a duty could consist either of an obligation to warn of the dangers of infection, or of an obligation to ensure that the infected patient does not come into contact with others at all, perhaps by keeping him or her in total isolation for the required period.[117] Of course, in individual cases, the imposition of such third party duties to protect will have to be reconciled with the defendant doctor's own professional duties of confidentiality

[114] [1970] AC 1004.

[115] See Lord Diplock's discussion and ultimate condemnation, in *Dorset Yacht* (at 1061 and 1069) of the decision in the earlier case of *Greenwell v Prison Commissioners* (1951) 101 *LJ News* 486 holding a prison authority liable for harm caused by an escaped prisoner on the grounds that it had been negligent in deciding to place him in an open prison system in the first place.

[116] See further, J Healy, *Medical Negligence: Common Law Perspectives* (Sweet & Maxwell, 1999), at pp 44–8, and MA Jones, 'Liabilities for psychiatric patients: setting the boundaries' (2000) 16 PN 3.

[117] See, eg, *Evans v Liverpool Corporation* [1906] 1 KB 160.

towards his patient.[118] Another likely scenario, one that has indeed already been litigated in Canada, is failing to advise patients suffering from certain medical conditions about the dangers of partaking in certain activities, such as driving with epilepsy, with the result that an accident occurs in which others are harmed.[119] Obviously, similar responsibilities would attach to the prescription of medication with potentially dangerous performance-inhibiting side effects.

As indicated above, however, it is the position of mental health professionals that warrants the most attention here, given that their work with a category of patients who pose particularly high levels of risk to others makes them prime targets for third party liability actions. That the actual harm-doers in these cases will also be morally designated as irresponsible will undoubtedly be seen to lend weight to the third party argument in this context. However, while a bare obligation to control the actions of a psychiatric patient may be readily founded upon the nature of the relationship existing between the defendant doctor and the patient, the case law on the matter would indicate that this will be transformed into a common law duty of care, such as to found an action in negligence, only where it is accompanied by knowledge of a specific threat to a specific individual. In other words, a special relationship of close proximity also needs to be established between the defendant and the victim before the defendant will be legally required to act affirmatively to protect the victim by controlling the conduct of the patient. Thus in *Palmer v Tees Area Health Authority*,[120] it was held by the Court of Appeal that a health authority owed no duty of care to a child in respect of her abduction, abuse and subsequent murder by an outpatient with a history of violence and sexual abuse, on the grounds that the child had not been individually identified to the authority as being at a specific risk of harm from this patient. Although the patient had threatened to murder a child, and the young girl in question lived close by, this was not enough to give her a special status.[121] Where there is evidence of a specific threat to an identified individual, such as in the well-known Californian case of *Tarasoff v Regents of the University of California*,[122] in which a patient confessed to his therapist about his feelings of violence towards a particular female who was also personally known to the therapist, it is likely that the duty will consist either of an obligation to alert the authorities about the potential threat, or if such individuals powers exist, to have the patient committed under the Mental Health Act 1983.[123] The standard *Bolam* test[124] will then obviously apply to determine breach.

[118] Note *W v Edgell* [1990] Ch 359.

[119] *Spillane v Wasserman* (1992) 13 CCLT (2d) 267.

[120] [1999] Lloyd's Rep Med 351.

[121] In light of this finding, the much earlier decision in *Holgate v Lancashire Mental Hospitals Board* [1937] 4 All ER 19 to hold a hospital board liable in respect of the actions of a patient in attacking a member of the public must be called into doubt.

[122] 551 P 2d 334 (1976).

[123] On this point, see also, F Morris and G Adshead, 'The liability of psychiatrists for the violent acts of their patients' (1997) 147 NLJ 558.

[124] As qualified by *Bolitho v City and Hackney Health Authority* [1997] 4 All ER 771.

While health authorities will also owe duties to prevent psychiatric patients under their care from committing acts of self-harm,[125] the courts have made it clear that they will not sanction an extension of these duties to further encompass the protection of such patients from the legal consequences of their own criminal behaviour. Thus in *Clunis v Camden & Islington Health Authority*,[126] an action for damages brought by a discharged psychiatric patient who had been convicted of manslaughter against the health authority charged with the statutory duty of providing after-care services for him, alleging a negligent failure to provide him with the required treatment that would have prevented him from carrying out the fatal attack, was dismissed by the Court of Appeal as being contrary to public policy. The court would not lend its aid to a claimant who relied on his own criminal or immoral act, and so the defence of *ex turpi causa non oritur actio* applied. Additionally, it was found that public policy also prevented a duty of care from being recognised on the facts, on the grounds that it would not have been fair, just, or reasonable.[127]

(iv) Education Authorities

The special position of authority and control occupied by those responsible for the running of schools has long been regarded as giving rise to third party affirmative duties to protect and control the pupils in their care. Consequently, schools are susceptible to two different forms of third party liability in respect of their pupils: (1) liability for harm that others inflict on their pupils;[128] and (2) liability for harm that their pupils inflict on others.[129] Thus, in *J (A Child) v Lincolnshire County Council*,[130] an LEA was held liable in respect of serious injuries sustained by one of its young pupils who was hit by a car after wandering off the school premises, while in *Carmarthenshire County Council v Lewis*,[131] an LEA was held liable to a motorist fatally injured in a road accident caused by an errant child. In both cases, liability was linked to the authorities' respective failures to provide adequate security to prevent very young pupils from making

125 *Hay v Grampian Health Board* [1995] 6 Med LR 128; *Walsh v Gwynedd Health Authority* unreported, 27 April 1998 (CC).

126 [1998] 3 All ER 1998. For further discussion of the decision see MA Jones, 'The violent mentally disordered patient: who cares?' (1998) 14 PN 99.

127 There was a previous case in which a claimant had been allowed to recover damages in respect of his conviction of a criminal offence. In *Meah v McCreamer* [1985] 1 All ER 367, the claimant, who had undergone a personality change after suffering a head injury in a road accident, was held to be entitled to damages in respect of his subsequent conviction of two offences of rape. In *Clunis*, however, the Court of Appeal refused to recognise this decision, stating that it could not be regarded as authoritative of the issue as it had been made without any consideration of the public policy question. As such, it is highly unlikely that *Meah* could ever be relied upon by future claimants.

128 See, eg, *Wilson v Governers of Sacred Heart RC School* [1998] 1 FLR 663.

129 See, eg, *Marvier v Dorset County Council* unreported, 4 April 1997 (CC).

130 [2000] ELR 245.

131 [1955] AC 549.

unauthorised exits from the premises. The applicable standard of care in such cases is said to be that of the 'careful parent'.[132]

A more controversial aspect of such liability is the extent to which schools may be held responsible for bullying. It is almost certain that schools have a duty to take reasonable care to prevent bullying from taking place within their own grounds, primarily through the implementation and execution of sensible disciplinary policies and procedures. Moreover, the Court of Appeal has recently stated that, in exceptional circumstances, this duty may even extend to bullying taking place outside the school premises, such as where a teacher actually witnesses one pupil attacking another just outside the school gates.[133] However, the courts have shown themselves particularly unsympathetic to claimants who try to recover damages for an alleged failure of this duty, in one case actually informing a claimant that the bringing of the case had caused her more suffering than the alleged bullying in respect of which she was suing.[134]

IV. CONCLUSION

Fundamental misunderstandings about the proper nature and scope of the ratio of *X v Bedfordshire County Council* have resulted in the courts adopting an entirely misguided and overly restrictive approach to the tortious liability of public authorities. As regards the tenability of third party liability actions against public authorities, it is argued that the principal determinative factor has to be the primary function of the actual body concerned in each individual case. Some public authorities, such as the police authorities and the prison authorities, are by the very nature of their designated statutory roles in society, inherently susceptible to third party liability arguments. In general, this is because their primary functions relate directly to the care and control of risk-producing third parties. Where third party liability actions against these particular authorities arise, special control mechanisms can be applied to exclude all but the most exceptional cases. At the duty of care stage, such mechanisms already exist in the form of a requirement that there exist two special relationships of close proximity: one as between the defendant and the third party harm-doer and another as between the defendant and the victim. At the breach of duty stage, it is submitted that a simple lowering of the relevant standard of care would constitute a suitable and

132 *Ibid* at 561 per Lord Goddard. See also *Barnes v Hampshire County Council* [1969] 1 WLR 1563.

133 *Bradford-Smart v West Sussex County Council* [2002] EWCA Civ 7. For a commentary on the case, see J Elvin, 'The Liability of Schools for Bullying' [2002] CLJ 255.

134 *Walker v Derbyshire County Council* (1994) *The Times*, July 16. Note also that the claim in *Bradford-Smart* ultimately failed on the grounds that the school had not been in breach of its duty of care.

highly effective measure in this respect.[135] One way of effecting this would be to simply transfer the requirement of *Wednesbury* unreasonableness from the duty of care inquiry, where it is currently applied under *X v Bedfordshire*, to the breach of duty inquiry. Alternatively, an approach similar to that taken by the French administrative courts could be followed whereby, as will be seen in the next chapter, a special test of 'gross' fault, as opposed to 'ordinary' fault, would apply to public authority actions.[136]

[135] See also Andenas and Fairgrieve, above n 101.

[136] Such a suggestion was indeed made a number of years ago by S Bailey in 'Beyond the call of duty' (1987) 50 MLR 956.

7

Liability for the Acts of Others: A French Perspective

A STRIKING FEATURE of the French legal system is its victim-oriented approach to questions of liability for unlawfully inflicted harm.[1] In pursuit of the principal goal of compensation for victims, the French courts are quite prepared to target peripheral defendants in cases in which the actual perpetrator of the harm, for whatever reason, either cannot be sued or is not worth suing. Moreover, they are indifferent in this respect to the status of defendants, in terms of whether they are public authorities or private law defendants. For the English lawyer, what is perhaps most remarkable of all, however, is that such third party liability is often imposed on an entirely no-fault basis. Indeed, in recent years, there have been dramatic developments in the law in this respect, particularly as concerns private law defendants, to the extent that it could now be argued that the French system has implemented a general regime of no-fault liability for the acts of others. Significantly, however, in terms of the actual application of its principles of third party liability, direct correlations can be drawn with the existing categories of such liability in English law.

I. THIRD PARTY LIABILITY OF PUBLIC AUTHORITIES IN FRANCE

In France, legal actions against public authorities do not come before the ordinary courts. Rather, in accordance with a strict interpretation of the doctrine of separation of powers, France operates an entirely separate court system, staffed by its own body of specialist judges, to deal exclusively with legal matters concerning the activities of the administration. Thus it is before these 'administrative courts' that any actions invoking the tortious liability of a public body will be brought. Crucially, these special courts also administer their own separate and distinct body of law which, unusually for a codified regime, is almost entirely judge-made. In essence, the law as regards the administration is effectively

[1] F Lambert-Faivre, 'L'évolution de la responsabilité civile d'une dette de responsabilité à une créance d'indemnisation' RTDciv.1987.1.

whatever the *Conseil d'Etat*, the highest administrative court, deems it to be. That French law recognises no doctrine of binding precedent, moreover, means that the substantive law in this respect is subject to change over time, for the *Conseil d'Etat* is free to change its position on any matter and does, as a matter of practice, frequently depart from its own previous decisions.[2] Such flexibility, which is characteristic of French law generally, has engendered, as will be seen, a judicial tendency towards creativity.

The first point to make about the tortious liability of public bodies in France is that, in stark contrast to the English approach in this respect, the administrative courts take an extremely broad approach to the concept of fault, and will, in principle, classify as an administrative tort any kind of conduct on the part of a public body that results in harm being unfairly inflicted upon a member of the public, thus entitling the victim to compensation. Indeed, even where the conduct cannot be construed as unlawful in any sense, a particular individual who shoulders the burden of works carried out in the public interest will still be entitled to compensation under the principle of 'equality before public burdens'. From a third party liability perspective, an interesting application of this liberal fault interpretation is to be found in the context of claims based upon the notion of a *faute de service*. A *faute de service* refers essentially to some kind of failure in the operation of a public service, and it is often invoked by claimants as a way of circumventing the restrictions imposed by the doctrine of vicarious liability, in order to make public service employers primarily liable for harm occasioned through the personal fault of their employees committed *outside* the scope of their employment. The argument runs to the effect that the public service is at fault in providing the conditions for the commission of the harm by the employee: for example, by providing the public vehicle that is used by the employee to make a private and unauthorised journey during which harm is inflicted on another.[3] Until recently, such an argument would undoubtedly have been frowned upon by English lawyers as stretching the boundaries of the fault principle just a little too far. However, as a result of the recent decisions of the House of Lords in *Lister v Hesley Hall Ltd*,[4] and the Court of Appeal in *Majrowski v Guy's and St Thomas's NHS Trust*,[5] which have dramatically expanded the doctrine of vicarious liability, the English law in this respect is no longer very different to its French counterpart.

While this liberal approach to public authority liability holds for most actions for damages before the administrative courts, there are some public activities that are afforded special protection in recognition of their particularly difficult or sensitive nature. Such protection is bestowed in the form of a modified standard of care requirement that deems as unacceptable only conduct that is capable of

[2] See LN Brown and JS Bell, *French Administrative Law* (Oxford, Clarendon Press, 1998), p 176.

[3] See *ibid*, pp 185–88.

[4] [2002] 1 AC 215.

[5] [2005] EWCA 251.

being characterised as gross fault (*faute lourde*). The activities of the police are a prime example of the kind that would fall into this category. In practice, this lowering of the standard of care appears to work very well as a control mechanism,[6] a fact that undoubtedly lends great support to the suggestion raised in the previous chapter that a similar approach be followed in all public authority actions in English tort law.

At the other extreme again, however, there are a number of public activities in respect of which the administrative courts operate a principle of no-fault liability, generally based upon the theory of risk. For present purposes, it is significant that the relevant 'risk-producing' activities often relate to the care and control of third parties, and thus give rise to a number of instances of no-fault state liability for the acts of others. The most well-established instances of such liability may be divided into two categories, both of which, significantly, have already been encountered in the English context: (i) third party liability in respect of harm caused by prisoners; and (ii) third party liability in respect of harm caused by mentally disordered patients in state care.

(i) Third Party Liability in Respect of Harm Caused by Prisoners

This form of no-fault liability on the part of the state is based upon the implementation of what Brown and Bell term 'liberal penal measures',[7] which most often refers to the operation of 'open' prison systems, and applies in respect of the conduct of both adult prisoners and young offenders. As regards adult prisoners, Brown and Bell provide, as an example, the decision of the *Conseil d'Etat* in *Garde des Sceaux c Banque Populaire de la Région Economique de Strasbourg*,[8] to the effect that the Minister for Justice was responsible for the actions of three criminals in robbing a bank, on the grounds that one of the perpetrators was a prisoner on home leave at the time, another was being held on a special regime of 'semi-liberty' which allowed him to work outside the prison during the day, and the other had just been granted parole. The contrast with the English position here is stark, for it is clear that such policy decisions would be deemed non-justiciable by the English courts.[9]

As regards young offenders, the potential for no-fault third party liability to arise on the part of the state on the grounds of risk theory is even greater, given that the French courts have long pursued a policy of applying educative solutions wherever possible to problems of juvenile delinquency.[10] Such solutions are designed as alternatives to traditional penal measures, and are aimed specifically

[6] See BS Markesinis, J-B Auby, D Coester-Waltjen, and S Deakin, *The Tortious Liability of Statutory Bodies* (Hart Publishing, 1999).
[7] Above n 2, p 196.
[8] CE, 9 avril 1987.
[9] *X & ors v Bedfordshire County Council & ors* [1995] 3 All ER 353.
[10] The French law governing juvenile delinquency is contained in the Order of 2 February 1945.

at the rehabilitation of young offenders.[11] They most commonly take the form of what may be termed 'open environment measures', whereby the child continues to live with his or her parents, but under the supervision and assistance of a court-appointed youth worker.[12] Often, however, an order will be made for the child to be placed in a specialist institution, particularly where it is thought that the child's home life may be a contributing factor in his or her criminal tendencies. Where such institutions are state-run, then liability for any harm caused by the child to others will automatically fall on the state. Interestingly, where the institution in question is a privately run concern that has been licensed by the state to receive young offenders on rehabilitation programmes, it appears that no-fault liability will arise on the part of both it and the state jointly, and that the claimant will have to bring two separate actions: one before the administrative courts against the state, and another before the ordinary civil courts against the private institution.[13] That the third party liability of the private institution may be invoked in such situations is a very significant recent development that will be discussed in detail in the next section.

Until very recently, the nature of the state's third party liability in respect of young offenders was to be contrasted with that arising on its part in respect of harm committed by children who have been taken into state care under child protection measures.[14] The latter used to be based on a presumption of fault, rebuttable by proof of lack of fault, and gave rise to a form of strict liability for the acts of others.[15] However, in February 2005, the *Conseil d'Etat* unified the two positions by deciding that harm caused by minors in protective state care would now also give rise to the no-fault liability of the state. This move was uniformly welcomed by French legal academics.[16]

(ii) Third Party Liability in Respect of Harm Caused by Mentally Impaired Patients in State Care

Persons with mental impairments are the other main category of supposedly 'dangerous' individuals in respect of whom special regimes of no-fault third party liability have been implemented in administrative law. It is a firmly established principle of French law, dating from the landmark *Thouzellier*[17] decision of the *Conseil d'Etat* in 1956, that the state will be held liable automatically for any

[11] See further, C Blatier, 'Juvenile Justice in France: The Evolution of Sentencing for Children and Minor Delinquents' (1999) 39 *British Journal of Criminology* 240.

[12] A comparison may perhaps be made here with 'supervision orders' in English criminal law.

[13] See, eg, Civ 2e, 9 déc 1999, JCP 2000, IV, 1163. See also comments made by G Viney, JCP 2000, I, 241.

[14] See Art 375 *et seq* of the Civil Code.

[15] See, eg, CAA Bordeaux, plén, 2 févr 1998, Cts Fraticola, Rdpubl 1998, p 579, concl D Peano.

[16] CE, 11 févr 2005, JCP 2005, II, 10070, concl C Devys, note M-Ch Rouault; JCP 2005, I, 149, chron G. Viney.

[17] CE, 3 févr 1956, D.1956.596, note Auby.

harm caused by a mentally impaired patient of a public hospital. This decision did, however, create a huge disparity between the legal positions of public and private hospitals in this respect, for it was limited to harm caused by patients of public hospitals. Indeed, the liability of private hospitals for the acts of their patients remained fault-based right up until 1991 when, as will be seen in the next section, the *Cour de Cassation* radically transformed the private law on third party liability.

II. THIRD PARTY LIABILITY OF PRIVATE LAW DEFENDANTS IN FRANCE

The French equivalent of the law of tort is contained in just five articles of the Civil Code. Articles 1382 to 1386 set out general principles of law providing for all cases of delictual liability. The principle of liability for personal fault is set out in Article 1382, which provides quite simply that: 'Any human deed whatsoever which causes harm to another creates an obligation in the person by whose fault it was caused to compensate it.'[18] For present purposes, the most relevant provision is Article 1384. By contrast to the brevity of Article 1382, this provision contains eight separate paragraphs and is fairly long and detailed. Not only does it govern all the various instances of third party liability in French civil law, but it also sets out a general principle of 'liability for the deed of things in one's keeping.' The significance of Article 1384 has increased dramatically over the last century. Conducive to judicial manipulation, it has been the subject of numerous substantive changes at the hands of the courts and is consequently associated with some of the greatest developments in the history of the French law of delict.

Paragraph 1 of Article 1384 states: 'One is responsible not only for one's own act, but also for that which is caused by the act of persons for whom one is responsible or by the things which one has in one's care.' It was originally intended as a mere introduction to the subsequent provisions, with the reference to responsibility for the acts of others functioning as a preface to the specific instances of third party liability set out in paragraphs 4 to 8, and the reference to liability for things in one's care relating to Articles 1385 (liability for animals) and 1386 (liability for buildings). Through a process of judicial interpretation, this particular paragraph has been adapted to meet perceived changes in social needs. In 1896,[19] in response to the rise in the number of accidents caused by machines as a result of the industrial revolution, it was dramatically reformulated by the French Supreme Court, the *Cour de Cassation*, to include a general principle of strict liability for the deed of things in one's keeping. This very famous example

[18] Translation taken from J Bell, S Boyron and S Whittaker, *Principles of French Law* (OUP, 1998), p 355.

[19] Civ, 16 juin 1896, D.1897.I.433, note Saleilles, concl Sarrut; S.1897.I.17, note Esmein.

of judicial law-making is illustrative of the adventurousness of the French courts and demonstrates the relative ease with which they can create new legal rules. What is more important for present purposes, however, is that it may be regarded as having paved the way for a further reinterpretation of paragraph 1 in recent times which has had the effect of extending the scope of liability for the acts of others. In 1991, in a decision that constituted a complete departure from it previous, firmly entrenched, legal position, the *Cour de Cassation* held that the principle of liability for the acts of others contained in paragraph 1 was not limited to the specific instances set out in the subsequent paragraphs and that it could be applied more generally to long-term relationships of authority and control.[20] On this basis, it then held a centre for occupational therapy civilly responsible for harm that had been caused by one of its mentally impaired patients. Moreover, by failing to delineate in any precise way the exact sphere of application of the principle, the *Cour de Cassation* also left open the possibility that the principle could be extended to other contexts. Not surprisingly, this soon happened. Before charting the progress of this 'general' principle of liability for the acts of others based on paragraph 1 of Article 1384, however, it is instructive to look at the specific instances of such liability set out in paragraphs 4 to 8.

There are four separate relationships detailed by paragraphs 4 to 8 as giving rise to a form of third party liability:

— parent and child (paragraphs 4 and 7)
— master and servant (paragraph 5)
— teacher and pupil (paragraphs 6 and 8)
— craftsman and apprentice (paragraphs 6 and 7).

Interestingly, each relationship gives rise to a different form of third party liability. Employers are subject to a regime of vicarious liability, while teachers can be held liable only on the basis of ordinary proven fault,[21] and craftsmen are bound by a presumption of fault. The position of parents in this respect is of particular interest given that the basis of their liability for the acts of their children has undergone several major transformations in recent times, developing from a system of ordinary fault-based liability into a system of quasi-strict liability and then into a rather extreme form of no-fault liability, operating on a policy of automatic compensation. Indeed, parental liability has now become the single most important instance of third party liability in French law, and its impact on the principles of civil liability generally has been considerable. Moreover, it is clear that there are direct correlations between the developments in relation to parent liability and those in respect of the 'general' principle of liability for the acts of others. This makes it prudent to look in detail at the

[20] Arrêt *Consorts Blieck*, Ass plén, 29 mars 1991, D.1991, p 325, note Larroumet; JCP 1991, II, 21673, concl Dontenwille, note Ghestin.

[21] New regime introduced by the Law of 5 April 1937. Prior to this, liability was based on a presumption of fault.

evolution of the principle of parental liability, before moving on to look at the developments in relation to paragraph 1.

(i) The Liability of Parents for the Acts of their Children based on Article 1384, paragraph 4

It is possible to identify three 'staging-posts' marking the main developments in parental liability:

— the *Gesbaud*[22] decision in 1966;
— the *Fullenwarth*[23] decision in 1984;
— the *Bertrand*[24] decision in 1997.

Before discussing the changes effected by these decisions, it is necessary to consider the legal position existing prior to 1966.

(a) The Legal Position before 1966

Paragraph 4 of Article 1384, as created by the Law of 4 June 1970, provides that the father and mother, to the extent that they exercise parental authority,[25] are jointly liable for damage caused by their minor children living with them.[26]

Paragraph 7, which was inserted into Article 1384 by the Law of 5 April 1937, states that such liability applies unless the father and mother prove that they could not prevent the act which gave rise to liability.[27]

While it does not contain specific wording to that effect, until 1997, paragraph 7 was always interpreted as creating a rebuttable presumption of fault as the basis of parental liability. Such a presumption was said to relate to a failure on the part of parents to carry out their duties to supervise and educate their children as set out in Article 371-2 of the Civil Code adequately.[28] Located in the section of the Code that deals with parental authority, this Article, at that time, provided that: 'The authority belongs to the father and mother to protect the child in its security, health and morality. They have, with regard to the child, the right and duty to keep, supervise and educate.'[29] The notion of a duty to educate is to be construed in a very broad sense as relating to the general upbringing of the child. This is clearly a wide-ranging duty that is open to an infinite number of

22 Civ 2e, 10 févr 1966, D.1966.332, concl Schmelck.

23 Ass Plén, 9 mai 1984, D.1985.525, concl. Cabannes, note Chabas.

24 Civ 2e, 19 févr 1997, D.1997.265, note Jourdain.

25 Term inserted by the Law of 4 March 2002. Prior to that, reference was to the exercise of a right of custody.

26 Prior to 1970, the mother only became responsible upon the death of the father.

27 This provision also applies to artisans.

28 A Bénabent, *Droit Civil, Les Obligations* (Montchrestien, 1995), p 569.

29 The wording of Article 371-2 has since been changed, in line with the recent developments in parental liability. See below p 151.

subjective interpretations. In consequence, it has given rise to difficulties for parents as regards discharging the burden of proof.

The function of the requirement set out in paragraph 4 that the child be living with the parents at the time the harm was caused was to ensure that liability would be imposed only on parents who were in a position effectively to supervise and educate their children. In practice, however, the courts always took a rather broad approach to the operation of this criterion of liability, for fear that it would be used too easily by irresponsible parents as a means of avoiding liability, and their firm stance was always that, in cases where the child was not living with either parent at the time the damage was caused, or, alternatively, was living with only one parent, absence from the family home would only have precluded application of Article 1384(4) to the non-resident parent where there was a legitimate reason for his or her absence, and must not have been due to what could have been construed as any fault on the part of that parent. For instance, the fact that one parent may have moved out of the family home due to a marital separation or the initiation of divorce proceedings, or the fact that the child was not living in the family home at the relevant time because he or she had run away would not have been regarded as legitimate explanations.[30]

A very important point to be made is that the system of liability as applied at this time was designed only to impose liability on parents for the *torts* of their children. Conduct of a child resulting in harm but not amounting to a tort did not give rise to an action in parental liability based on Article 1384(4). The presumption of fault on the part of the parents was, therefore, conditional upon proof of fault on the part of the child. When the presumption did come into play, the theory was that it would operate to effect a reversal of the burden of proof. The idea was that the commission of the tort by the child would presuppose that the parents had failed to carry out their parental duties properly and this would give rise to a prima facie finding of negligence. The parents would then be given the opportunity to rebut the presumption by attempting to establish that they had adequately supervised and educated the minor so that they could not have prevented the harm.

Such a system was designed to benefit victims by relieving them of at least some of the difficulties inherent in establishing fault and placing the burden instead on the parents to prove that they had not been negligent. At the beginning, however, this is not how the doctrine was implemented in practice. Up until about 1979, the courts merely paid lip-service to the presumption without actually applying it and, in most cases, the victim was required to furnish proof of actual negligence on the part of the parents. By way of example, in one 1960 decision,[31] in which a 19-year-old boy[32] crashed into the claimant while riding his moped at night and without any insurance, the finding of the Court of Appeal

[30] Cf Civ 1re, 4 déc 1963, D.1964.159, note Voirin (separation); Crim 21 août 1996, D.1996.IR.235 (divorce); Civ 2e, 24 nov 1996, Bull Civ II, no 922 (runaway).

[31] Civ 2e, 2 nov 1960, D.1961.770.

[32] In 1960 in France the age of majority was 21. It was not lowered to 18 until 1974.

that it could be inferred from the facts that the boy's father had not adequately supervised or educated his son was quashed by the *Cour de Cassation.* It held that the Court of Appeal should have directed its attention as to whether, in the circumstances, the father had behaved as a reasonable man, which is a clear application of the ordinary fault principle. It further held that the fact that a parent allows a child to use a particular object which subsequently causes harm will constitute fault on the part of the parent only if, by reason either of the age, inexperience or intellectual incompetence of the child, or of the poor condition or dangerous character of the object, or of the abnormal circumstances in which the child was using it, an accident was foreseeable. The approach of the French courts at this point to the issue of parental liability may thus be compared to the current UK system of parental liability.

In another case in the following year, the *Cour de Cassation* took the same course and quashed the finding of the Court of Appeal that the commission of harm by a 13-year-old boy who fired a pellet gun at his friend and hit him in the eye was sufficient proof, in itself, that the boy's father had failed in his duty to educate. The case was sent back to be retried.

Commenting on these two decisions, Rodière suggested that the legal consequence of this approach taken by the French Supreme Court was, effectively, the eradication of the principle of parental liability from the Civil Code.[33] He did, however, also intimate that the reasoning behind the first decision may have been the age of the youth involved, for the position is clear that as children become older the duties of parents become less onerous.[34] Nevertheless, both decisions illustrate the clear tendency of the courts at this stage to avoid the liability of parents in the absence of personal fault.

A third decision provides further persuasive authority to this effect.[35] It involved a claim for compensation for injuries sustained by the claimant in a large department store as a result of being hit by a stool which had been thrown over the railings five floors above by a two-and-a-half-year-old child. The Court of Appeal, quite remarkably, held that the shop was liable and did not even consider the question of the mother's liability. It found that the shop had a duty to supervise the child and that this duty was made particularly onerous by the fact that the child was located in the children's clothing department when the incident occurred. The reasoning behind this was apparently that this section of the shop constituted a particular allurement to young children. In quashing the decision, the *Cour de Cassation* resisted this attempt to dilute even further the duties placed on parents but, unfortunately, it did so by stating that the Court of Appeal should have established whether the mother had been personally at fault by determining whether she had been in a position to prevent the harm occurring, instead of imposing the presumption and leaving it up to her to submit such evidence in her defence.

[33] 'La Disparition de l'Alinéa 4 de l'Article 1384 du Code Civil', D.1961, chron 209.

[34] Civ 1re, 6 janv 1982, JCP 1982, IV, 107; Paris, 7e ch B, 12 juill 1990, JCP 1991, IV, 248.

[35] Civ 1re, 20 déc 1960, D.1961.141, note Esmein.

At this stage, therefore, it can be seen that the victim had a double hurdle to clear in establishing liability, being required to establish the fault of both the child and the parents. This position was redressed to some extent by the *Gesbaud* decision in 1966,[36] relative to the question of the child's liability.

(b) The Gesbaud *Decision*

Gesbaud marked the first step in the movement towards objective liability. It established that where harm had been caused by a child through the medium of an object, the liability of the child, from which the liability of the parents was to be derived, could be established on the basis of Article 1384, paragraph 1, rather than on the basis of Article 1382. In other words, instead of having to prove actual negligence on the part of the child in accordance with Article 1382, claimants could invoke the principle of strict liability for the deed of things in one's keeping contained in Article 1384(1). To satisfy the requirements of liability on this basis, all that needed to be proven was that the child had the use, direction, and control of the object that caused the harm. Given that, in most cases, the infliction of harm by children is to be attributed to their use of an object,[37] the impact of this decision was clearly far-reaching. In the majority of subsequent cases, the need for the plaintiff to establish fault on the part of the child perpetrator was dispensed with so that the presumption of parental negligence contained in Article 1384(4) could be brought into play practically automatically.[38]

It is significant that, at this stage, Article 1384(1) could not be used to give rise to an action in personal negligence against the child,[39] children having traditionally been exempt from such a regime of liability. Parental liability was thus evidently based on the objective negligence rather than the actionable negligence of the child perpetrator.[40]

The consequence of the *Gesbaud* decision was that in cases of harm caused by a child through the medium of an object, parental liability was based on two presumptions: the presumption of fault on the part of the parent based on the presumption of the child's liability.

[36] Civ 2e, 10 févr 1966, D.1966.332, concl Schmelck.

[37] This point is made by Warembourg-Auque in 'L'Irresponsabilité de l'Infans', RTDciv.1982.329. She suggests that this is because, otherwise, children do not generally have enough physical force to inflict significant harm.

[38] It was established by the famous *Jand'heur* decision, Ch Réunies, 13 févr 1930, D.1930.1.57, note Ripert, that Art 1384(1) implements a presumption of liability rather than a presumption of fault. The difference is that a presumption of liability may be rebutted only by proof of a *force majeure* or contributory negligence. This clearly operates to the advantage of claimants by guaranteeing a positive verdict in all but the most exceptional of cases.

[39] It was not until 1984 that Art 1384(1) could be used to impose liability on children: Ass plén, 9 mai 1984, D.1984.525, concl Cabannes, note Chabas.

[40] Although there was no formal legal rule to this effect contained in any French text, it was the opinion of leading jurists in this field that this was the state of the law as applied by the courts, such conclusions being drawn from a detailed study of the relevant case-law. Cf Warembourg-Auque, above n 37, and Puill, 'Les Caractères du Fait Non Fautif de la Victime', D.1980.chron 157.

However, an examination of the cases reveals that the courts continued for many years to disregard the presumption of negligence contained in Article 1384(4) and to require proof of fault on the part of defendant parents in order to impose liability. In one 1970 decision,[41] the *Cour de Cassation* stated that the claimant was required to prove that the defendant father had acted unreasonably, and it applied the increasingly familiar formula for determining negligence: that of inquiring whether by reason of the age or inexperience of the child, the state of the object used to cause the harm or the circumstances surrounding the activity, an accident was foreseeable.

A change in attitude may be identified as taking place around 1979, when the courts began to adopt a stricter approach to parental liability and actually started to apply the presumption in its intended form. Liability began to be imposed in circumstances in which, previously, parents would nearly always have been exonerated. In a decision of 7 November 1979,[42] the *Cour de Cassation* applied the presumption of fault to the father of a child who caused an accident while riding his bicycle in the street. It also held that evidence that the father had expressly forbidden the son to do so was insufficient to rebut the presumption.[43]

Two 1980 decisions reported together indicate that the courts had a tendency to treat evidence of the bad character of the child perpetrator as conclusive proof that the parents had failed in their duty to educate. In such cases the presumption became, to all intents and purposes, irrebuttable. In this way, the approach of the French courts at this stage may be compared with the current tendency of the common law courts to impose liability more readily in cases of reprehensible conduct.[44] In the first case,[45] the boy in question had aggressive tendencies which were assumed to have been known to his parents, and the incident which gave rise to this action involved him kicking a fellow pupil at school. The court held the father liable due to a breach of his obligation properly to educate his son, even though the boy was actually under the care and supervision of the particular educational establishment at the time. In the second case,[46] the boy in question had committed arson with malicious intent, and a similar decision was reached. In a commentary accompanying these two decisions it was suggested that basing liability on evidence of a poor upbringing was only a pretext for deciding that parents are generally responsible for the character of their children. A call was made at this early stage for the courts to state that parental liability was not based on a presumption of fault and that neither did it have anything to do with any notional duties to supervise and educate. It was argued that the courts should simply admit that parents are, in accordance with Starck's famous formulation of the '*obligation de garantie*', under an obligation to act as guarantors of

41 Civ 2e, 4 nov 1970, D.1971.205.

42 Civ 2e, 7 nov 1979, JCP 1980, IV, 27.

43 See also Crim 17 oct 1979, D.1980.IR.131, although in this case the court took a more lenient approach to the application of the presumption by holding the parents not liable.

44 See ch 2 above.

45 Civ 2e, 4 juin 1980, D.1981.IR.322.

46 Crim 18 juin 1980, D.1981.IR.322.

the character defects and unsociable traits of their children. It was also recognised at this stage that, if this were the case, there would no longer be any need for the requirement of cohabitation, given that it was specifically linked to the duties to supervise and educate.

Such a change in attitude prepared the way for the next major development in this area of the law, in the form of the *Fullenwarth* decision.[47]

(c) The Fullenwarth *Decision*

Fullenwarth was one of five[48] decisions examined and delivered together on the same day by the *Cour de Cassation* sitting in plenary session, a formation which lends even greater authority to the conclusions reached by the Court.

In *Fullenwarth*, a child aged seven fired an arrow from a homemade bow and arrow set in the direction of his friend and blinded him in one eye as a result. Having lost before the Court of Appeal, the defendant father brought his case before the *Cour de Cassation*, contending that the Court of Appeal had erred in its decision in not considering whether his son had sufficient understanding or awareness of his actions in order to establish liability on his part on the basis of fault. The position in French law until then had always been that, fault being an essentially moral concept based on blameworthiness, an individual could be capable of negligence in the legal sense only if he or she was fully aware of the import of his or her actions. Young children lacking reason were thus generally exempt from the regime of liability contained in Article 1382, with no particular age limit being fixed for the attainment of the so-called 'age of reason'. In this case the father was arguing that the presumption of negligence against him contained in Article 1384(4) came in to play only upon proof of the prior liability of the child tortfeasor, so that if the child was not liable then the presumption could not apply. This contention, although a perfectly accurate statement of the pre-existing law, was rejected by the *Cour de Cassation*, which held that to invoke the principle of parental liability as set out in Article 1384(4), it sufficed that the act committed by the minor was the 'direct cause' of the harm. The actual terminology used by the court was also significant in that it referred to a 'presumption of liability' rather than a presumption of fault, thereby reversing its previous position.[49] Only proof of a *force majeure* or contributory negligence would now suffice to rebut the presumption. Thus, from 1984 onwards, parental liability, as a mere causation-based liability, was no longer based on the prior liability of the child perpetrator.

An important observation to make here is that, at this point, the regime for establishing parental liability became even stricter than the corresponding doctrine of employer's liability, which continues to this day to require that the

[47] Ass plén, 9 mai 1984, D.1984.525, concl Cabannes, note Chabas.

[48] Of the five cases, *Fullenwarth* was the only one to concern the issue of parental liability. The other four decisions dealt rather with the related issue of the personal liability of children.

[49] Cf Civ 2e, 15 févr 1956, D.1956.410.

liability of the employee be established as a prerequisite to the application of its legal principles.[50] Moreover, *Fullenwarth* also operated to place those victims who had suffered at the hands of children in a more favourable position than those who had been injured by adults, for they were afforded the opportunity of suing the parent for the act of a child where, in ordinary cases, such an act would not give rise to the primary liability of an adult because it was simply not negligent according to ordinary standards of reasonableness.

The concern of the French judiciary at this time was clearly to improve the situation of victims. This was, no doubt, at least partly in response to the declaration of the Constitutional Council in 1982 that all persons who suffer harm at the hands of another have a constitutional right to receive compensation.[51] Also significant, in the sense of being indicative of the legal atmosphere of the time, is the law of 5 July 1985, which implemented a new system of liability in relation to road accidents in France. Operating largely on a no-fault basis and awarding to victims of road accidents an essentially automatic right to compensation, it constituted a major inroad into the fault doctrine. It is illustrative of how the notion of moral imputability was being supplanted by considerations of reparation, as the policy of automatic compensation adopted by the courts became an important method of determining questions of liability.[52]

In the light of these victim-oriented developments, it is not surprising that following the 1984 decisions many more calls were made for a radical overhaul of the regime, and the process of reforming this area of the law stepped up a gear. Commentators were more or less unanimous in the view that only the transformation of parental liability into a system of automatic liability based solely on the fact of parenthood and regardless of the actual conduct of the parent defendants would suffice to restore coherency to this area of law.[53] It was similarly envisaged that, in order to be financially sustainable, such a proposal would have to be based on the existence of compulsory liability insurance. Since specific insurance cover had already existed in this domain for many years and was already widely subscribed to, it was generally considered that the jump to compulsory indemnity policies would not be too traumatic. Many authors also pointed to the fact that the basis of the presumption as it then stood was, in most cases, entirely

[50] Civ 2e, 19 févr 1997, D.1997.265, note Jourdain.

[51] Déc no 82-144 du Conseil Constitutionnel du 22 oct 1982, *JO* 23 oct 1982, *Gaz Pal* 1982.2, *Bull Legisl* 764. It is to be noted that Art 62, para 2 of the Constitution of 1958 sets out that the decisions of the constitutional judge are binding on all public powers and on all administrative and judicial authorities.

[52] For a discussion of the French law on road accidents see TA Downes, 'French Lessons on Motor Accident Compensation', in R White and B Smythe (eds), *Current Issues in European and International Law* (1990), p 173, and R Redmond-Cooper, 'The Relevance of Fault in Determining Liability for Road Accidents: The French Experience' (1989) 38 ICLQ 502.

[53] G Viney, 'La réparation des dommages causés sous l'empire d'un état d'inconscience: un transfert nécessaire de la responsabilité vers l'assurance', JCP 1985, I, 3189; B Puill, 'Vers une réforme de la responsabilité des père et mère du fait de leurs enfants?', D.1988, chron 185; Fulchiron, JCP 1988, II, 21064.

fictitious.[54] Indeed, Fulchiron pointed out in this respect that while parental liability was then said to be based on the exercise of parental authority, such authority was actually made up of a bundle of rights and duties extending beyond supervision and education. The concept of the duty to educate, in particular, was the subject of further criticism because of its inherent ambiguity and the resulting inconsistencies in court decisions to which it gave rise.[55]

Initially, the courts responded to this surge of opinion by making the existing regime of parental liability stricter. The presumption of liability was more stringently applied[56] and the cohabitation requirement was broadened so that it was held to be satisfied for the purposes of Article 1384(4) even where the child perpetrator was temporarily in the care of a third party when the damage occurred.[57] It was not, however, until 1997, in *Bertrand*, that the *Cour de Cassation* took the opportunity to resolve definitively this much debated issue.[58]

(d) The Bertrand *Decision*

While the legal implications of *Bertrand* were to form the subject of innumerable commentaries and debates, the actual facts giving rise to the case could hardly have been more mundane. The claimant brought an action based on Article 1384(4) against the father of a 12-year-old boy who had collided with her while riding his bicycle. The Court of Appeal upheld her claim, and the defendant father brought the case before the *Cour de Cassation*, contending that the Court of Appeal should have considered the evidence submitted by him to the effect that he had properly carried out his duties to educate and supervise his son. The *Cour de Cassation*, rejecting his argument, held that the courts were no longer bound to take into account such evidence, because parental liability was no longer based on these duties to supervise and educate. It further held that, in future, the only defences that would be available to parents under Article 1384(4) would be those of *force majeure* and contributory negligence. The presumption of liability had been categorically replaced by a principle of automatic liability.

The overall reaction to the decision from legal quarters has been one of overwhelming support,[59] with many calling for further legislative intervention in order to make parental insurance cover compulsory. The view shared by the majority is that the imposition of no-fault liability is justified by sociological factors such as the strengthening of family links, with closer relationships developing between parents and children, and the fact that many children remain in

[54] Fulchiron, above n 53; Dagorne-Labbé, note D.1990.519; Jourdain, note D.1997.265.

[55] See, for example, H et L Mazeaud, *Traité théorique et pratique de la responsabilité civile délictuelle et contractuelle*, 6e ed, t1 par A Tunc ed, (Montchrestian, 1965), p 869, no 756; Jourdain, note D.1997.265; Vailard, note D.1990.207.

[56] Civ 2e, 3 mars 1988, JCP 1988, IV, 176; Civ 2e, 16 mai 1988, *Gal Pal* 1989.2.Somm.371; Lyon, 16 nov 1989, D.1990.207, note Vialard; Civ 2e, 16 janv 1991, JCP 1991, IV, 97.

[57] CA Nancy, 1re ch civ, 20 oct 1993, JCP 1994, IV, 2636; CA Paris, 9 avr 1996, D.1996.IR.128.

[58] Civ 2e, 19 févr 1997, D.1997.265, note Jourdain.

[59] Jourdain, D.1997.265; Radé, chron. D.1997.279; Mazeaud, somm D.1997.290.

the family home for longer due to the modern trend of embarking on extended periods of study, thus prolonging the period of dependency.[60]

It is also said that the availability of the sole defences of *force majeure* and contributory negligence is entirely consistent with the actual wording of Article 1384, paragraph 7, since it does not refer to fault at all but merely states that liability is to be imposed unless the parents prove that they could not have prevented the act of the child which gave rise to the harm. It has also been pointed out that the new interpretation of these provisions of Article 1384 is more reconcilable with Article 482, governing the legal position of parents in relation to children who have reached the aged of legal responsibility, for it sets out that 'parents are not automatically responsible for damage caused by an emancipated child subsequent to emancipation.'

Much criticism has since been directed at the cohabitation requirement, to the effect that it is totally inapplicable and out of step with the new regime of liability, given that its original purpose was to ensure that parents were in a position to exercise effective supervision of their children and that this consideration is no longer of any formal relevance. It has been pointed out, however, that it is not possible to simply remove or ignore this criterion for it is set out in black and white in Article 1384.[61] Thus, as a way of circumventing it, the courts have simply continued to apply to the concept an extremely liberal interpretation.[62]

That the wording of Article 371-2, in relation to parental authority, has now been changed, to the effect that the exercise of parental authority is no longer equated solely with the duties to supervise and to educate,[63] is arguably clear confirmation that the *Bertrand* approach has been fully embraced by the French legal community. More importantly, in the time that has passed since *Bertrand*, the French courts have demonstrated that they are prepared to continue to apply the principle of no-fault liability with its full rigour.[64]

The contrast with the corresponding English approach to parental liability is thus now very great. For while under both regimes the actual principles underlying such liability are the same, based as they are on the existence of a special relationship of authority and control, in practice the operation of these principles

[60] Jourdain, above n 59. Jourdain also contends that, while having a child cannot be said to constitute a fault, it is nevertheless a personal choice which is rather selfish. As such, the consequences of this choice should not be imposed upon others (above n 59 at 283).

[61] *Ibid.*

[62] See, eg, Civ 2e, 20 janv 2000, JCP 2000, I, 404; Civ 2e, 9 mars 2000, JCP 2000, I, 730; Cass Crim, 15 juin 2000, JCP 2000, I, 280, chron Viney; Cass Crim, 28 juin 2000; Civ 2e, 16 nov 2000, JCP 2001, I, 340, chron Viney; Cass Crim, 8 févr 2005, JCP 2005, II, 10049, note M-F Steinlé-Feuerbach.

[63] Amended by the Law of 4 March 2002. The new version sets out that: 'Each parent is to contribute, in proportion to their respective means and by reference to the needs of the child, to the maintenance and education of their children. This obligation does not lapse automatically upon the child's attainment of the age of majority' (author's own translation).

[64] Civ 2e, 4 juin 1997, D.1997.IR.159; Crim 25 mars 1998, D.1998.IR.152; Civ 2e, 1er avr 1998, D.1998.IR.120; Civ 2e, 2 déc. 1998, D.1999.IR.29; Civ 2e, 18 mai 2000, JCP 2000, IV, 2187; Civ 2e, 10 mai 2001, JCP 2001, II, 10613, note Mouly. See also G Viney, chron JCP 2002, I, 124; Ass Plén, 13 déc 2002, JCP 2003, II, 10010, note A Hervio-Lelong.

could not be more different, insofar as the English courts will go to great lengths to avoid parental liability, even in instances of clear fault.[65]

(ii) Liability for the Acts of Others based on Article 1384, paragraph 1

Prior to 1991, the *Cour de Cassation* had always presented itself as extremely hostile to the idea of using Article 1384(1) to create new categories of third party liability.[66] Then, in 1991, presumably in response to mounting pressure from the academic community, it dramatically reversed its position on the issue, and decided, in the case of *Blieck*,[67] that the four specific relationships detailed in Article 1384 did *not* constitute an exhaustive list of the domain of application of the principle of third party liability set out in Article 1384(1), after all, and that the principle could rather be applied in other particular circumstances. What these particular circumstances were, however, it did not define in any precise fashion. That it not to say that the *Cour de Cassation* was necessarily just being careless in this respect, for it has a noted tendency to be deliberately vague in circumstances in which it is unsure about a new principle, thus leaving itself the scope to go back on its decision should it wish to.[68] In the event, however, it appeared to lose any reservations that it might have had about the decision, for it ended up going to the other extreme and sanctioning a number of further extensions to the principle, to the point that it now has a sphere of application far beyond what could ever have been initially anticipated. Indeed, the court is now more likely to be accused of overzealousness, for it has effected one particular extension that is totally out of step with the rest and that cannot be reconciled at all with the original grounds for *Blieck*. For present purposes, however, the existence of this particular extension is highly significant in that it may be compared directly with an existing English law category of third party liability. Indeed, there exist a number of other striking similarities between the two regimes in this context, to the point that, in terms of the foundational principles of third party liability, their respective approaches may be regarded as broadly comparable.

(a) The Evolution of the Blieck *Principle of Third Party Liability*

The legal action in *Blieck* arose out of the actions of a mentally impaired individual in setting fire to the claimant's forest. The individual in question was a resident patient at the defendant's nearby centre for occupational therapy, and at the relevant time he had been undertaking some work outside the centre. The

[65] See, eg, *Donaldson v McNiven* [1952] 2 All ER 691 and *Gorely v Codd* [1967] 1 WLR 19, discussed in ch 2 above.

[66] See, eg, Civ 2e, 24 nov 1976, D. 1977.595, note Larroumet.

[67] Ass plén, 29 mars 1991, D. 1991.324, note Larroumet.

[68] T Le Bars and K Buhler, 'Responsabilité civile du fait d'autrui: une dérive à la jurisprudence Blieck', D.1996.453.

work had been organised by the centre, as part of its programme of 'supervised freedom', whereby patients would be allowed total freedom of movement during the day but at night would be supervised in a protected environment. The *Cour de Cassation* held that the defendant association was liable for the harm caused by its patient in this instance, on the grounds that it had 'accepted the responsibility of organising and controlling the life of this person on a permanent basis.' On the basis of this particular formula, it is thus possible to discern three separate elements to the *Blieck* principle:

(i) the acceptance of responsibility;
(ii) the existence of authority to organise and control the day-to-day conduct of the harm-doer; and
(iii) the exercise of such authority on a long-term or permanent basis.

Some commentators have further interpreted the decision as having been based also on some degree of risk theory, on the grounds that the court referred specifically in its judgment to the fact that the centre had operated on an 'open' basis[69] and that this arrangement obviously created a risk for the public.[70]

The first real extension of this *Blieck* principle was one that took many people by surprise. In 1995, the *Cour de Cassation* decided, in two cases heard simultaneously, that sporting associations could be held liable for the actions of their members in the course of a sporting event, on the basis of a similar, though not identical, formula to that set out in *Blieck*. Both cases involved harm caused by unidentified rugby players during the course of a match, and in both cases the liability of the respective rugby clubs was said to arise from the fact that their missions were to 'organise, lead and control the activities of their members in sporting events in which they take part.' Immediately, two distinctions from the *Blieck* formula may be identified: first the permanency criterion has been dropped altogether; and second, the position of authority and control in this instance is said to relate to the *activities* of the individual harm-doers in a particular context, rather than to their general day-to-day conduct. In the immediate aftermath, these decisions were heavily criticised on the grounds that they did not constitute an appropriate application of *Blieck*. However, it would appear that by this stage the French Supreme Court was already beginning to reason more in terms of general principles of third party liability, and had simply identified the grounds for liability in these cases as sufficiently compelling to warrant an extension of the *Blieck* principle. Moreover, it has subsequently affirmed its position in this respect by delivering several more sports liability decisions to like effect,[71] although in what may perhaps be seen as a concession to the critics, the Court has made it clear that liability requires that prior fault be established on the part

69 P Jourdain, 'La reconnaissance d'une responsabilité du fait d'autrui en dehors des cas particuliers énoncés dans l'article 1384', RTDciv.1991.541.

70 On this basis, a comparison can then be made with the equivalent administrative law regime for such liability.

71 Civ 2e, 3 févr 2000, JCP 2000, II, 10316, note Mouly.

of at least one of the defendant club's players, thus creating an obvious distinction with the parental position in this respect.[72] Clearly there is an analogy to be drawn here between these cases and the English sports liability cases, and it is submitted that it is one that actually lends greater support to the latter decisions. For arguably, the English approach of targeting referees and sports governing bodies rather than the actual clubs or associations is more directly justifiable in terms of the actual control that these defendants can exercise over the conduct of the harm-doers and their consequent ability to prevent harm.

Interestingly, the rather anomalous further extension of third party liability alluded to earlier[73] occurred in a decision that was delivered on exactly the same day as the first two rugby club decisions. In this particular instance, the *Cour de Cassation* decided that liability based on Article 1384(1) could be imposed on a building owner for harm caused by squatters. The men in question had started a fire in the defendant's building, which had then spread to neighbouring property. Liability was said to be based on the fact that the defendant had known that the men were there, that they had been engaging in aggressive and anti-social behaviour, and that they had previously been lighting dangerous fires in the building. Crucially, the defendant was also considered to have had the ability to remove the men. The *Blieck* formula itself was not even referred to, which is significant in that it suggests that the Court was perhaps even trying to break away from the constraints of this principle and conserve for itself total freedom in the development of general principles of third party liability. Once again, a striking similarity between the French and English regimes presents itself, for in respect of this particular French decision, the English cases of *P Perl v Camden London Borough Council*,[74] *King v Liverpool City Council*,[75] and *Smith v Littlewoods Organisation*[76] automatically spring to mind. The conclusion reached in respect of these cases, when they were examined in conjunction with other related ones, was that they perhaps established a principle of third party liability based upon a defendant's positive contribution to the creation of the circumstances giving rise to harm, combined with the existence of a high degree of likelihood of the harm occurring, and this would appear to be borne out in many ways by the adoption of a very similar French approach. At the very least, it indicates that such a principle of liability has intrinsic value of universal appeal. However, just as happened with the English cases, the existence of this French decision has provoked a rather reactionary response,[77] and as yet the principle of liability that it would appear to establish has not been developed any further.

From then on, the courts reverted to the *Blieck* formula in developing further categories of no-fault third party liability, and concentrated particularly on

[72] Civ 2e, 20 nov 2003, JCP 2004, II, 10017, note J Mouly; Civ 2e, 21 oct 2004, D.2005, note J-B Laydu.

[73] At p 152 above.

[74] [1984] 1 QB 342.

[75] [1986] 3 All ER 544.

[76] [1987] 1 AC 241.

[77] T Le Bars and K Buhler, above n 68.

instances of harm caused by children. Indeed, it will be seen that the most significant extensions of the principle have been in the context of harm by children and, moreover, that many of these extensions have been effected only very recently. The first application of *Blieck* in this context was against private care homes as regards the conduct of 'problem' children in their care. Such children would be either young offenders who had been sent by the courts to the home on a rehabilitation programme, under the Order of 2 February 1945,[78] or else minors who had come to the attention of the authorities as being potentially anti-social and who had been taken into care as a pre-emptive action under civil protection measures.[79] The latter are commonly referred to in France as '*enfants en danger*'. In these cases, the courts have reinstated the original *Blieck* formula, and founded the liability of these private institutions on their 'acceptance of the responsibility to organise, direct and control the day-to-day conduct of the children in their care on a permanent basis.'[80] That the courts are prepared to invoke the liability of these institutions even in situations in which the child perpetrator is not in their de facto care at the time the harm is caused,[81] either because the child is on a temporary home visit, or has been placed by the care home with a foster family, or else has run away, is a clear indication that such liability is based primarily on the exercise of *legal* authority over the harm-doer.

Initially, it was thought that this extension of the *Blieck* principle would be limited only to 'problem' children, as they were readily recognised as high risk-creators. To begin with, the *Cour de Cassation* obviously thought so too, for it continually rejected attempts to make relatives and guardians responsible for the acts of children in their care on the basis of Article 1384(1).[82] However, it would appear that, after the *Bertrand* decision in relation to parents in 1997, the court became concerned about the great disparity that had been created between the positions of victims injured by children living with their parents, and those injured by children not in the care of their parents. Thus in 2000, the court effected a further complete turnaround, and decided that guardians would now be liable for the actions of minors[83] in their care on a no-fault basis under Article 1384(1).[84] Following that decision, the Court of Appeal of Paris then imposed

[78] It is to be noted that that the joint liability of the state will also be engaged in respect of the conduct of young offenders.

[79] Art 375 Code Civil.

[80] Cass Crim, 10 oct 1996, JCP 1997, II, 22833, note Chabas; Civ 2e, 9 déc 1999, JCP 2000, IV, 163; Civ 2e, 20 janv. 2000, JCP 2000, IV, 1403. See also, T Le Bars and K Buhler, above n 68.

[81] CA Pau, 1er ch, 2 déc 1999, JCP 2000, IV, 2571. Civ 2e, 6 juin 2002, D.2002.IR.2028 et 2029.

[82] Civ 2e, 18 sept 1996, D.1998.Jur.118, note Rebourg; Civ 2e, 25 févr 1998, JCP 1998, II, 10149. See also AM Galliou-Scanvion, 'L'Article 1384, alinéa 1er, et la responsabilité du fait d'autrui: un fardeau non-transférable sur les épaules du tuteur', D. 1998. chron 240. Some commentators also interpreted this refusal as meaning that the Art 1384(1) principle was only to be applied against legal entities and not against natural persons: W van Gerven, J Lever and P Larouche, *Tort Law* (Hart Publishing, 2000), p 519.

[83] It is probably still the case that guardians of incompetent *adults* are not subject to Art 1384(1), their role being distinguishable from that of guardians of children.

[84] Cass Crim, 28 mars 2000, JCP 2001, II, 1045, note Robaczewski.

Article 1384(1) liability on a non-profit-making association running a children's holiday camp in respect of harm caused to a child during a sporting activity there. The formula used was similar to that invoked in the rugby club cases, relating as it did to the responsibility of the defendant for 'organising, directing and controlling the *activities* of its members' for the duration of the camp.[85] This last decision has been criticised by Geneviève Viney, an extremely influential academic in this field and an ardent supporter of the other Article 1384(1) developments, on the basis that the defendant's authority over the child perpetrator in this case was merely contractual in origin. Viney argues that, for the purposes of Article 1384(1), a distinction should be made between authority conferred by contract and authority conferred by a court order, and that in the case of the former, application of the no-fault principle should be limited to paid professionals.[86] The *Cour de Cassation* does appear to have taken account of this concern to some extent, however, in the sense of allowing some concessions to be made in non-commercial contractual contexts, for in a recent case involving a mentally impaired youth carrying out a sexual assault at a train station on his way back to his special school, it held that the liability of the school[87] could not be engaged on the basis of Article 1384(1) in this instance because, at the relevant time, it did not have de facto control of the boy.

This development in French law of a general principle of third party liability for the acts of children in one's care demonstrates the potential scope of the English law principle of liability based upon the existence of a relationship of authority and control over an irresponsible other.[88]

III. CONCLUSION

While the French law regime of third party liability is clearly much more radical than the corresponding English regime, particularly in terms of its very rigorous application of a general theory of no-fault liability, as regards the actual foundational principles governing the various existing instances of third party liability, there are some striking similarities. In particular, both would appear to recognise general principles of third party liability based upon:

(1) the long-term occupation of a position of general authority and control over the day-to-day conduct of an irresponsible other; and

[85] CA Paris, 9 juin 2000, JCP 2001, I, 340, chron Viney.

[86] *Ibid.*

[87] The regime of ordinary fault-based liability set out in Art 1384, paras 6 and 8, applies only to individual schoolteachers.

[88] See ch 3 above.

(2) the occupation of a position of authority and control over specific risk-producing activities of identified third parties for the duration of the activities in question.

Moreover, it is submitted that the second principle is more legitimately implemented in English law than in France. Furthermore, there would also appear to be some limited support in the French case law for the recognition of the proposed English law principle of third party liability based upon a positive facilitation of the commission of harm by a third party, combined with a high degree of likelihood of the harm occurring.

Conclusion

AT A TIME when serious concerns are being raised about the future viability of the English tort system, and extra vigilance needs accordingly to be employed in vetting all new legal developments that are likely to result in further expansions of the boundaries of tortious liability, the instinctive reaction to the current trend towards expanding the categories of third party liability is bound to be one of resistance and rejection. Notwithstanding that some of the existing manifestations of this trend would tend to fuel such a reaction, it is submitted that the recognition of a number of specific and strictly limited instances of third party liability in tort can be legally justified. Our innate hostility to the very idea of making one person liable for the acts of another is directed at its incongruity with our basic notions of justice and fairness, particularly as concerns our deep-rooted attachment to the corrective justice principle of individual moral responsibility and the general rule against imposing liability for omissions. However, this objection does not apply to the instances of third party liability that have been defended in this book. They are to be distinguished insofar as they can be presented not only as legitimate exceptions to the omissions rule, but also as forms of liability linked directly to the personal responsibility of the defendant, in that they stem from the nature of his or her relationship with either the victim of the harm or the third party perpetrator.

The *Dorset Yacht* principles of third party liability apply to persons occupying a position of authority and control over an irresponsible other. Of most obvious application to the parent/child relationship, the case law nevertheless demonstrates that parental liability will generally be precluded on policy grounds. It is submitted that such third party liability arguments are more likely to succeed in the context of other relationships of authority and control, such as that existing between non-parental carers and children, and that they would relate either to a responsibility to control the irresponsible other or to a duty to protect that other from foreseeable risks.

In nuisance, special duties to abate nuisances created by third parties arise on the part of occupiers of property simply by virtue of the fact of their occupation. It is argued, however, that the existence of such duties is only justifiable in respect of third party nuisances taking place *within* the defendant's property. As regards third party negligence actions against property owners, the analysis of the relevant case law resulted in the formulation of a general principle of third party liability based on a defendant's positive facilitation of the commission of harm by another in circumstances involving a high degree of likelihood of harm occurring. Although such a principle would not be confined specifically to property owners, it is envisaged that, through a strict interpretation of the relevant 'likelihood' requirement, it would be applied in only the most exceptional of circumstances. Some support for the recognition of such a general principle is, moreover, to be found in the French system and its implementation of a strikingly similar formula for liability.

In the context of sport, two separate grounds for the imposition of third party liability may be identified:

(1) the occupation of a position of immediate authority with a resultant power of immediate and effective control, as in the case of a referee; and
(2) the occupation of a position of general authority and indirect control in which there has been an express assumption of responsibility with concomitant reliance, as in the case of a rule-making body.

In both cases, the affirmative duties of care can be further justified by the existence of two special relationships of close proximity: one of protection as between the defendant and the victim; and another of control between the defendant and the harm-doer. While third party sport liability is also recognised in France, the French approach is to target sports clubs and associations, rather than referees or sports governing bodies. Insofar as the English principles are based upon more concrete notions of control, they are arguably more defensible than their French counterparts.

Lastly, as regards public authorities, it is argued that third party actions may legitimately be brought in respect of certain public functions relating to the care and control of risk-producing third parties. Examples of such functions would be those exercised by the police and the prison authorities, to name but two. Such liability would generally be invoked vicariously in respect of the torts of individual employees. By way of control mechanisms, the affirmative duty of care in these cases is already subject to a requirement that there be established two special relationships of close proximity, and it is submitted that, at the breach of duty stage, liability could be limited even further through a simple lowering of the standard of care. This would certainly appear to have operated as an effective control mechanism for the French.

Apart from the suggested general principle of liability based on positive facilitation of third party harm and a high likelihood requirement, the foundational principles identified are obviously highly context-specific. That they are so disparate in nature, however, serves merely to reinforce the validity of the general rule against holding one person liable for the acts of another, and the consequent exceptional status of the existing law on third party liability. It is submitted that if the above-formulated principles are applied in a strict and controlled manner, then not only will the English law on third party liability be transformed into a more coherent and legitimate body of law in its own right, but appropriate boundaries will also be imposed upon its development. Failure to proceed on such a rigorous basis will result in additional and irreparable damage being done to the integrity of this area of tort law, the early warning signs of which are arguably already being provided by the mounting case law on third party liability in respect of the intoxicated.

Bibliography

Books

Atiyah, PS, *The Damages Lottery* (Hart Publishing, 1997).
—— *Vicarious Liability in the Law of Torts* (Butterworths, 1967).
Bell, J, Boyron S, and Whittaker, S, *Principles of French Law* (Oxford University Press, 1998).
Bénabent, A, *Droit Civil: Les Obligations* (Montchrestien, 1995).
Brown, LN and Bell, JS, *French Administrative Law* (Oxford, Clarendon Press, 1998).
Cane, P, *The Anatomy of Tort Law* (Hart Publishing, 1997).
—— *Atiyah's Accidents, Compensation and the Law* (Butterworths, 1999).
Cane, P and Stapleton J (eds), *Essays for Patrick Atiyah* (Oxford, Clarendon Press, 1991).
—— *The Comparative Law of Obligations: Essays in Honour of John G. Fleming* (Oxford, Clarendon Press, 1998).
Craig, P, *Administrative Law* (Sweet & Maxwell, 2003).
Ehrenzweig, AA, *Negligence Without Fault* (University of California Press, 1951).
Englard, I, *The Philosophy of Tort Law* (Dartmouth, 1992).
Fleming, JG, *The Law of Torts* (Sydney Law Book Co, 1998).
Giliker, P and Beckwith, S, *Tort* (Sweet & Maxwell, 2004).
Grubb, A (ed), *Principles of Medical Law* (Oxford University Press, 2004).
Healy, J, *Medical Negligence: Common Law Principles* (Sweet & Maxwell, 1999).
Howarth, D, *Textbook on Tort* (Butterworths, 1995).
Jaffey, AJE, *The Duty of Care* (Dartmouth, 1992).
Jones, MA, *Textbook on Torts* (Oxford University Press, 2002).
Livingstone, S and Owen, T, *Prison Law* (Oxford University Press, 1999).
Lunney, M and Oliphant, K, *Tort Law: Text and Materials* (Oxford University Press, 2003).
Markesinis, BS, Auby, J-B, Coester-Waltjen, D and Deakin, S, *The Tortious Liability of Statutory Bodies* (Hart Publishing, 1999).
Markesinis, BS and Deakin, SF, *Tort Law* (Oxford, Clarendon Press, 1999).
Mowbray, A, *The Development of Positive Obligations under the European Convention on Human Rights by the European Court of Human Rights* (Hart Publishing, 2004).
Murphy, J, *Street on Torts* (LexisNexis UK, 2003).
Owens, DG (ed), *Philosophical Foundations of Tort Law* (Oxford, Clarendon Press, 1995).
Rogers, WVH, *Winfield & Jolowicz on Tort* (Sweet & Maxwell, 2002).
Tunc, A (ed), *Mazeaud & Mazeaud, Traité Théorique et Pratique de la Responsabilité Civile* (Montchrestien, 1965).
van Gerven, W, Lever, J and Larouche, P, *Tort Law* (Hart Publishing, 2000).
Weinrib, EJ, *The Idea of Private Law* (Harvard University Press, 1965).
Wright, J, *Tort Law and Human Rights* (Hart Publishing, 2001).

Articles

Alt-Maes, F, 'La Garde, Fondement de la Responsabilité du Fait du Mineur', (1998) *JCP* 1367.

Andenas, M and Fairgrieve, D, 'Sufficiently Serious? Judicial Restraint in Tortious Liability of Public Authorities and the European Influence' in M Andenas (ed), *English Public Law and the Common Law of Europe* (Key Haven Publications, 1998).

Artus, D, 'Le Mineur Placé en Application des Articles 375 et Suivants du Code Civil et le Contentieux de la Responsabilité Devant le Juge Administrative', D.2001.Chron.18.

Atiyah, PS, 'Personal Injuries in the Twenty-First Century: Thinking the Unthinkable' in P Birks (ed), *Wrongs and Remedies in the Twenty-First Century* (Oxford, Clarendon Press, 1996).

Atkin, B and McLay, G, 'Suing Child Welfare Agencies – A Comparative View from New Zealand' [2001] *CFLQ* 287.

Bagshaw, R, 'Proximity's Siren Song: Negligence Liability of Fire Brigades in England' (1998) 6 *Tort LR* at 109.

—— 'The Duties of Care of Emergency Service Providers' [1999] *LCMLQ* 71.

—— 'Private Nuisance By Third Parties' (2000) 8 *Tort LR* 165.

Bailey, S, 'Beyond the Call of Duty' (1987) 50 *MLR* 956.

Bailey, SH and Bowman, MJ, 'The Policy/Operational Dichotomy – A Cuckoo in the Nest?' (1986) 45 *CLJ* 430.

—— 'Public Authority Negligence Revisited' (2000) 59 *CLJ* 85.

Bailey-Harris, R and Harris, M, 'The Immunity of Local Authorities in Child Protection Functions – Is The Door Now Ajar?' [1998] *CFLQ* 227.

—— 'Local Authorities and Child Protection – The Mosaic of Accountability' [2002] *CFLQ* 117.

Bamforth, N, 'The True Horizontal Effect of the Human Rights Act 1998' (2001) 117 *LQR* 34.

Baker, C, '*Phelps v Hillingdon LBC*' (1999) 143 *SJ* 85.

Barker, K, 'Unreliable Assumptions in the Modern Law of Negligence' (1993) 109 *LQR* 461.

—— 'NHS Contracting: Shadows in the Law of Tort?' (1995) 3 *Med LR* 161.

Blanc, G, 'A Propos de la Responsabilité des Grandparents' D.1997.Chron.327.

Blatier, C, 'Juvenile Justice in France: the Evolution of Sentencing for Children and Minor Delinquents' (1999) 39 *British Journal of Criminology* 240.

Blyth, T, 'Hotelier and Social Host Liability for Alcohol Related Harm – A Review of the Law in Australia' (1999) *Murdoch University Electronic Journal of Law*, vol 6, no 3.

Bowman, MJ and Bailey, SH, 'Negligence in The Realms of Public Law – A Positive Obligation to Rescue?' (1984) *PL* 277.

—— 'Public Authority Negligence at the Waterfront' (2001) 9 *Tort LR* 7.

Bright, S, 'Liability for the Bad Behaviour of Others' (2001) 21 *OJLS* 311.

Bright, S and Bakalis, C, 'Anti-Social Behaviour: Local Authority Responsibility and the Voice of the Victim' [2003] *CLJ* 305.

Brodie, D, 'Pursuing the Police' [1995] *Jur Rev* 292.

Buckley, RA, 'Negligence in the Public Sphere: Is Clarity Possible?' (2000) 51 *NILQ* 25.

—— 'Public Authorities – Negligence Actions – Control Devices' (1998) 18 *LS* 1.

Cane, P, 'Suing Public Authorities In Tort' (1996) 112 *LQR* 13.

—— 'Corrective Justice and Correlativity in Private Law' (1996) 16 *OJLS* 471.

—— '"What a Nuisance!"' (1997) 113 *LQR* 515.

—— 'Vicarious Liability for Sexual Abuse' (2000) 116 *LQR* 21.
Carnwath, R, 'Welfare Services – Liabilities in Tort After the Human Rights Act' [2001] *PL* 475.
Chamberlain, E, 'Alcohol Provider Liability in Canada and the United Kingdom: Legal and Cultural Influences' (2004) 33 *Common Law Word Review* 103.
Coe, R, 'A New Test For Vicarious Liability?' (2001) *NLJ* 1154.
Convery, J, 'Public or Private? Duty of Care in a Statutory Framework: *Stovin v Wise* in the House of Lords' (1997) 60 *MLR* 559.
Craig, P and Fairgrieve, D, '*Barrett*, Negligence and Discretionary Powers' [1999] *PL* 626.
Cullen, W, 'The Liability of the Good Samaritan' [1995] *Jur Rev* 20.
de Burca, G, 'Proportionality and *Wednesbury* Unreasonableness: The Influence of European Legal Concepts in UK Law' (1997) 3 *European Public Law* 561.
Downes, TA, 'French Lessons on Motor Accident Compensation' in R White and B Smythe (eds), *Current Issues in European and International Law: Essays in Memory of Frank Dowrick* (Sweet & Maxwell, 1990), p 173.
Doyle, J and Redwood, J, 'The Common Law Liability of Public Authorities: The Interface Between Public and Private Law' (1999) 7 *Tort LR* 24.
Dugdale, AM, 'Public Authority Liability: To What Standard?' (1994) 2 *Tort LR* 143.
Elvin, J, 'The Liability of Schools for Bullying' (2002) 61 *CLJ* 255.
Fairgrieve, D, 'The Human Rights Act 1998, Damages and Tort Law' [2001] *PL* 695.
—— 'Pushing Back the Boundaries of Public Authority Liability: Tort Law Enters the Classroom' [2002] *PL* 299.
Fairgrieve, D and Andenas, M, 'A Tort Remedy for the Untaught? – Liability for Educational Malpractice in English Law' [2000] *CFLQ* 32.
Feldthusen, B, 'Failure to Confer Discretionary Benefits: The Case for Complete Negligence Immunity' (1997) 5 *Tort LR* 17.
Fleming, JG, 'Injury Caused by Stolen Motor Vehicles' (1994) 110 *LQR* 187.
Fordham, M, 'Liability for the Criminal Acts of Third Parties' (2001) 117 *LQR* 178.
Foster, S, 'Prisons and the Duty of Care' (1999) 149 *NLJ* 799.
Fridman, GHL, 'Non-Vicarious Liability for the Acts of Others' (1997) 5 *Tort LR* 102.
Galliou-Scanvion, AM, 'L'Article 1384, Alinéa 1er, et la Responsabilité de Fait d'Autrui: Un Fardeau Non-Transférable Sur les Epaules du Tuteur' D.1998.Chron.240.
Gearty, CA, 'Unravelling *Osman*' (2001) 64 *MLR* 159.
—— '*Osman* Unravels' (2002) 65 *MLR* 87.
George, J, '*Watson v British Boxing Board of Control*: Negligent Rule-Making in the Court of Appeal' (2002) 65 *MLR* 106.
Giliker, P, '*Osman* and Police Immunity in the English Law of Torts' (2000) 20 *LS* 372.
Glover, N, '*Bolam* in the House of Lords' (1999) 15 *PN* 136.
Greenfield, S and Osborn, G, 'The Referee's Fear of a Penalty' (1996) 12 *PN* 63.
Grubb, A, 'Medical Negligence: Duty of Care and *Bolam*' (1998) 6 *Med LR* 120.
Haberfield, L, '*Lowns v Woods* and the Duty to Rescue' (1998) 6 *Tort LR* 56.
Hall, M, 'The Liability of Public Authorities for the Abuse of Children in Institutional Care: Common Law Developments in Canada and the United Kingdom' (2000) 14 *IJLPF* 281.
—— 'After Waterhouse: Vicarious Liability and the Tort of Institutional Abuse' (2000) 22 *JSWFL* 259.
Hamad, A, 'The Intoxicated Pedestrian: Tortious Reflections' (2005) 15 *Tort LR* 14.
Handford, P, 'Trimming the Wings of Vicarious Liability' (2001) 9 *Tort LR* 97.

Hartshorne, J, 'Suing the Saviours – The Liability in Negligence of the Fire Service' (1996) 12 *PN* 85.
—— 'The Liability in Negligence of The Fire Service – The Court of Appeal Decides' (1997) 13 *PN* 53.
Hartshorne, J, Smith N, and Everton, R, '*Caparo* Under Fire: A Study into the Effects Upon the Fire Service of Liability in Negligence' (2000) 63 *MLR* 502.
Hoffmann, Lord, 'Human Rights and the House of Lords' (1999) 62 *MLR* 159.
Honoré, T, 'Responsibility and Luck: The Moral Basis of Strict Liability' (1988) 104 *LQR* 530.
—— 'Are Omissions Less Culpable?' in P Cane and J Stapleton (eds), *Essays for Patrick Atiyah* (Oxford, Clarendon Press, 1991), p 33.
Horder, J, 'Tort and the Road to Temperance: A Different Kind of Offensive Against the Drinking Driver' (1988) 51 *MLR* 735.
Howarth, D, 'Negligence After *Murphy*: Time to Rethink?' (1991) 50 *CLJ* 58
—— 'My Brother's Keeper? Liability for the Acts of Third Parties' (1994) 14 *LS* 88.
—— 'Three Forms of Responsibility: On the Relationship Between Tort Law and the Welfare State' (2001) 60 *CLJ* 553.
Hoyano, L, 'Policing Flawed Police Investigations: Unravelling the Blanket' (1999) 62 *MLR* 912.
Jaconelli, J and Jaconelli, A, 'Tort Liability Under the Mental Health Act 1983' (1998) 20 *JSWFL* 151.
Jones, MA, 'Multiple Causation and Intervening Acts' (1994) 2 *Tort LR* 133.
—— 'The Violent Mentally Disordered Patient: Who Cares?' (1998) 14 *PN* 99.
—— 'Liabilities for Psychiatric Patients: Setting the Boundaries' (2000) 16 *PN* 3.
Josselin-Gall, M, 'La Responsabilité du Fait d'Autrui Sur le Fondement de l'Article 1384, Alinéa 1er: Une Théorie Générale est-elle Possible?' JCP.2000.I.268.
Jourdain, P, 'La Reconnaissance d'une Responsabilité de Fait d'Autrui En Dehors des Cas Particuliers Enoncés dans l'Article 1384' RTDciv.1991.541.
Keeler, J, 'Thinking Through the Unthinkable: Collective Responsibilities in Personal Injury Law' (2001) 30 *CWLR* 349.
Kidner, R, 'Resiling From the *Anns* Principles: The Variable Nature of Proximity in Neglience' (1987) 7 *LS* 319.
Kirk J and Trichardt, A, 'Sports, Policy and the Liability of Sporting Administrators' (2001) 75 *ALJ* 504.
Lambert-Faivre, F, 'L'Evolution de la Responsabilité Civile d'une Dette de Responsabilité à une Créance d'Indemnisation' RTDciv.1987.1.
Lawson, R at (1998) 142 SJ 1064.
Le Bars, T and Buhler, K, 'Responsabilité Civile du Fait d'Autrui: Une Dérive à la Jurisprudence *Blieck*' D.1996.453.
Lewis, R, 'Insurance and the Tort System' (2005) 25 *LS* 85.
Linden, A, 'Rescuers and Good Samaritans' (1971) 34 *MLR* 241.
Lippke, RL, 'Torts, Corrective Justice and Distributive Justice' (1999) 5 *Legal Theory* 149.
Logie, JG, 'Special Relationships, Reasonable Foreseeabilities and Distinct Probabilities: The Duty to Prevent Damage to the Property of Others' (1988) *Jur Rev* 77.
—— 'Affirmative Action in the Law of Tort: The Case of the Duty to Warn' (1989) 48 *CLJ* 115.
Lunney, M, 'Don't Play With Matches' (1998) 114 *LQR* 377.
Markesinis, B, 'Negligence, Nuisance and Affirmative Duties of Action' (1989) 105 *LQR* 104.
Martin, R, 'Further Thoughts on the Liability of Rescuers' (1998) 6 *Tort LR* 113.

McIvor, C, 'Expelling the Myth of the Parental Duty to Rescue' [2000] *CFLQ* 229.
—— 'Liability in Respect of the Intoxicated' (2001) 60 *CLJ* 109.
—— 'Police immunity and the legacy of Hill Chief Constable of West Yorkshire' (2005) 21 PN 201.
McLean, H, 'Negligent Regulatory Authorities and the Duty of Care' (1988) 8 *OJLS* 442.
Miles, J, '*Z and Others v United Kingdom; TP and KM v United Kingdom.* Human Rights and Child Protection' [2001] *CFLQ* 431.
Monti, G, '*Osman v UK* – Transforming English Negligence Law into French Administrative Law' (1999) 48 *ICLQ* 757.
Morgan, E, 'Police Immunity, Public Policy and Proportionality' (1999) 149 *NLJ* 13.
Morgan, J, 'Nuisance and the Unruly Tenant' (2001) 60 *CLJ* 382.
Morris, F and Adshead, G, 'The Liability of Psychiatrists for the Violent Acts of Their Patients' (1997) 147 *NLJ* 558.
Mouly, J, 'Les paradoxes du droit de la responsabilité civile dans le domaine des activities sportives' JCP 2005, I, 134.
Mullender, R, 'Negligence, the Public Interest and the Proportionality Principle' (1997) 5 *Tort LR* 9.
—— 'Negligence, the Policy/Operational Distinction and the European Convention on Human Rights' (1999) 7 *Tort LR* 98.
—— 'Negligence, Public Authorities and Policy-Level Decisions' (2000) 116 *LQR* 40.
—— 'Corrective Justice, Distributive Justice and the Law of Negligence' (2001) 17 *PN* 35.
Mullis, A, '*Barrett v Enfield London Borough Council.* A Compensation-Seeker's Charter?' [2000] *CFLQ* 185.
—— '*Phelps v Hillingdon London Borough Council.* A Rod for the Hunch-Backed Teacher?' [2001] *CFLQ* 331.
Murphy, J, 'Children in Need: The Limits of Local Authority Accountability' (2003) 23 *LS* 103.
Osode, PO, 'The Modern Hospital and Responsibility for Negligence – Pointing Canadian Courts in the Right Direction' (1993) 22 *Anglo-American Law Review* 289.
O'Dair, R, 'Liability in Tort for the Transmission of Aids: Some Lessons From Afar and Prospects For the Future' (1990) 43 *Current Legal Problems* 219.
O'Sullivan, J, 'Negligence Liability of Auditors to Third Parties and the Role of Assumption of Responsibility' (1998) 14 *PN* 195.
—— 'Nuisance. Local Authorities and Neighbours From Hell' (2000) 59 *CLJ* 11.
Phillipson, G, 'The Human Rights Act, "Horizontal Effect" and the Common Law: A Bang or a Whimper?' (1999) 62 *MLR* 824.
Pickford, V, 'Playing Dangerous Games' (1998) 6 *Tort LR* 221.
de Prez, P, 'Proportionality, Symmetry and Competing Public Policy Arguments: The Police Force and Civil Immunity' (1999) 15 *PN* 217.
—— 'Liability for Failure to Prevent Acts of Self-Destruction: The House of Lords' Decision in *Reeves v Commission of Police of the Metropolis*' (2000) 16 *PN* 113.
—— 'The Enemy Within: Reflections on Human Rights in Tort Law' (2001) 9 *Tort LR* 178.
Puill, B, 'Les Caractères du Fait Non-Fautif de la Victime' D.1980.Chron.157.
—— 'Vers une Réforme de la Responsabilité des Père et Mère du Fait de Leurs Enfants?' D.1988.Chron.185.
Redmond-Cooper, R, 'The Relevance of Fault in Determining Liability for Road Accidents: The French Experience' (1989) 38 *ICLQ* 502.
Reid, E, 'Liability for Dangerous Activities: A Comparative Analysis' (1999) 48 *ICLQ* 731.

Reynolds, FMB, 'Causal Delegation' (2001) 117 *LQR* 180.
Robinson, J, 'Schools, LEAs and Damages' (1997) 141 *SJ* 80.
Rodière, M 'La Disparition de l'Alinéa 4 de l'Article 1384 du Code Civil' D.1961.Chron.209.
Silberberg, H, 'The Intoxicated Patron: A Re-Appraisal of the Duty of Care' (1974) 20 *McGill LJ* 491.
Smith, JC, and Burns, P, '*Donoghue v Stevenson*, The Not So Golden Anniversary' (1983) 46 *MLR* 147.
Solomon, R and Payne, J, 'Alcohol Liability in Canada and Australia: Sell, Serve and be Sued' (1996) 4 *Tort LR* 188.
Sprince, A and Cooke, J, 'Article 6 and Immunity in Tort: Let the Facts Speak for Themselves' (1999) 15 *PN* 228.
Stapleton, J, 'In Restraint of Tort' in P Birks (ed), *The Frontiers of Liability*, vol 2 (Oxford University Press, 1994), p 84
—— 'Tort, Insurance and Ideology' (1995) 58 *MLR* 820.
—— 'Duty of Care: Peripheral Parties and Alternative Opportunities For Deterrence' (1995) 111 *LQR* 301.
Stauch, M, 'Risk and Remoteness of Damage in Negligence' (2001) 64 *MLR* 191.
Sugarman, SD, 'Judges as Tort Law Un-Makers: Recent California Experience with "New" Torts' (1999) 49 *Depaul Law Review* 455.
Todd, S, 'Liability of Agents in Tort' (1998) 14 *PN* 136.
Trichardt, A and Cilliers, C, 'Rugby Administrators Take Note – A Recent Development in Antipodean Law' (1999) 15 *PN* 153.
Vines, P, 'Fault, Responsibility and Negligence in the High Court of Australia' (2000) 8 *Tort LR* 130.
Viney, G, 'La Réparation des Dommages Causés Sous l'Empire d'un Etat d'Inconscience: Un Transfert Nécessaire de la Responsabilité Vers l'Assurance' JCP.1985.I.3189.
—— 'Vers un Elargissement de la Catégorie des "Personnes Dont On Doit Répondre": La Porte Entrouverte Sur une Nouvelle Interprétation de l'Article 1384, Alinéa 1er, du Code Civil' D.1991.Chron.157.
—— Chronique, JCP.2000.I.241.
—— Chronique, JCP.2002.I.124.
Vos, G, 'Linking Chains of Causation: An Examination of New Approaches to Causation in Equity and the Common Law' (2001) 60 *CLJ* 337.
Vranken, M, 'Duty to Rescue in Civil Law and Common Law: Les Extrêmes Se Touchent?' (1998) 47 *ICLQ* 934.
Waller, PL,'Visiting the Sins of Children – The Liability of Parents For Injuries Caused By Their Children' (1963) 4 *Melbourne University Law Review* 17.
Warembourg-Auque, F, 'L'Irresponsabilité de l'Infans' RTDciv.1982.329.
Weinrib, EJ, 'The Case for a Duty to Rescue' (1980) 90 *Yale LJ* 247.
Weir, T, 'Suicides in Custody' (1998) 57 *CLJ* 241.
Whippy, WP, 'A Hospital's Personal and Non-Delegable Duty to Care for its Patients – Novel Doctrine or Vicarious Liability Disguised?' (1989) 63 *ALJ* 182.
Wightman, J, 'The Limits of the Rules on Recovery for Psychiatric Damage in the United Kingdom' (2000) 8 *Tort LR* 169.
Williams, K, 'Medical Samaritans: Is There a Duty to Treat?' (2001) 21 *OJLS* 393.
Williams, R, 'Remoteness: Some Unexpected Mischief' (2001) 117 *LQR* 30.
Wright, J, 'Negligent Parenting. Can My Child Sue?' (1994) *Journal of Child Law* 104.

—— 'Local Authorities, the Duty of Care and the European Convention on Human Rights' (1998) 18 *OJLS* 1.

—— '"Immunity" No More: Child Abuse Cases and Public Authority Liability in Negligence after *D v East Berkshire Community Health NHS Trust*' (2004) 20 *PN* 58

Yeo, S, 'Am I My Child's Keeper? Parental Liability in Negligence' (1998) *Australian Journal of Family Law* Lexis 12.

—— 'The Infallibility of Rule-Making Sporting Bodies' (2001) 9 *Tort LR* 104.

Index

www.ingramcontent.com/pod-product-compliance
Lightning Source LLC
LaVergne TN
LVHW011803200926
848484LV00003B/772
9781841135526